POP DREAMS
Music, Movies, and the Media in the 1960s

Archie K. Loss
Penn State Erie, The Behrend College

Harcourt Brace College Publishers

Fort Worth Philadelphia San Diego New York Orlando Austin San Antonio
Toronto Montreal London Sydney Tokyo

This book is for Suzanne—
semper te amo

Publisher	Earl McPeek
Acquisitions Editor	David Tatom
Product Manager	Steve Drummond
Project Editor	Laura J. Hanna
Art Director	Candice Clifford
Production Manager	Diane Gray

ISBN: 0-15-504146-0
Library of Congress Catalog Card Number: 98-72416

Address for Orders: Harcourt Brace College Publishers, 6277 Sea Harbor Drive, Orlando, FL 32887-6777. 1-800-782-4479

Address for Editorial Correspondence: Harcourt Brace College Publishers, 301 Commerce Street, Suite 3700, Fort Worth, TX 76102

Web site Address: http://www.hbcollege.com

Printed in the United States of America

9 0 1 2 3 4 5 6 7 8 066 9 8 7 6 5 4 3 2 1

Harcourt Brace College Publishers

PREFACE

This book attempts, in a concise form, to show the relationship between the most important social and political events of the American 1960s and the popular arts and media. As such, it synthesizes certain aspects of the cultural history of the postwar period that, more typically, are treated separately. This approach is particularly useful because of the close connection in this period between historical trends and events and the arts and media. In general, this relationship is best described as dialectical, each side impacting with equal force and influence on the other.

This text is not aimed at specialists, but rather the general student or reader who is approaching the material for the first time. It will be of special use in American Studies and history courses that deal with, or touch on, the 1960s. Hopefully, it will lead its readers to pursue the subject in greater depth. Because the 1960s are still with us in many ways, with numerous issues as yet unresolved and events still open to interpretation, what is written here will in some respects necessarily be incomplete or undefinitive. Thirty years is a short time in history, too short for anyone to say that ultimate truths have emerged about so striking a decade. The best one can do—and this has been my aim—is to interpret it as objectively as possible, acknowledging both the limitations imposed by nearness in time and the probability of historical revisionism in the future.

Each chapter begins with an italicized passage that summarizes the thrust of its main argument. The chapters are organized around certain themes that are important to a consideration of the decade. These include the civil rights and antiwar movements, the counterculture, the conservative resurgence, women's liberation and special identity politics, and various legacies of the sixties. These movements or trends overlap in time but are best understood when studied separately. In addition to the preceding, there are chapters devoted to the concept of popular culture itself and to important postwar developments, through the end of the 1950s, with special impact on the decade of focus.

Following the initial summary, each chapter reviews important historical developments related to its subject, then goes on to consider their relationship to the popular arts and media. Given the wide variety of possibilities, I have had to be highly selective in my choice of examples. In general, my operating principle has been to use musical, movie, and media examples that are demonstrably popular and most indicative of major trends in sixties and post-sixties thinking. I have tried to avoid a technical approach to musical interpretation, as well as any terminology, slang or otherwise, that might confuse or put off the reader. When special terms are introduced in the text, they are usually followed by a definition or are contextualized in such a way that their meaning should be plain.

I must acknowledge many debts for what follows: its mistakes, of course, are mine alone. First of all, I want to thank my editors, Gerald D. Nash and Richard W. Etulain of the University of New Mexico, for many helpful comments and suggestions. My colleagues in history, John Rossi and Dan Frankforter, have given much time and patience to reading the book in its various drafts; I owe them many thanks as well. Wendy Eidenmuller of our staff did the hard work required in preparing the manuscript in its final form—as always, with great patience and skill. Norma Hartner handled permissions and other details equally with tact. I am much indebted to them both.

I must thank my students in American Studies 105: American Popular Culture, whose continuing interest and enthusiasm for this subject provided the primary motivation for this book, and my teaching assistants, whose work with their break-out groups has made such a difference to a class that has grown gradually larger and larger. Thanks also to Roberta Salper, director of the School of Humanities and Social Sciences, for encouraging me to teach the course in the first place and supporting my research for this book in many different ways, and to John Lilley, provost of Behrend College, for creating an environment in which teaching and research can coexist so well.

In addition, I want to give special thanks to my research assistants, whose help on this project has been invaluable: Pat Bruce, Steve Ceriani, Jon Clark, Jason Giersch, and Brian Kitchen. Of this group, Pat and Jon worked longest and deserve special mention for their unflagging support. In addition, Scott Naigle was extremely helpful in designing the visuals.

Finally, I must thank my wife Suzanne and children Emma, Christopher, and Lucinda, all of whom read and commented in depth on various aspects of the text and were, as usual, patient with me at times when I probably didn't deserve it.

Archie K. Loss

CONTENTS

Chapter 1

Introduction: Popular Culture in 1960s America

For many students, the 1960s in America inspire much curiosity. Why, of all decades in recent history, do you hear so many references to the events and personalities of the sixties? If you read the newspaper regularly, you find stories about the 1960s almost every week—anniversaries of important events, the reviving of old questions, obituaries of people who were well-known then. If you follow music, you recognize certain musicians, like Bob Dylan or the Rolling Stones, as 1960s survivors still popular today. Or perhaps, like Eddie Vedder of Pearl Jam, the Seattle alternative group, you may admire the music of an artist like Neil Young, who has strong roots in the 1960s. If you follow movies, you may have seen *Forrest Gump*, one of the most popular films of the last decade, in which Tom Hanks plays the role of a person with a borderline I.Q. and special needs who mysteriously becomes part of some of the major events of this most turbulent decade. In addition, through a host of documentaries on John F. Kennedy and his family, Martin Luther King and the civil rights movement, American involvement in the war in Vietnam, and the social and cultural history of the period—including the history of rock 'n' roll—you've gotten glimpses of the 1960s that you may never have seen before.

If you follow politics, you have heard in recent years much criticism of ideas current in the sixties and government policies that were implemented then. For many politicians elected, or returned, to office in the watershed off-year election of 1994, when the Republican party regained control of both houses of Congress for the first time in 40 years, these criticisms constituted a major part of their campaign rhetoric and subsequent legislative agenda, the so-called "Contract with America." But students interested in these developments may know more about the criticisms leveled against government policies dating from the 1960s and early 1970s than about their history and origin. Similarly, they may know more about what people think is wrong with sixties ideas—often summed up under the general rubric of "the counterculture"—than the reasons why the original proponents of such ideas thought they were so right.

Differences of opinion over the sixties abound among current political and cultural commentators and professional historians. Recent studies by some of the latter have revised many long-held views of the sixties and helped to place the events of the period in the greater continuum of American history. Among those who lived through the period and played a role in its events, similar differences exist. Consider the following comments, all from people of the sixties generation wanting to share their point of view with the present generation:

> This was it. This decade made the greatest difference for me. I went into it, like most of my friends, with the outlook of the suburbs where I grew up—sports, mom and dad, apple pie. I came out of it seeing American society as rotten to the very core.

> I don't think there was ever a decade in the history of the country that did more to pervert fundamental American values— of the family as well as society. That was when everything started going wrong in colleges and universities. The inmates started running the asylum.

> I had no political views at all [before the shooting incident at Kent State]. I was strictly a sorority girl, an onlooker at a few rallies, and that was it. But then I saw my sorority sister shot down—she was there just by chance that day, on her way to class, and had nothing to do with any of the demonstrations on campus—and that changed it all for me. In one instant in time I became politicized.

> I remember how we started out in the sixties, our sisters and brothers working together to knock down old Jim Crow. All

through the time of the Freedom Riders, and the Freedom Summer in Mississippi, and the Freedom Democratic party—that word says it all, doesn't it? Freedom was what we wanted, freedom was what we were working for. And then Martin Luther King was shot down in Memphis, and we all began to ask what the hell we thought we'd achieved, if that was what the result would be.

I was out on the field and they came to me and said this was it, you're done, and I hopped on a chopper, rode it out to Saigon, flew on to Manila, spent a day or two in Honolulu, and ended up in San Francisco, where I was back in civilian life, but still in uniform, after three or four days at the Presidio. Now, can you believe that? After 31 months in 'Nam, I was back in the States within a week and out on the street. Man, it was like a different world. (Author's files)

For the last speaker, 31 months had created a world of difference in American society. The 1960s was a decade of conflicts and contrasts, in which it seemed that any reconciliation of differences—military, political, racial, or personal—would be the least likely outcome. The 1960s saw the development of a host of alternative lifestyles and viewpoints that threatened to splinter American society forever. At the same time, however, the decade brought significant changes in the political process and the hopes of large groups of Americans. African Americans and women came closer to the centers of power in American society, and other special groups—Native Americans, Hispanics, gays and lesbians—saw the beginnings of their own movements toward greater acceptance.

These changes and conflicts were reflected profoundly in our popular culture. It is here that we can often see most directly and immediately the blueprint of what was to follow for American society after the 1960s. This book attempts to show the correlation between the major events of the decade and certain crucial elements of American popular culture. This was a dialectical relationship, in which events shaped culture and culture shaped events. By the beginning of the 1970s, a new sensibility had emerged—viewable in music, movies, and the communications media—in the lifestyle of a whole generation. By the same point in time, however, a major segment of the population reasserted and sustained certain values regarded as "traditional" in politics and in popular culture. In this conflict between tradition and change lay the seeds of the decades that were to follow, up to the present time. From this, too, come questions that have persisted ever since: Did the sixties change our lives in any positive way? Did this decade represent the beginning of something new or the end of something good?

WHAT IS POPULAR CULTURE?

One thing that the field of cultural studies teaches us is that culture is not merely what is found in libraries, museums, and opera houses. Understanding popular culture entails a broader view. It includes folk, rock, and pop music, as well as symphonic music and opera. It encourages us to rummage through the junk shop as well as tour the museum—to see movies, not just "cinema" or "film," to watch reruns of "Star Trek" and "I Love Lucy," not just the latest offerings on "Masterpiece Theatre." It is egalitarian in spirit and more complicated than it may appear at first glance. It is what makes possible courses in such recent cultural phenomena as the social significance of the slacker, the films of Keanu Reeves, and the development of rap music. It considers culturally significant not merely what we read or see or hear, but also what we wear, what we eat, and what we drive. It has given rise to an important body of critical writing—much of it European in origin—which has done much to legitimize cultural studies as an intellectual discipline.

About the beginnings of popular culture there is some debate. Many scholars, like Ray Browne of Bowling Green University (one of the primary centers for the study of popular culture in the United States), argue that popular culture has always been with us, developing at some point in the past from folk culture and maintaining historically a complex relationship to it. Other scholars, like Russel Nye, see popular culture emerging at a specific historical moment in Western civilization, toward the end of the eighteenth century. For Nye, popular culture is linked inextricably with the concurrent development of industrialization, mass communication, and an affluent middle class.

However it is viewed historically, popular culture in our time in the United States is undeniably commercial, self-replicating, and all-pervasive. It is all around us, from the fast food chains that line our busiest streets, to the malls where popular movies—often sequels of other popular movies—are shown and where the CDs of the hottest new groups are sold. We are so much a part of this culture, in fact, and it is so much a part of us, that we have trouble reading it for what it is. Unlike more hierarchical societies, in which taste is determined primarily by social or hereditary factors, contemporary popular culture in the United States forms the large, middle part of a continuum. The remnants of folk or ethnic culture are on one side of it and more elite cultural forms on the other. Drawing from both sides, and to a large extent cutting across class lines, popular culture has become a dominant factor forming taste, opinions, and values in modern American society. In addition, because it has been exported widely throughout the world, it has become a phenomenon of international importance. For this reason, some countries—mainland China, for instance—have seen it as a political threat. Indeed, rock 'n' roll has frequently been viewed that way in this country, from its beginnings, when it was linked with the so-called communist threat, to the present day, with widespread attempts to censor the lyrics of many rock or rap groups. Inevitably, popular culture both shapes and reflects the political climate of the society where it occurs. When that political climate is divided, as it was in this country in the 1960s, then popular culture can become like the Roman god Janus, looking forward and backward at the same time.

POPULAR CULTURE IN THE 1960S: HISTORICAL FACTORS

The events of the American 1960s are rooted primarily in the period following the end of the Second World War. Indeed, we cannot properly understand what happened in the 1960s without looking closely at the entire postwar period. First and foremost, the economic boom that extended till the end of the 1960s was especially friendly to the development of the elements of popular culture emphasized in this study. During this period, from 1947 till 1960, the gross national product (GNP) increased by 56 percent, reaching $439.9 billion. In the words of Robert M. Collins, "The postwar affluence took hold of the American imagination." Soon writers were finding metaphors for abundance in all aspects of American culture, and expansiveness became a key political concept. Meanwhile, sociologists were beginning to define the characteristics of the new professional middle class that emerged from the boom period. Some saw a fundamental shift in values forming in the traditional middle-class work ethic. One major result was a focus on leisure activities—of profound importance to American popular culture.

The demographic change of greatest significance to the 1960s was the birth of the baby boomers, the offspring of those couples who married and had children in the postwar period. The low birthrate and late marriages of the Depression era gave way by the mid-1940s to earlier marriages and more children. As a result, by 1964 there were more people who were 17 years old than any other age group in this country. By 1965, 41 percent of the population would be under 20 years of age.

While this group divided along lines of color, class, and income, it shared enough experience and values to make many young people feel that they constituted a special group older Americans could not, *would* not, understand. This group soon came to be known by the general term "youth culture." Born into a society in which consumerism had become a common denominator and delayed gratification a rapidly disappearing concept, young people also shared a richly developed taste for the products of American popular culture. For this group, movies, music (especially folk and rock), and the media (especially radio and television) would become integral to their experience of growing up.

FORMS OF POPULAR CULTURE: THE ARTS AND THE MEDIA

None of the forms of the popular arts or media that dominated the 1960s actually saw their beginnings during the decade. Movies had become an important popular cultural form in American life even before the 1920s. Television, while a much younger medium, took a central place in the popular imagination in the 1950s, superseding radio in general popularity and ultimately, through competition, pushing both movies and radio in new directions. And rock music, frequently associated with the political protests and countercultural trends of the 1960s, had emerged as an identifiable cultural phenomenon of immense attraction to young people, both here and abroad, by the latter half of the 1950s. Nevertheless, all of these forms of popular culture underwent significant, sometimes even wrenching, changes during the 1960s. These changes reflected the dominant social and political trends of the decade, as well as its technological developments.

Of all the popular art forms, rock music was most closely identified with the youth culture. With roots primarily in African-American music—especially in gospel, blues, and jazz—by the 1960s rock music had become the preferred musical expression of white middle-class youth in rebellion against the more conservative values of their parents and edicts of their society. During the civil rights movement early in the decade, folk music played a similar historic role for whites and blacks both. For another segment of white American society in the 1960s, however, country music and rock would be blended together to express values thought to be more traditional. For radical and conservative alike, radio and concerts became important means of transmitting the musical message.

Movies, like music, took advantage of the greater freedom of expression of the decade. Legally, this freedom was provided by the United States Supreme Court decision in the *Fanny Hill* case (1966), liberating the language of the arts from the constraints of government-imposed censorship. In their use of four-letter words and their graphic depiction of sex and violence, many movies took on new expression and form in the later years of the 1960s, reflecting the changing tastes and values of movie producers and the moviegoing audience. Increasingly, that audience was drawn from the youth culture. Generally, however, the majority of movies of the decade reflected mainstream American values and avoided political controversy. For this reason, no significant film was made about the American experience in Vietnam until the 1970s.

Of all the popular media, television arguably had the greatest direct influence on popular culture in the decade of the 1960s. Not only did the medium demonstrate its ability to capture a huge segment of the mass audience with its regular entertainment programming, but television news also became a major factor in the political sphere. Advances in technology, coupled with relative freedom from censorship, allowed TV to play an important, some thought decisive, role in shaping public opinion on American involvement in Vietnam and on the civil rights movement. No one who lived through the decade and its chaos will ever forget certain images, impressed indelibly on our collective memory by the TV screen: the young John Kennedy, Jr., saluting the coffin of his dead father; the American forces in Saigon scrambling to defend the American Embassy during the Tet offensive of January 1968; the solemn march of civil rights leaders and Robert Kennedy to the grave site of Martin Luther King in Atlanta; the equally solemn movement of the train bearing the body of Kennedy himself past row upon row of mourners a few months later; the violence of the inner-city riots and the antiwar demonstrations at the Chicago Democratic Convention in August of 1968. To these images many more can be added. All of them had an incalculable influence on our social and political thinking for years to come.

In evaluating the influence of television, however, it is important not to forget other important elements of the media establishment that played a major role in shaping popular opinion in the 1960s. Newspapers and magazines had their own share of indelible images of the civil rights movement, the war in Vietnam, and the reaction, both positive and negative, to that war on the home front. Such images also provide a telling record of how much the mere appearance of people, especially of American youth, changed in the course of a very few years. But newspapers and magazines also provided commentary, both reasoned and impassioned, that had a major impact on public opinion. Such editorial comment was easier to provide in print than in the more ephemeral medium of television. Certain publications had their origins in the antiwar movement and played a special role in presenting that viewpoint to their readership. However, the press was chiefly important in reflecting opinion in the great center of American society.

Ultimately, all forms of a culture reflect and shape the history of a decade. Popular culture of the 1960s was charged by the social and political struggles of the day to an extent that may be difficult to believe in today's more homogenized environment. This gave the popular arts and the media a special significance in describing and defining public taste and opinion during that period, especially among the young people who found themselves rebelling against the laws and values of mainstream American society.

Chapter 2

SEARCHING FOR A CENTER: CONFORMITY AND CONSENSUS IN POSTWAR AMERICA

To realize fully the extent of the rebellion among young people in the 1960s and the importance of various events of that decade, we need to understand the major historical developments of the postwar years. These include the suburbanization of the white middle class, the idealization of the nuclear family, the baby boom, and the new emphasis on consumerism and leisure time activities. By the middle of the 1950s, the civil rights movement would become an equally important development among black Americans. As American society was changing, its popular art forms and communication media were changing, too. By the end of the 1950s, rock 'n' roll had become the most popular form of music among American youth, and Hollywood movies had begun to reflect the questioning of parental and institutional authority that was to be a dominant theme of the sixties. Television, meanwhile, was becoming the most important communications medium. In general, its programming would reflect the values of the dominant white middle-class culture of suburban America, financed by the economic boom of the postwar period.

The United States was the only major nation to emerge from the Second World War stronger economically than it went in. To the GIs returning from that war, this country offered an abundance of material opportunities unprecedented in its history—indeed, in the history of the world. The period of extraordinary affluence that resulted fed the development of our popular culture and set the stage for the 1960s.

An important aspect of the era of abundance that began in the postwar period was the GI Bill of Rights (1944). An entitlement passed by a Congress and presidency grateful for the contribution of its servicemen, the GI Bill became the cornerstone of prosperity for the white middle class. For one thing, it opened the door of educational opportunity to many veterans. Colleges and universities were changed permanently by the large influx of new students, many of them older and more experienced than the typical undergraduate of the prewar period. The bill also made it possible for many of these veterans to own their own homes, with loans requiring low down payments and interest rates. Very soon, the dream of home ownership became a reality for hundreds of thousands who had never had that opportunity before.

For those located in or near large cities, the home they would buy was likely to be in a suburban development. The economic boom of the postwar period together with low mortgage rates led to home construction on a scale larger than ever before in American history. One result was planned communities like Levittown, the brainchild of real estate entrepreneur Bill Levitt, who felt that housing should be affordable and replete with all the conveniences that modern technology could provide. With the Levittowns in this period would come a network of new roads, culminating in the development of the interstate system in the 1950s, as the urban community spread itself across the American countryside.

NUCLEAR FAMILIES IN A NUCLEAR AGE

The ideal family unit of this suburban community consisted of a working father, a homemaking mother, and two to four children who would grow up with their social peers in the controlled environment such developments provided. By the beginning of the 1950s, after a brief spurt in the divorce rate at the end of the Second World War, it seemed that the home-centered existence with clearly defined family roles was here to stay. In the history of the American family, the idealization of the nuclear unit was relatively new. Gone were not only the various dislocations caused by the war, but also the extended family units of earlier decades. The nuclear family was supposed to be a self-sufficient social and economic enterprise, in which the division of labor between husband and wife was clearly defined. Material possessions and children provided the primary focus of their attention.

For the white middle class—soon to be called the "baby boomers" because of the increasing birthrate among them—the suburban ranch-type home with its picture window, new appliances, and open interior space would become a symbol of a whole way of life, a new frontier in American history. With automobility and consumerism as two of its principal features, this lifestyle was touted as a new world standard in the popular media.

The upper, professional end of the new middle class became the subject of much intellectual and scholarly speculation. One of the most important and influential studies appeared only five years after the war, David Riesman's *The Lonely Crowd* (1950). In this book, whose title would be a phrase that stuck, Riesman defined the values of the new class in contrast with those of an earlier, more individualistic period. America's original values, which had historical roots in the Renaissance, he called "inner-directed." They characterized the explorer, the inventor, the entrepreneur. The values of the modern professional, on the other hand, were "other-directed," determined more by his sense of what was expected by his peers and by the organizational slot he occupied than by his own personal desires and aspirations.

Sociologist C. Wright Mills of Columbia University expanded on these ideas, approaching them by a somewhat different historical route, in his *White Collar* (1954). Like Riesman, Mills thought the new middle class had moved away from earlier American ideals. With jobs offering no internal satisfactions, only whatever motivation salary and status could provide, Mills saw the new middle-class life increasingly emphasizing leisure time activity:

> What is psychologically important in this shift to mass leisure is that the old middle class work ethic—the gospel of work—has been replaced in the society of employees by a leisure ethic, and this replacement has involved a sharp, almost absolute split between work and leisure. Now work itself is judged in terms of leisure values.

One result of the split Mills saw at the beginning of the 1950s was that "popular goals and daydreams" began to form around movie star and baseball heroes rather than business or professional types: "the faculties of reflection, imagination, dream, and desire . . . do not now move in the sphere of concrete, practical work experience."

Many other books of the period popularized these ideas in various forms, helping to create the image of what William H. Whyte called, in his best-selling study, *The Organization Man* (1956). Sloan Wilson, meanwhile, in his semiautobiographical novel *The Man in the Gray Flannel Suit* (1955), depicted through the personal dilemmas faced by his characters the frustration and emptiness of the life of the new professional class. The key element in all of these descriptions, fictional and nonfictional, is conformity. The price paid for the material rewards of middle-class society was a considerable sacrifice of personal freedom. Conforming to the requirements of one's professional or personal role was more important than any individual preference.

Another problem with the new suburban life was that it did not include African Americans and other minority groups. Developments of the Levittown type were specifically aimed at whites; persons of color were excluded outright or steered away. As a result, in the influx of approximately 1 million southern blacks to northern industrial cities in the 1940s—one effect of the economic boom of the war years and afterward—virtually all of the new population would join the older black community in the inner city. Increasingly, city and suburb became polarized social and ethnic units, though the suburban developments frequently had a more diverse national mix than the old ethnic neighborhoods of the city. However, for African Americans, despite improvements in income and social class, the suburban Edens were an impossibility.

Yet another problem of the new suburban lifestyle stemmed from the concept of the nuclear family itself. Though the space of the ranch home was open, the roles in the family were closed. As a result, mothers, fathers, and children frequently experienced a sense of isolation. What happened when the mother became tired of being constantly responsible for the children? What if she began to feel underutilized or stultified by the role she was supposed to play? And what of the father who worked long hours—sometimes at two jobs—to maintain the economic standard by which the new middle class lived? With many fathers overworked, and many moth-

ers feeling unhappy with their activities on the home front, dissatis-
factions could grow beneath a surface of material contentment.
How widespread such feelings were is a matter of debate, but the
evidence suggests that they were more than just a minor phenomenon.

One effect of such negativity among the children was a greater
reliance than ever upon peer relationships—in this case their social
and economic peers—and a growing number of questions about
adult authority. The first of these (a natural feature of childhood
and adolescence) was only intensified by the lack of work, or defined roles of labor, for children in the new suburbia. Theirs was to
a large extent a life of leisure in a heavily child-focused environment. In addition, the degree of conformity in the life of the new
middle class—one result of people moving upward socially and trying to fit into new standards of right and wrong—ended by alienating many of the children. Questions about authority were their response to the repression such conformity required. Both
dependence on peer culture and a feeling of alienation from adults
were to have profound results in the 1960s, when this generation
of children reached college age. These problems of the baby
boomer generation were only exacerbated by the culture of the
Cold War that dominated the American political scene in the postwar period.

Despite the prosperity and relative calm of the eight years of
the Eisenhower presidency (1952–1960) (the slogan of the 1956
Eisenhower campaign was "Peace, Prosperity, and Progress"), a
powerful, often virulent, anticommunism characterized American
foreign policy and domestic politics of the time. Following the so-
called domino theory, the United States adopted strong policy
stands and invested millions in the development of a defense system that was to end up second to none. In the process, however,
the strength of the Soviet defense system was constantly overesti-
mated by Cold War policy makers.

Domestically, the effect of anticommunism reached its greatest
extreme during the so-called "McCarthy era" of the early 1950s.
Senator Joseph McCarthy of Wisconsin headed the Senate Committee on Government Operations and its investigations subcommit-
tee. Under McCarthy, this committee engaged in a reckless witch-
hunt of major proportions, accusing unnamed individuals in various
government agencies, including the Departments of State and the
Army, of close connections with the Communist party. In fact,

McCarthy was a demagogue who made unsubstantiated claims for his own political gain. Ultimately repudiated by the Senate itself when his agenda became even too reckless for his supporters to bear, McCarthy represented the anticommunism of American politics in the postwar period at its worst. Unfortunately, the effects of McCarthyism continued long after the man who gave it his name had been condemned for his reckless acts.

THE BEGINNING OF THE CIVIL RIGHTS MOVEMENT

Both the paranoia and the conformity that the anticommunist politics of the period engendered were reflected in the reaction to another major domestic development of the 1950s: the civil rights movement. The problem of slavery was never resolved in the early days of the republic, and the civil rights of black Americans became one of the major issues in the War Between the States of 1861-65. African Americans were freed from slavery by the Emancipation Proclamation of 1863 and the Thirteenth Amendment, and their civil rights were protected by two additional amendments to the Constitution (the fourteenth and fifteenth). During the Reconstruction period (1865-77), African Americans fought for and, to a degree, received equal political rights in the South. However, in the decades following the end of Reconstruction, they were faced with an increasing number of restrictions that came to be known collectively (from a stereotype of the black male) as the Jim Crow laws. Essentially the legal means to deny African Americans political equality and to enforce the separation of black and white Americans in the South, these laws were declared constitutional by a number of conservative U.S. Supreme Court decisions. In particular, *Plessy* v. *Ferguson*, 1896, established the legitimacy of the "separate but equal" doctrine that was their foundation. Soon, however, groups like the National Association for the Advancement of Colored People (NAACP), formed in 1909, targeted for review the laws that established separate and very unequal public school systems and denied blacks equal voting rights.

In a celebrated decision of 1954 in the case of *Brown* v. *Board of Education* (of Topeka, Kansas), a previously divided United States Supreme Court, under Chief Justice Earl Warren, an Eisenhower appointee, decided unanimously that segregation in the public schools was unconstitutional. "To separate [black children] from others of similar age and qualifications solely because of their race," the ruling read, "generates a feeling of inferiority as to their status in the community that may affect their hearts and minds. . . . We conclude that in the field of public education the doctrine of 'separate but equal' has no place."

This landmark decision became the opening wedge in the campaign of the newly invigorated civil rights movement. Many school districts in border states complied, but the immediate reaction on the part of southern states was anger, incredulity, and resistance. One result, in 1957, was a crisis in Little Rock, Arkansas, in which federal troops were reluctantly called in by President Eisenhower to restore order and allow nine black students to attend the public high school. In Prince Edward County, Virginia, the public schools were closed altogether.

By 1955, in Montgomery, Alabama, the movement had spread to public transportation, in particular city busing, when Rosa Parks refused to take a seat in the back of a city bus. (A Supreme Court decision of 1946 had ruled against segregation in interstate transportation, though the practice persisted.) By the end of the decade, the movement began to focus primarily on the voting rights of southern blacks. By then also, the Reverend Martin Luther King, Jr., of Atlanta, had become its most important national leader and the organization he headed, the Southern Christian Leadership Conference, its most important group. Although the major aims of the civil rights program would not be fully realized for some time and its severest critics even alleged connections with the "Communist Conspiracy," the movement achieved major impetus in the 1950s and became the inspiration for similar antiestablishment movements of the next decade.

SOCIAL DEVIANCY IN AN AGE OF CONFORMITY

Another exception to the rule of conformity in the 1950s was the so-called "beat generation," a group of writers, artists, intellectuals, and their hangers-on clustered primarily in major cities like San Francisco and New York and known popularly (in a spin-off of the Russian *Sputnik*) as "beatniks." For this group, which anticipated the counterculturalists of the 1960s, American capitalism and militarism were repugnant. Advocating sexual freedom and experimentation with drugs, especially marijuana and LSD, the beats suggested an alternative to mainstream American values but no program to give that alternative much substance. As a literary movement, beat ideals were heralded by literary spokesmen like Allen Ginsberg (his *Howl*, 1956, was the major poem of the movement) and Jack Kerouac (his *On the Road*, 1957, was the major novel). Ginsberg was to become prominent in the counterculture of the 1960s.

Another significant group to deviate from middle-class standards were so-called "juvenile delinquents." These were adolescents, many of them the children of the new middle class, who indulged in antisocial, often illegal, behavior. In many respects they were imitating what they took to be lower-class values and freedoms in the behavior they adopted. In doing so, they separated themselves from the middle-class norms represented by their parents and attracted major attention in the media and American popular culture. In some respects, they were the first wave of a development that was to culminate by the end of the 1960s in a whole set of alternative values associated with the young.

TELEVISION AND THE NEW LEISURE TIME

With home-centered leisure time activities an increasingly important part of the daily life of the middle class, it is scarcely surprising that television should have become such a popular medium during the decade of the 1950s. It would replace radio and movies as the foremost entertainment and information source for millions of Americans.

One reason for the success of television was its place in the home. The suburban lifestyle was not only family-centered, it was home-centered. The new suburban homes, ranch-type or otherwise, were designed to be automobile, appliance, and TV friendly. That is, the very design of the houses, and the subdivisions of which they were a part, accommodated and encouraged the new technology. Streets were widened for a greater number of automobiles; garages became a more prominent feature, now attached to homes. Inside, houses provided space for the new kitchen appliances and the television set in the living room. In fact, the Levittown homes eventually included a dishwasher and a television set as standard incentives to purchasers.

The pattern of living was set: Father leaves for work early in the morning, comes home in the late afternoon or early evening. Mother meanwhile has tended to the kids and the housework. Dinner done (without bothering Dad with anything too disturbing), the family ends up in the living room, in front of the TV. Soon, throughout the country, the TV habit set in, despite serious objections of various kinds to its potentially negative effects. At first, in most parts of the country, programming began in the late afternoon or early evening. However, as TV became increasingly popular, a long-lasting formula was fixed. Daytime programming was aimed at women and younger children, late afternoon and evening at older children and adults.

The statistics chart the triumph of TV. In 1950, at the beginning of the decade, there were 2,061 commercial AM radio stations in the country, most of which had affiliations with major networks like NBC or CBS. Total AM revenue from advertising and other sources was $605.4 million dollars, and 94.7 percent of American families had one or more radio sets in their homes. FM radio stations (733 total) added an additional $2.8 million in revenue. By contrast, there were only 98 commercial television stations, all but two with network affiliations, with a total industry revenue of a mere $170.8 millions. Only 9 percent of American homes boasted TV sets.

By 1960, at the beginning of the next decade, there were 515 commercial TV stations, of which 96 percent had network affiliations, with a combined revenue of more than 1.5 billion dollars, with 87.1 percent of American families owning TV sets. By 1960, 3,431 commercial AM radio stations reached radio sets in 95.6 percent of American homes and generated revenues of $692.4 million. Even adding in FM revenues (by 1960, 688 stations—down from 733 in 1950—with $9.4 million in revenue), the commercial predominance of television is clear: Radio revenues were only 43 percent those of TV. The importance of TV as a medium is largely attributable to its commercial clout; no other branch of the broadcasting industry could reach so many people so quickly with so much message.

This is not to say, however, that radio, AM at least, suffered a serious decline in the 1950s and later. As a matter of fact, the statistics show the opposite to be true. The number of AM radio stations

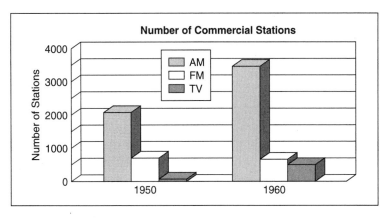

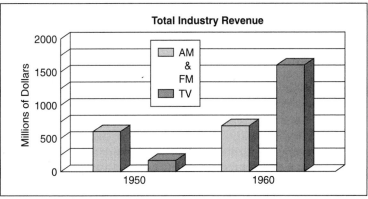

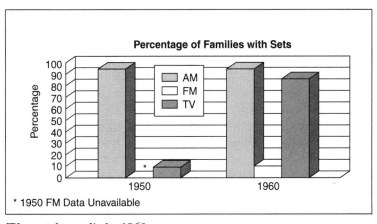

TV overtakes radio by 1960

(Source of data: Sterling and Kittross, *Stay Tuned*, 2d ed., 1990)

increased in the ten-year period of 1950 to 1960 by 66.5 percent, and total revenues (AM and FM together) rose by more than 15 percent. TV revenues in the same period, however, increased so much more—an 852 percent increase, nearly nine times as much as radio's. In addition, the number of commercial TV stations increased by 425.5 percent. (The number of noncommercial stations by 1960 was 44.)

Another way of looking at it is to say that AM radio had peaked by the beginning of the 1950s. Though FM radio was to flourish in the 1960s and 1970s, radio as a whole would never match the commercial power of TV. Eventually, TV would preempt much of the traditional programming of AM radio, as AM and FM radio moved into new terrain.

During the postwar period, radio remained nearly as important a source of news information as television, but increasingly its programming was devoted to music. As early as 1946, immediately after the war, according to a reliable survey, fully 41 percent of all AM radio programming was recorded music, chiefly of the popular and dance variety. While musical types differed somewhat by region (with country and western more important in the South and West, classical in the East and in major cities), the overall emphasis in music was popular. As the 1950s progressed and radio programming became more specialized, the music programming reflected the growing taste for rock 'n' roll.

In most respects, television programming of the 1950s both reflected and promoted the dominant cultural values of the white middle class. The most popular categories of shows—comedy, drama, and variety—all aimed, one way or another, to capture the attention of this affluent, upwardly mobile social group, clustered largely in the suburbs. The highest ratings fell to comedy, variety, and dramatic shows during the early to mid-1950s, with westerns becoming extremely popular toward the end of the decade. Between October 1958 and April 1959, for instance, western dramas occupied seven out of the ten top spots in the Nielsen ratings, with four of them—"Gunsmoke," "Wagon Train," "Have Gun—Will Travel," and "The Rifleman"—in the top four positions. (The first three maintained these positions for three years running.) These shows reflected conformist patriarchal values, depicting a world divided between right and wrong in which males were always in authority. They also projected Cold War values onto the old frontier: The hero was prepared to fight the enemy at all times.

"I Love Lucy," with Lucille Ball and Desi Arnaz, was the most popular comedy show of the fifties—at #1 in the Nielsen ratings from October 1952 to April 1955, and again from October 1956 to April 1957. It had enormous audience appeal, based largely on the slapstick comic style of its star. In 1952, when Lucille Ball became pregnant in real life, her experience was incorporated into the show in a way that made Lucy's madcap situations seem more human and endearing to her ever-growing audience. It also broke ground in subject matter for network television.

Family comedies like "The Adventures of Ozzie and Harriet," "Father Knows Best," and "Leave It to Beaver" were not among the most popular shows, but they had very loyal audiences and frequently were the shows most watched in their time slots. However, these programs provide a good sense of the idealized "family values" of the period. They have in common a fixation on a largely patriarchal, nuclear family unit in well-to-do suburban settings often quite remote from the real conflicts and tensions of American society of the period. (By contrast, "I Love Lucy" had an urban setting and was never, in the sense in which the term applies to these later developments in programming, "family" comedy.) These were comedy shows for a middle-class white audience, expected to respond to jokes about children, family life, and pet animals. Blacks, when they appeared in such shows, were in traditional servant categories—cook, handyman, maid—not on the same level as the protagonists. The shows also projected a respect for authority, especially that of fathers and the institutions that comprised the social setting of the episodes. Mothers were regularly reduced to scheming behind their husbands' backs or finding some devious means to get what they wanted. The message to children seemed to be that the way to accomplish something in middle-class family life was to seek it indirectly and never to acknowledge your true feelings. The resolution of most problems, with a moral message of special significance to the family unit, would often rest with the father or some other paternal figure in the plot.

TV broadcasting in the informational category accounted for as much as one third of all programming during this period. As such, it became an important element in the political process in the 1950s. TV covered campaigns, provided an increasing amount of advertising for political candidates, and spotlighted important political events that helped to shape public opinion on various issues. One of the first and most important of these was the Kefauver hearings on organized crime in 1950, which elevated a relatively un-known senator from Tennessee into national prominence and sec-ond place on the Democratic ticket in the presidential election campaign of 1952. Another was the Army–McCarthy hearings of 1954, which resulted in the political demise of Senator Joseph Mc-Carthy. Yet another occurred during the political campaign of 1952, when Eisenhower was running for his first term with Richard Nixon as his running mate. Nixon was accused of improperly ac-cepting gifts from wealthy Texas donors and found his political ca-reer at risk. In a speech on national television that came to be known as the "Checkers" speech because of a sentimental refer-ence to the family dog (also a gift), Nixon managed to repudiate his critics and save his political career. The speech showed how influ-ential television could be under such circumstances.

Less fortunate for Nixon, however, were his debates with John F. Kennedy during the 1960 presidential campaign. For the first time, two major presidential candidates faced off in a series of live debates on national television. Kennedy lacked Nixon's advantage of having been the two-term vice president of a popular president, and the further disadvantage of being Roman Catholic and clearly associated with what was called the "Eastern establishment." Fur-thermore, in many respects, despite party differences, Kennedy's positions on the issues were not far removed from those of his op-ponent. However, Kennedy's self-assurance and poise, along with his command of the medium of television, carried the day. In none of the four debates between Richard Nixon and Kennedy did Nixon emerge the victor in the eyes of the viewing public, though the first was especially damaging. (To those who heard the first debate on radio, however, Nixon won.) While not the only deciding factor in a tight race, the debates between the two candidates demonstrated again the potential force of television in opinion shaping.

These debates came at a time when television was trying to demonstrate its worthiness as a medium in the wake of a series of scandals involving one of the more popular categories of program-ming in the late fifties, the quiz show. The most watched program in the season of 1955-56, in fact, was "The $64,000 Question." However, it was revealed that another popular quiz show, "Twenty-One," rigged its results by providing questions in advance to contes-tants. One contestant embarrassed by these disclosures and the dis-honesty they displayed was Charles van Doren, son of a renowned Columbia University professor. Van Doren's public humiliation marked the climax of an episode that made many among the viewing public begin to wonder whether they could trust what they were watching on TV.

PRINT MEDIA IN THE TV AGE

TV's growing popularity and importance notwithstanding, no account of the role of the media in American popular culture should scant the importance of print media, especially the daily newspaper, in determining how people feel on a whole variety of issues. In the same era that saw the growing popularity of TV and the continuing popularity of radio, millions of Americans read newspapers every day in thousands of towns and cities. By the early sixties, these newspapers, of various social and political persuasions, collectively amassed advertising revenues of some $4-5 billion, with subscription revenues of $1.25 billion.

It is possible to argue that the newspaper Americans put by their breakfast coffee or evening dessert had more influence on their opinions than any other segment of the communications media. That influence was not always to be measured merely by circulation figures. A newspaper like the *New York Times*, for instance, had a daily circulation well below that of a tabloid like the *New York Daily News*, but its influence on the course of history in the period covered by this book was more profound.

Besides newspapers, large circulation weekly magazines were also a major influence on public opinion. Magazines like *Life* and *Look* covered major events and also provided "human interest" coverage, feature articles that often increased readers' understanding of the main events of the news. *Life*, which began publication in 1936, was especially noted for its pictorial coverage, while magazines like *Time* and *Newsweek* covered stories in greater depth. The monthly *Reader's Digest* acquired a large readership by reprinting articles from other magazines. It had considerable appeal in what would be called in the sixties "middle America."

The decade of the 1950s also saw the first publication of one of the most popular men's magazines, *Playboy*. The brainchild of a former *Esquire* staffer, Hugh Hefner, *Playboy*, which debuted in late 1953, soon became a symbol of a hedonistic lifestyle that seemed especially well suited to the economic boom of the decade and the leisure time of its more conspicuous consumers. Among so-called "special interest magazines," including many aimed at women, *Playboy* set a trend that others were soon to follow as a new sexual and personal ethos began to define itself. *Playboy* had special appeal to affluent young males.

A major development in book publishing in the postwar period was the increasingly larger paperback market. Paper-covered books had existed for a long time—though, in this country at least, they were primarily reprints. By the late 1930s, mass-market paperback publishers had acquired a large readership nationwide. During the Second World War, paperback books—published according to wartime standards—were widely distributed as reading matter for servicemen. After the war, paperback publishing became a major segment of the book publishing trade, with some authors—like the popular Mickey Spillane, author of the Mike Hammer detective series of the 1950s—achieving sales in the millions.

POPULAR MUSIC: TASTE AND TECHNOLOGY IN THE POSTWAR PERIOD

Popular music of the postwar period, well into the 1950s, reflected the taste of previous decades, and record sales, especially in the late forties, were generally flat. Romantic ballads, dance music (particularly of the "big band" variety common to the thirties and forties), and novelty tunes dominated the charts. Crooners like Frank Sinatra and Bing Crosby, bands like the Dorsey brothers' or Artie Shaw's, and novelty groups like the Spike Jones band were popular favorites. Singers with hit records in the early fifties included such names as Tony Bennett, Rosemary Clooney, Perry Como, Patti Page, Eddie Fisher, Joni James, Dean Martin, and Vic Damone. Featured on the musical and comedy variety shows of radio and early television, the work of these performers and others like them defined the popular music category of the time.

Until the advent of the long-playing vinyl record, popular music was recorded by an electrical process at 78 revolutions per minute (rpm) onto masters from which were pressed shellac disks measuring 10 inches across, with approximately two and a half minutes of music per side. The sound of 78 rpm recordings was often very good, but the surfaces were almost always noisy and the disks themselves highly breakable. Manufacturers—the major ones in this country were RCA Victor, Columbia, Decca, and their subsidiaries—

sometimes experimented with vinyl materials, but generally, in their makeup, 78 rpms remained what they had been since the first disk recordings were introduced in the early years of the century.

The new technology appeared first in the form of 33⅓ rpm vinyl recordings (both 10″ and 12″) introduced by Columbia Records in 1948. The long-playing microgroove recording, as it was called, required a special phonograph Columbia also marketed. RCA Victor countered with its own version of the LP, the 45 rpm disk introduced the following year. This disk measured only seven inches across and had a large hole in its center. Its recording capacity equalled that of the 78 rpm disk, though eventually, in competition with the long-playing Columbia disk, RCA increased it. This later version became known as "Extended Play" (EP). Like Columbia, RCA marketed its own small phonograph with a large spindle on which their seven-inch disks could be played. The 45 disks were color-coded: red for classical, aquamarine for country and western, and so on. Historically, changes in recording technology or packaging have always been accompanied by innovations in players and other marketing ploys.

For a time the two giants competed unsuccessfully for the entire market. Columbia issued a seven-inch version of the LP to compete with the 45, and RCA issued multi-disk albums much as they had for the old 78s. Eventually the issue was resolved with LPs taking the album market and 45s the single, with EPs somewhere in between. The technology of the LP had great importance to the classical music industry, in that whole symphonies and concertos could now be recorded on single disks. As rock music developed in the 1960s, LPs also proved attractive to performers who felt constrained by the old time limits. (An even slower speed—16½ rpm—would serve for the "talking book," another new product of this period.) The 45 became the home of the popular single, for which teenagers of the fifties and sixties were the primary market. Both 45 and 33⅓ rpm recordings were considerably cheaper to record and manufacture than were the old 78s. When the technique of recording masters on tape was perfected with the introduction of Ampex machines in the late forties, the process became even less expensive and at the same time more faithful to the original sound.

In the late forties and early fifties, however, the most important development in popular musical taste actually began on 78s, on small independent labels or offshoots of major ones. It was not the changes in recording technology but the fact that there existed by then a young, affluent buying public eager for new music that explains why, in the first place, rock 'n' roll became what it did. However, its ultimate commercial success on 45s and LPs was also attributable to the need of the recording industry to find a new sound to move its new products. The triumph of this marketing strategy would mark a turning point in the history of American music. With the advent of rock 'n' roll, the locus of power in the music industry would shift from the music publishers, who until that time profited more than anybody else from new music, to the recording industry, which operated through TV and radio networks as well as sales outlets nationwide.

SHAKE, RATTLE, AND ROLL: THE ROCK 'N' ROLL REVOLUTION BEGINS

Much of the early popularity of rock 'n' roll came from the disk jockeys who played recorded music on the air. The very term *rock 'n' roll* (in blues music a synonym for sexual intercourse) was first introduced by a white disk jockey in Cleveland, Ohio. Alan Freed was urged by a friend to begin playing what had hitherto been considered Negro or "race" music on the radio because young white kids were eagerly buying it. In the summer of 1951 Freed started "The Moondog Show" on a 50,000 watt station that reached an audience extending well into the Middle West. Soon other stations began to do the same thing, and, before long, the airwaves were saturated with the sound.

Like other areas of American life, the music world had long been subject to de facto segregation. Music identified as "Negro" was not marketed in white stores nor played on white radio stations. This was particularly true for the category of music called "rhythm and blues" (R & B). Like traditional blues, R & B frequently had lyrics considered too "racy" or sexually explicit for a white audience. It was recorded on independent specialty labels like Chess or King and distributed primarily to stores that had a black clientele. R & B had its own chart of hits separate from the pop and country categories. (*Billboard* magazine, the statistical bible of the music business, had begun charting popular music in 1940.)

Occasionally black artists would make the crossover into the white music world and find acceptance there. Instrumentalists and singers like Louis Armstrong, Nat "King" Cole, Billy Eckstine, and

Lena Horne or vocal groups like the Ink Spots had all been accepted by mainstream white audiences long before rock 'n' roll, but not by performing R & B. The great Louis Jordan would come close, but his version of R & B was partly a variation on the swing style popular in the forties. Straight R & B artists, including the many vocal groups that made up the roster of artists on the small labels, did not find themselves so widely accepted.

Despite the difficulties in hearing or buying it, young white kids were attracted in increasing numbers to black music, and the major draw was the rhythm in R & B. This attraction, felt so strongly by young people who had been brought up to regard such music with suspicion, marked a major turning point in the history of American popular culture. But given the nature of the music and recording business in the early fifties, no black performer was able to popularize the style on a wide scale. What would confirm the music's appeal, solidify its audience, and eventually mainstream it in American musical taste was the emergence of a major white performer who could do R & B.

ELVIS PRESLEY: THE WHITE NEGRO

In 1952, a small-time Memphis musical entrepreneur named Sam Phillips, who had been recording black R & B and straight blues performers for race labels like Chess, formed his own recording company named Sun Records. As a sideline in his studios he created the Memphis Recording Services, where anyone could record a demonstration record for a mere four dollars. In the summer of 1953 a young truck driver named Elvis Presley recorded two songs there. By the following summer, Presley had made other recordings, none completely successful, but by then Phillips had decided that Presley had a voice and manner that should be cultivated. He was, in Phillips' words, "a white man with the Negro sound and the Negro feel."

The breakthrough recording for Presley—and a watershed event in American musical history—was "That's All Right (Mama)," a relatively undistinguished song in blues style by Arthur "Big Boy" Crudup. It was Presley's first hit, followed in 1955 by his recording of Junior Parker's classic "Mystery Train," which became a #1 hit on the country chart.

Presley's background contributed to his feeling for black music. Born in Tupelo, Mississippi, in 1935, deep in the South of de jure segregation, Presley was an only child whose twin brother died at birth. Living close to the poverty line, Presley's family moved to Memphis in 1948, where he attended high school. He also spent time hanging out on Beale Street in the black section of town, where blues performers like B. B. King could be heard. Presley had owned a guitar since his eleventh birthday and was always listening to blues music on the radio and picking out tunes. In Memphis, he got to hear the music firsthand.

Memphis had a significant musical tradition and was the locus of WDIA, the first black-owned and -operated radio station in the South. It was also a city in which race relations were more relaxed than they were in the Deep South. The sound that Presley developed in his first recordings, however, owed as much to country music, the preferred white southern musical form, as it did to black R & B. From this connection came the term sometimes applied to it, "rockabilly."

In fact, an entire group of artists that Sam Phillips gathered together at Sun Records, including Carl Perkins, Jerry Lee Lewis, and the young Johnny Cash, had in common a musical style that mixed in varying degrees elements of blues and country. Presley's Sun recordings epitomize the rockabilly style, with vocals featuring country-style whoops and hollers, lead electric guitar with acoustic backup, and slapstyle bass. Rockabilly can be heard not only in Presley's sides for Sun, but also in Carl Perkins's "Blue Suede Shoes" (1956). This recording made Perkins the first rockabilly artist to cross over from the country to the R & B chart (Presley's version came later). Jerry Lee Lewis's familiar "Whole Lot of Shakin' Goin' On" (1957) is in the same style.

By 1956, Presley had already become a nationally recognized artist. Under the managerial care of Colonel Tom Parker, who had successfully managed country artists like Eddy Arnold and Hank Snow and who fully understood Presley's commercial potential, Presley signed with RCA Victor, which bought his contract from Sun for a mere $35,000 plus $5,000 in back royalties.

What followed was a meteoric rise in popularity, with a long string of hit singles, including (by the end of 1957) nine #1 hits: "Heartbreak Hotel," "I Love You," "Hound Dog," "Don't Be Cruel," "Love Me Tender," "All Shook Up," "(Let Me Be Your) Teddy Bear," "Too Much," and "Jailhouse Rock," the last three of which shared #1 status simultaneously on the pop, country, *and* R & B charts. Presley also began to appear regularly on national television,

Elvis after signing with RCA

including three appearances on Ed Sullivan's, "Toast of the Town" weekly variety show though his pelvic movements (hence the name "Elvis the Pelvis") were so controversial that in his third appearance he was shot only from the waist up. He also began to appear in places like Las Vegas, though initially without success. His first movie role, in *Love Me Tender*, also dates from 1956. It began a series of increasingly popular film ventures for the young singer, with significant financial rewards. Elvis was the first rock 'n' roll performer to become a true movie star, setting a trend which the Beatles and others were to follow in the 1960s. At a later time in his career, when he had abandoned public appearances, it was movies and recordings that sustained his popularity with the public.

At the crest of this enormous wave of popularity, Presley was drafted into the U.S. Army in December of 1957, though his period of service did not begin until March of the following year. Recordings continued to be released during his two years as a soldier, but the career of Presley after his army service was to prove somewhat different from what came before.

What did Presley bring to American music? First of all, it is important to judge that contribution on the basis of his entire career. However, if by chance that career had stopped in 1958, his contribution would still have been enormous. Presley was not a singer-songwriter of the kind to become more standard in American music by the mid-1960s. However, he did much more than simply perform songs that black musicians had done better, a practice all too common among many white singers. Whatever Presley sang, he shaped to his own artistic requirements. His source material included R & B, gospel, and country, sometimes fused skillfully into a single mix. His very earliest recordings were an irresistible and highly original blend of these elements. They created and defined the rockabilly style and set a new standard for the romantic ballad.

Elvis's performing manner—spontaneous, flamboyant, frankly sensual—was easily as important to American music as his singing. It served to liberate white performers from their cultural straitjacket. It also made it possible for more black musicians to be accepted on their own terms by the way it popularized their moves, and their music, for a wider audience. Finally, it struck a chord with young white kids who themselves were seeking a form of liberation, personal and sexual, that they had not yet completely defined. Elvis's very look, with long hair trained back in a ducktail, sideburns, tight jeans, and leather jacket, personified the "bad boy" look sought by so many young males of the late fifties. In short, the performing style and personal appearance of Elvis Presley marked a significant turning point in the cultural life of this country, after which nothing was ever quite the same again.

COVERS AND CROSSOVERS: ROCK 'N' ROLL HITS THE CHARTS

Rockabilly would not remain important for long in this country, though it was to have a more extended life in England. Presley himself largely abandoned it after he began to record for RCA. In its purest form, it was regional, southern, white. Groups like Bill Haley and the Comets would achieve enormous success with songs like "Shake, Rattle and Roll" (1954) and "Rock Around the Clock" (in the 1955 release), both basically rockabilly in style (Haley had begun as a country musician). However, the dominant rock 'n' roll style in the late fifties and early sixties was something else: a blander, more homogenized version by white musicians—some of extremely modest talent—of music first written, performed, and recorded by blacks. In the process, lyrics were toned down and performing styles modified to suit the assumed requirements of a white audience. It was in fact an old story, though one soon to be revised: appropriation of the work of black musicians for the profit of whites.

"Cover" records were already common by the year Elvis did his version of Crudup's "That's All Right (Mama)." A *cover* is a version of a song not performed by the artist who originally recorded it. Some covers may actually improve on their originals, though, in the period we are discussing, this didn't happen very often. Haley and the Comets' "Shake, Rattle and Roll" was a cover of a song written and first recorded by black blues musician "Big" Joe Turner. Pat Boone, one of the most popular white singers of the fifties, covered songs by Fats Domino ("Ain't That a Shame," #1 in 1955), Ivory Joe Hunter ("I Almost Lost My Mind," #1 in 1956), and many others. Popular singer Georgia Gibbs, also white, took LaVern Baker's "Tweedle Dee" (for which Baker sued), and Kitty Kallen took the Dominoes' "Little Things Mean a Lot." Elvis was as guilty as anybody else, though he did more with the material than most. Of his best-known early recordings, not only "That's All Right" and "Mystery Train," but also "Good Rocking Tonight" and, most popular of all, "Hound Dog" were covers of music first recorded by black artists.

While this practice was in some respects deplorable, two things can be said in its defense. First, duplication of this sort was common. Competitive versions of the same song frequently appeared among white performers, often in the form of "crossovers," songs that moved from one hit chart to another. In his study of the emergence of rock 'n' roll in American music, Philip Ennis documents the phenomenon extensively. In 1950, for instance, there were *eight* versions of the popular song "Rag Mop" on the pop, R & B, and country charts, *seven* versions of "Mona Lisa" on the same three charts, *seven* versions of "Goodnight, Irene" on the same three charts, and so on. There were so many, in fact, that it is difficult to ascertain which were "covers" and which originals. Two-market crossovers were even more common. With the exception of songs on the R & B chart, virtually all of these competing versions were recorded by white artists.

A second, and more important, defense of the practice of covers is that it fed the growing taste for the rock 'n' roll sound and eventually led listeners back to the originals. One sign that this was happening occurred in 1954 when the Chords's popular R & B number "Sh-Boom" (an example of what was called "doo-wop," because its lyrics consisted of sounds, not words) became a #1 hit on the pop chart of 1954 in the cover version by a white group, the Crewcuts. (Direct crossovers occurred as early as 1951, though a more significant one was 1953's "Crying in the Chapel" by the Orioles, which moved from first place on the R & B chart to #11 on the pop chart.)

The development of Top Forty radio—programming that emphasized the most popular music of the day—was critical to the growing taste for rock 'n' roll. The efforts of Alan Freed (who moved from Cleveland to New York in 1954 to become a disk jockey—first at WINS, then at WABC) and other pioneers brought the attention of the young white audience to the work of black musicians by playing their music and also by providing these musicians with the opportunity for personal appearances on their shows. In 1955, Freed was to hold his first Rock 'n' Roll Party stage show at the St. Nicholas Arena in New York, bringing in some 15,000 people to hear the likes of Joe Turner, Fats Domino (a black musician from New Orleans who achieved his own crossover popularity in the late fifties with songs like "Blueberry Hill" and "I'm Walkin'"), as well as various black vocal groups. The audience for these events was racially mixed. This was not unique in New York and certain other major cities by this date, but was far from standard nationwide. These events would anticipate the large venue concerts to become popular in the sixties, but, more immediately (like the coffeehouse circuit popular with the beats), they would give many white kids their first exposure on a direct, personal level to blacks. Freed also became involved in a number of film ventures that added to the growing list of movies featuring black artists. In 1956 he went national (on CBS) with his radio show, "Rock 'n' Roll Dance Party."

Freed's career was to end tragically, however, after the so-called "Payola" investigations beginning in 1960. These congressional inquiries into payments to disk jockeys by record companies and promoters, part of the new commercial alliance between the recording and broadcasting industries, followed on the revelations about major scandals on broadcast quiz shows. Freed was fired from WABC for refusing to testify to the matter and later faced legal action from, among others, the Internal Revenue Service. He died in 1965 at the age of 43.

Another major force among disk jockeys, still active in the music world today, was Dick Clark, whose "American Bandstand" show was to become a television staple from the late 1950s on. Debuting on ABC in 1957, Clark's show featured teenagers dancing to recorded music as guest artists performed or lip-synched their own music. "American Bandstand" made an important contribution to the growing popularity of rock 'n' roll among white teenagers. Although the teenagers featured on the show were white, the musical guests were frequently black. "The Dick Clark Saturday Night Show," a spinoff of the weekly late afternoon show, debuted the following year. Like Alan Freed, Clark also faced payola charges, but, by selling out his interests in various record companies, he gave himself a clean bill before his appearance to testify.

While disk jockeys like Freed and Clark were popularizing rock 'n' roll on the airwaves, a growing number of white musicians were adopting the idiom of R & B in their own compositions. In this trend, one of the true groundbreakers was Buddy Holly.

Buddy Holly and the Crickets had a career of only two years, from 1957 to 1959, when Holly was killed in an airplane accident. Their music, their instrumentation, and their technique of recording had a major influence on future developments in rock 'n' roll, as did Holly's singing style, partly derived from Elvis Presley's. While basically a rockabilly group when they first started, the Crickets soon moved away from that style in their own musical direction. First of all, they did their own compositions, some of which have become rock standards (for instance "Peggy Sue" and their first hit, "That'll Be the Day"). They used two guitars, electric and acoustic, in the rockabilly manner. With additional bass and drums, they created a lineup of instruments that set a standard. They experimented with studio recording techniques, including *double tracking* (using more than one track to produce the recorded sound) and other devices soon to be popular. Holly's vocal style, which moved from normal tones to very high (falsetto) and included hiccups and other rockabilly mannerisms, influenced countless vocalists after him, including Bob Dylan and Paul McCartney.

However, such innovations notwithstanding, the more typical rock 'n' roll music of the late fifties and early sixties was somewhat less exciting. There were the teen idols, many of them imitators of Elvis, singers like Frankie Avalon and Bobby Darin and Bobby Rydell and Fabian and Pat Boone (who had 38 Top Forty hits, many of them covers, in the mid-fifties), who were attractive to their audience as much for their looks as for their singing ability. Ricky Nelson, of TV's "Adventures of Ozzie and Harriet" fame, was one of the first of these teen idols, singing on the Nelson show beginning in 1957. (Though he was originally grouped in the pretty boy category, Nelson eventually became a respected musician whose style fell fundamentally into the rockabilly track.)

There were the girl groups of the early sixties—the Shangri-Las, the Shirelles, the Ronettes, and others—who produced an appealingly innocent sound and sang simple songs about high school sweethearts and loves lost to their friends or to car and motorcycle crashes. There were the dance crazes—especially the one that grew out of Chubby Checker's "The Twist" (1961). There was the surfer sound, from California, with its guitar riffs heavily derived from those of black rock 'n' roll musician Chuck Berry (whose "Maybelline" launched his career in 1955), celebrating the surfer lifestyle. Surfer rock was first popularized by Jan and Dean, whose number one hit "Surf City" appeared in 1963. Later the Beach Boys, headed up by Brian Wilson (who co-wrote "Surf City") would prove to be the most important single group associated with this style, with hits like "I Get Around" (1964), "California Girls" (1965), and the highly original "Good Vibrations" (1966). But these songs take us, as they took the Beach Boys, into new terrain that belongs more to the sixties than it does to the fifties. By that point, the commercial viability of rock 'n' roll was firmly established, and the shift in power from the music publishers to the recording and broadcasting industries (often, as in the case of RCA Victor, the same) was complete.

JAZZ AND FOLK IN THE FIFTIES

Two more categories of music were important to many young people in the fifties, though they were less commercially potent than rock 'n' roll. One of these was jazz, which, like rock 'n' roll, was in most respects a black musical form, both in origin and in practice.

Jazz grew from the same roots as rock 'n' roll, beginning in New Orleans around the turn of the century, then spreading to cities like Memphis, St. Louis, Kansas City, and Chicago, all of which developed their own distinctive jazz styles. Fundamental to jazz musical structure, as to rock 'n' roll, was the blues, a 12-bar musical form in which one line of the lyric is repeated (A-A-B) against a progression of three chords in a tonic-subdominant-dominant sequence. The second stanza from the traditional "Joe Turner Blues" illustrates the lyric pattern:

He come wid fo'ty links of chain *Oh Lawdy*   (A)

Come wid fo'ty links of chain *Oh Lawdy*   (A)

Got my man an' gone   (B)

Almost from the first, jazz music was attractive to white musicians (among the earliest jazz recordings are those of the so-called Original Dixieland Jazz Band, an all-white group recorded in New York in 1917 and 1918), who appreciated its rhythmic drive and creative spirit. Those most appreciative included classical composers as well, names like Ravel, Stravinsky, and Shostakovich abroad, and, in this country, Virgil Thomson and Aaron Copland, who were equally attracted to the idiom.

By the mid-1940s, small group jazz, overshadowed in the thirties by the big bands, once again became popular among jazz musicians and their audience. It was in these small combos that so-called "modern jazz" was born and the work of important musicians like alto saxophonist Charlie Parker and pianist Thelonious Monk was recorded.

In the 1950s, many young white people, especially college students and young professionals living in urban America, were attracted to this music and followed it closely on record and in concert. Several popular TV series, including the detective show "Peter Gunn," with a jazz-based theme by Henry Mancini, featured jazz music regularly, as did Steve Allen (himself a jazz pianist), first host of NBC's "Tonight" show. By the 1950s, jazz music had also become fully interracial, at least in the North, and so had its audience. This was an important development in American music at a time when many other aspects of musical life still remained segregated.

Jazz music of the modern or "cool" school was also the preferred musical form of the beats. In the coffeehouses of San Francisco and Chicago and New York, where members of the beat generation gathered to read their poetry and rap, jazz was frequently played live or in recorded form. The fundamental improvisatory style of jazz performance became an inspiration for writers like Kerouac, who claimed that he created his novels as the jazz musicians did their music, never revising, taking it as it came.

Another popular musical form among the beats, and generally among the political left, was folk music. The link between folk music and populism was forged early in the century, during the labor union movement, and continued into the period of the Depression, from which a number of major folk singers and composers emerged. Chief among these was Woody Guthrie, son of a poor Oklahoma family, who left home at an early age to roam the country and write and perform folk music, including the well-known "This Land Is Your Land."

Guthrie eventually settled in New York and became acquainted with Pete Seeger, the son of a Columbia University musicologist. Together, Guthrie and Seeger were to have a major influence on the development of folk music in the forties, fifties, and early sixties. They found themselves blacklisted during the McCarthy era—that is to say, prevented from performing because of their Communist sympathies—in spite of the popularity of a number of songs recorded by Seeger's group, the Weavers, including "On Top of Old Smoky" and "Goodnight, Irene."

The association of folk music with political radicalism was to carry over into the sixties and the music of Phil Ochs, Joan Baez, and Bob Dylan, on whom Guthrie exerted a great influence, together with other young folk musicians. Furthermore, the popular success of the Weavers in the early 1950s anticipated a significant general revival of interest in folk music by the end of the decade.

Harry Smith's "Anthology of American Folk Music," issued by Folkways Records in 1952, was one major reason for this revival. Fundamentally a collection of personal favorites of Smith, who was a folklorist and anthropologist, this collection revealed to young folk musicians then developing their own personal styles the breadth and depth of American music in this idiom. Among those to feel most deeply the music in this collection were Dylan, Baez, and Ochs.

HOLLYWOOD: THE HUAC INVESTIGATIONS AND THE DECLINE OF THE STUDIO SYSTEM

Just as music and the communications media reflected numerous changes in American life occurring in the period after the Second World War, so did movies. Long associated with the name of Hollywood and certain major studios like Metro-Goldwyn-Mayer, Twentieth Century Fox, and Warner Brothers Pictures, the film industry in the postwar era began to move in new directions partly in response to the competition posed by the developing medium of television, partly in response to social demographics and political threats. The result, by the decade of the 1960s, was a significantly changed industry in which actors, writers, producers, and directors were able to operate with a greater degree of independence, both economic and artistic, than they had ever been able to achieve under the old studio system. But, as a result of McCarthyism, there were still stringent political limits to this independence.

Under the terms of the studio system, developed in the 1920s and 1930s, movie personnel, from actors to writers and directors, were under contract to studios that oversaw all aspects of their careers and even, in the case of the biggest stars, their personal lives. While the financial rewards from such arrangements were great, so were the limitations on freedom to pursue independent projects or personal whims.

Supporting this system were networks of fan clubs, movie magazines, and film distributors which saw to the publicizing and showing of the film projects of the major studios. One of the greatest fears of many actors and directors was that somehow their work would become so unpopular that they would no longer be considered important to the studio they depended on for their livelihoods. Very few could operate independently of such concerns. For everybody in the industry, the gradual shift in funding to eastern banks and investors in the postwar period only increased the feelings of insecurity.

For this reason, the investigations of Hollywood launched by the House Unamerican Activities Committee (actually, the House

Committee on Un-American Activities) in 1947 were especially threatening. HUAC, the first congressional committee to become prominent during the postwar Red scare, included some of the most openly racist and deeply conservative congressmen, among them the young Richard Nixon, whose pursuit of Alger Hiss, a State Department functionary accused of Communist connections, became a *cause célèbre* in 1948. The Hollywood investigations began in 1947, when the Red scare was reaching its height. As a result of HUAC's investigations, ten major Hollywood figures, including a number of prominent screenwriters, were blacklisted. "The Ten," as they were called, ultimately faced prison terms for contempt of Congress and a loss of employment extending over many years.

Although the Ten were defended by some of the most prominent Hollywood stars, including such names as Humphrey Bogart and Katharine Hepburn, in the end conformity prevailed. The message was clear: Cooperate or you may lose your job. In the second wave of investigations, during the McCarthy period in the early fifties, many film people caved in to the demands of the committee and their studios and provided names and other information sought by investigators. Among these was one of the best known and most successful directors of both films and stage plays in the postwar era, Elia Kazan. In the end, some 200 people were blacklisted, some on the flimsiest of evidence. In addition to destroying careers, this episode in Hollywood's history virtually eliminated the possibility of doing films that questioned the social or political order. The studios, fearful of government censorship or restrictions, censored themselves heavily thereafter. All the media felt the impact of the HUAC/McCarthy campaigns, which led to a decline in the range of issues open for political debate in any form. In the more liberal political atmosphere that developed by the late sixties and early seventies, scars that had not healed from the blacklisting period contributed to the ultimate demise of the studio system.

The studio system weakened itself by its actions during the blacklisting period and afterwards, but other developments external to the industry were also important in the changes that came. Principal among these was the development of the television industry, which, for the first time, brought a form of entertainment and information based on visual imagery directly into the home.

Movie attendance, which had reached a peak in the mid-1940s, by the next decade had begun to slide noticeably as a result of TV. In 1946, a total of 467 new releases brought 90 million patrons into the nation's theaters each week with an average ticket price of 40¢. Box office receipts totalled $1.692 billion, or 1.5 percent of all corporate profits in the United States. By 1957, 533 new releases brought only 45 million people into the theaters every week—a drop of one half in attendance in slightly more than a decade. Receipts were also down, despite the fact that ticket prices were higher. At an average 51¢ per ticket, receipts came to $1.126 billion, which represented, in the burgeoning economy of the period, a much smaller share of corporate profits than in the mid-1940s.

As movie attendance declined, the industry tried various ploys to bring people back. One of these—which began in Camden, New Jersey, in 1934, but soon spread nationwide—was the drive-in theater. Located in areas outside of the cities, convenient to the new subdivisions, these theaters, with their rows of parking spaces each with its own speaker system, became popular throughout the country in the postwar period, taking away more and more of the audience that used to go to the large downtown movie "palaces." Popularly nicknamed "passion pits," drive-ins were favorite make-out places for teenagers who found they could do a lot more than just watch movies in the comparative privacy of their cars. A second area of expansion of the movie industry in response to declining attendance was the suburban shopping mall, which, by the 1960s, began to feature movie theaters along with other stores and ser-

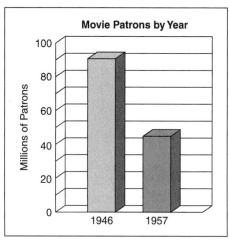

Movie attendance shrinks as TV triumphs
(Source of data: Gene Brown, *Movie Time*, 1995)

vices. By 1964, there were some 7,600 shopping centers throughout the United States.

Another important response was technological. Hollywood began using technicolor more than ever before (television in the fifties was limited to black and white) and also began filming in Cinemascope, a widescreen film process especially well suited to epic-style films. Another experiment, largely unsuccessful, was 3-D movies, for which the audience was obliged to wear special glasses for the three-dimensional effect.

MOVIE GENRES AND POSTWAR POLITICS

Few changes occurred in the kinds of movies that were being made, however. The genres of popular film were fixed long before. Family dramas, romantic comedies, war films (especially important in the 1940s), westerns and crime stories, musical comedies, cartoons, and biblical or historical epics were the standard ones. Subgenres, often the products of the lesser studios like Monogram or Republic Pictures, included science fiction, horror films, serials, and short features. Television would imitate most of this subject matter in its own programming. In the fifties especially, it would carve out a special niche (one of the most innovative aspects of early TV programming) in live comedy and drama, where some major stars and writers would get their start.

"Serious" Hollywood films tended to be conservative, reflecting the dominant trends of postwar American politics. One group of films from the late forties and early fifties dramatized the anticommunism which by then had become a major political force. These included *The Iron Curtain* (1948), *I Married a Communist* (1949), and *I Was a Communist for the FBI* (1951), all of which came from major studios and featured well-known stars. These films stressed the sinister quality of the Communist "movement" and its willingness to do anything to achieve its ends.

War films supported the argument for a strong defense being voiced by many in Congress and throughout the nation that was to result in the arms buildup of the fifties and sixties. During the Second World War, a huge wave of patriotic films was released in support of the war effort. This trend continued after the war with films such as *Command Decision* (1948) and *Sands of Iwo Jima* (1949).

Adapted from a stage play, the first of these featured a large cast headed by the popular Clark Gable. It stressed the difficulties the military faced during the Second World War in achieving strategic goals because of their necessary dealings with politicians. *Sands of Iwo Jima* starred the popular John Wayne and dramatized the war actions of the Marines in the Pacific theater. *Strategic Air Command* (1955), starring the equally popular James Stewart (himself a brigadier general in the Air Force), issued at the height of the Cold War period, presented an inside picture of the main nuclear strike force of the United States. Patriotic in theme and propagandistic in intent, it showed this country poised to attack the enemy in Moscow.

Less common in the 1950s were films showing the negative side of war, either real or projected. Two such films came from the hand of one major director, Stanley Kubrick—*Paths of Glory* (1957) and *On the Beach* (1959). The first of these, a strong statement of an antiwar theme, is set during the First World War. The second, based on a popular novel by Nevil Chute, takes place after a major nuclear attack. The latter film was criticized when it was released for the way it minimized the effect of nuclear war, but, in a period when civil defense was a major thrust and schoolchildren were taught to lie under their desks to protect themselves against such an attack, *On the Beach* suggested that any defense against nuclear war was ultimately ineffective.

Strange objects or attacks from outer space provided the subject matter for another group of films that became popular during the fifties. From very early in the history of film, science fiction subjects had appealed to filmmakers because of the capacity the medium provided for creating the illusion of space. The special effects possible in filmmaking by the fifties encouraged the making of such escapist films, and their plots often had Cold War overtones.

George Pal's *When Worlds Collide* (1951), one of the best of these films in terms of its special effects, is based on the premise of an imminent disaster: A planet from another solar system has penetrated our universe and is about to crash into the earth. In *The Thing from Another World* (1951), scientists at a research station in the Arctic discover a spacecraft buried in the ice. When they bring the frozen pilot back to their station and he thaws out, disaster strikes. In *It Came from Outer Space* (1953), a mysterious fireball comes down near a mine. Mysteriously, people who have contact with the strange object return behaving in strange ways, clearly affected by their contact with aliens.

The War of the Worlds (1953), based on the classic science fiction novel by H. G. Wells, premises an alien invasion that is stopped only by a common virus to which the invaders are not immune. Like *When Worlds Collide*, this was a film notable for the quality and scope of its special effects. Wells's novel had also served as the basis of a famous radio dramatization of 1938 by Orson Welles and the Mercury Theater. Mass hysteria occurred among its listeners when people thought they were hearing actual reports of an alien invasion. In *Them!* (1954), cities in the southwestern United States are threatened by gigantic mutant ants which have developed as the result of nuclear tests in the Nevada desert.

These films and others in the same genre reflected many of the preoccupations and fears of the Cold War period. The social concerns of the same period are dramatized in another, more realistic set of films reflecting the growing sense that American youth had entered a troubled phase.

NEW KIDS ON THE BLOCK: HOLLYWOOD AND THE NEW YOUTH CULTURE

With juvenile delinquency a major social concern of the 1950s and with a major youth audience to play to, Hollywood began to give serious attention to the new American youth culture by the middle of the decade. Because conservatives often linked juvenile delinquency, like the growing taste for rock 'n' roll, to "international communism," movie makers trod cautiously, especially in the wake of the HUAC investigations. Nonetheless, 1954 saw the release of *The Wild One* with Marlon Brando, who in the same year turned in an outstanding performance in Elia Kazan's exposé of labor union corruption in *On the Waterfront*.

Set in California, where motorcycle gangs like the notorious Hell's Angels had begun to attract attention, *The Wild One* tells the story of one such gang, the Black Rebels. They crash a motorcycle race, steal a trophy, and then ride into a small town where their presence creates uneasiness and fear. When another motorcycle gang (the Beetles) rides in later on, trouble breaks out, and with it the violence always associated with such groups. Though the stated intent of the film was not to glorify them, audience sympathy is clearly directed toward the gangs. As in Hollywood biblical epics, where sadism was allowed in the name of religion, *The Wild One* sensationalizes its subject while pretending to view it critically.

The local bar is owned by the sheriff, who is only too eager to sell the Rebels drinks, and a romantic subplot develops between Johnny (Brando's character) and the sheriff's daughter, who works at the restaurant behind the bar. At one point someone asks Johnny what he's rebelling against. "What've you got?" he replies. With certain overtones of the western film—especially the kind that romanticizes the outlaw—*The Wild One* was extremely popular with younger moviegoers, particularly teenagers, when it was released.

The Blackboard Jungle (1955) was notable in music history of the fifties for being the first film to use a rock 'n' roll number as theme music. "Rock Around the Clock" by Bill Haley and the Comets is played at the beginning and end of the film. It later became the first such soundtrack number to become a national hit. Based on a novel by Evan Hunter, the movie deals with the problems of juvenile delinquents in an urban, all-male high school to which an idealistic young teacher (Glenn Ford) comes, hoping to reach out to such students. In dealing with this theme, *Blackboard Jungle* is the first of a number of films to be made in succeeding years showing the problems teachers face in dealing with troubled adolescents. In a prominent role as one of the students in the class, Vic Morrow (as West) shows the pathology of delinquent behavior while Richard Dadier (Ford), though he occasionally loses his self-control, proves the redemptive power of sincerity and patience. The young Sidney Poitier—who would become the leading African-American film actor of his generation—also plays a key role. As Miller, he ultimately comes to the defense of Dadier when he is attacked by West and one of his goons. Generically, *The Blackboard Jungle* has roots in films about New York gang life in the Depression era (for instance, *Angels with Dirty Faces* [1938], featuring Leo Gorcey and Huntz Hall as the East Side Kids, later known as the Bowery Boys). However, it does a serious, in fact, sometimes preachy, take on this subject suitable to the new concern of the 1950s with deviant behavior among American youth.

The most important Hollywood film of the fifties to deal with teenage rebellion was also one that helped to create an enormous popular following for its male lead. *Rebel Without a Cause* (1955) with James Dean, from Warner Brothers, became the first major statement from Hollywood on the subject of middle-class delinquency.

Dean's emotional intensity as an actor epitomized the naturalistic American style of "method" acting also practiced by Marlon Brando. Dean's brooding good looks, his comparative youth (he was only 24 when *Rebel* appeared), and his tragically short career have made him into one of the major cult figures in recent American movie history, inspiring a posthumous adulation comparable to that bestowed in the silent era on the popular Rudolph Valentino, who also died prematurely. As Jim Trask in *Rebel*, Dean gave a whole generation of white teenagers a character whose frustrations with life they could all too easily identify with. Elvis Presley idolized Dean in this role and reputedly saw the film a dozen or more times.

The language of the trailer, or preview, for *Rebel* made it clear that the film was not about the social outcasts of *The Wild One* or the lower-class slum kids of *Blackboard Jungle*. "Teenage terror torn from today's headlines," it began, "Warner Bros.' challenging drama of today's juvenile violence! . . . and they both [Dean's character and Judy, played by Natalie Wood] came from 'good' families!"

Sensitive to the fact that they were dealing in controversial subject matter, and anxious to avoid the charge of outright sensationalism, Warner Brothers gave the film a long preview in addition to the standard one in which Dean, then making his final film, was interviewed. (Dean was to die in an automobile accident just after completing his role in George Stevens's *Giant*, based on the novel by Edna Ferber.) At one point, as this preview begins, the commentator remarks that this movie is about teenagers who live in houses like these, as the camera pans outside to give the audience a view of a middle-class suburban subdivision of the kind by then common throughout the country.

The story, however, is set in a decidedly upper-middle-class suburb near Los Angeles, where Jim and his parents have just moved, apparently as a result of some never-detailed trouble of Jim's at their previous residence. In his effort to fit into the affluent neighborhood, Jim tries to befriend Judy, but, though attracted to him, she is constrained by peer pressure from her group. He is befriended, however, by another outcast, Plato (Sal Mineo), and ultimately the three of them, including Judy, who now sees Jim for what he is, form a triad that tries for a short time at least to live by its own code until reality, in the form of angry peers and the police, intervenes.

In developing the relationship between Jim and his parents, the film suggests that one of Jim's major problems is that his father (Jim Backus, a comic actor who here takes a serious role) is weak and passive in his relationship with Jim's mother. In one of the strongest scenes of the film, as Jim begs his father to tell him what to do and the older man does not come through, it is clear that the idea of paternal authority is the issue. In fact, nowhere in the film is adult authority seen as positive or even influential in any way in the lives of the youthful characters, with the exception of the juvenile officer (Edward Platt), who shows an interest in Jim's problems early in the film, and Plato's mother's black maid.

In possibly the most famous scene of the film, just before the confrontation with his father, Jim is forced to take part in a game of "chicken" (two cars driven at top speed toward a cliff at the edge of the sea, with the loser the one who jumps out first) in competition with Judy's current boyfriend. This game, which leads to the boyfriend's death, dramatizes both the kind of peer pressure felt by many adolescents in their daily lives and also the ultimate futility of many of their pastimes. For Jim, for Plato (from a divorced family in which he is given material but not emotional sustenance), and for Judy (who has, by implication, a sublimated incestuous relationship with her father), nothing has any meaning except the possible happiness to be gained from personal relationships.

In the melodramatic conclusion to the film, Plato, gone berserk and in possession of a handgun, is mistakenly gunned down by the police, and Jim and Judy are left with only themselves and whatever love they can sustain to face the world. The note of reconciliation with their parents that one might expect is barely suggested as the last scene fades from view. They are both rebels without a cause.

If the purpose of *Rebel Without a Cause* was to draw attention to a social problem and treat it seriously, the romantic ending of the film seems somewhat implausible. At the same time, however, it suggests in fairly strong terms that the problems of many adolescents are caused by their parents' lack of values, not their own. It also manages to dramatize effectively in many scenes the strength and influence of peer relationships among teenagers of the day. Once these kids found a cause, as many did in the 1960s, their rebellion would take more specific forms.

In the end, the popular arts and media suggest a probable truth: that the culture of the 1950s was not entirely the uniform thing it is sometimes described as being. The tone of American life, including its popular culture, was certainly more conservative in most respects than it was to prove in the sixties. Nonetheless, the 1950s provided a greater sense of variety than is sometimes supposed, though the pressures toward consensus and conformity were strong and the appreciation of minority rights modest at best. At any rate, it is difficult to imagine anything that occurred in the 1960s having happened as it did without the historical and cultural events preceding it in the 1950s.

Chapter 3

—

"WE SHALL OVERCOME": THE CIVIL RIGHTS MOVEMENT AND THE EARLY SIXTIES

The United States of the postwar period aspired to a national consensus, but the failure to provide adequate minority rights fractured that effort. The civil rights movement proved that the American dream was still limited primarily to whites. The early sixties would see the movement expand to include college students, black and white, who adhered to the principles of nonviolence espoused by the Reverend Martin Luther King, Jr. The same period would also see the emergence of an alternative approach known as black separatism, with Black Muslim leader Malcolm X as its primary spokesperson. Instead of the integration sought by King and the Southern Christian Leadership Conference, Malcolm proposed separation from the white community and, when necessary, violent action. After the assassination of John Kennedy, his successor, Lyndon Johnson, would push through Congress the most significant civil rights legislation in American history. Coverage of the civil rights movement by television proved to be one of the key factors in building public support for the African-American cause. It created sympathy and caused serious questioning of American democracy by many members of the white community, especially its young people.

Their questioning was soon reflected in American popular music, as the folk music revival took up the protest themes of the civil rights movement. Bob Dylan, Phil Ochs, Joan Baez, and others wrote and sang about the injustices faced by African Americans. Also as a result of the civil rights movement, black musicians and composers found themselves in a more favorable position than ever before in the American musical scene. One important measure of their progress was the formation of Motown Records in 1962. Motown was to become the most successful black-owned and -operated music business in the history of American popular music. Meanwhile, Hollywood dealt only minimally with the political and social transformations taking place in American society. One positive development, however, was the emergence of major African-American stars like Sidney Poitier, and another was the filming of Harper Lee's novel of segregation in the South of the Depression years, To Kill a Mockingbird.

The presidential election of 1960 brought to office a Democratic cold warrior. In a close contest, John Fitzgerald Kennedy, 43, became the youngest president ever elected and the first Roman Catholic to hold the office. By concentrating attention on votes in heavily populated states and urban areas, he squeaked by Nixon. In all, Kennedy took some 70 percent of Catholic and black voters with him.

He headed a party already facing major differences over domestic policies. Especially problematic for Kennedy would be the civil rights movement. Ever since 1948, the Democrats had been seriously divided on the segregation issue. In that election, in response to the generous civil rights plank approved for the Democratic platform, Strom Thurmond of South Carolina mounted a third-party campaign opposed to desegregation. Kennedy's success with black voters stemmed in part from his party's platform support for civil rights, though, as a senator, Kennedy had never taken strong positions on this issue. In general, his political record was conservative.

KENNEDY'S NEW FRONTIER AND THE CIVIL RIGHTS MOVEMENT

During the campaign, however, Kennedy and his brother Robert intervened on the behalf of Martin Luther King, Jr., who had been jailed in Georgia on a phony charge. As a result, King became a strong supporter of the Democratic ticket. As president, however, Kennedy would have to deal with senior southern politicians of his own party who held key committee posts in the House and Senate. This was to prove a major difficulty for him during the slightly more than one thousand days that comprised his term in office. His choice of vice president—Lyndon Johnson, a Texan with extensive experience in politics and the former speaker of the House—would prove to be of some help.

The tone of Kennedy's presidency was set in his often quoted inaugural address, in which he exhorted his fellow Americans to ask not what their country could do for them, but what they could do for their country. This theme of service and dedication had a Cold War context in Kennedy's speech (as did the entire concept of the New Frontier), but it struck home with many who had not found the second term of Kennedy's predecessor especially inspiring. Kennedy was not only young, he was also handsome, energetic, charismatic, and something of a war hero. With his young wife Jacqueline and their children Caroline and John, he brought to the White House a sense of common purpose which the older Eisenhower, popular as he was, had not been able to sustain through the second term of his presidency.

Young people were especially drawn to Kennedy, in part because of his age, but also because he seemed to speak for the young when he discussed the challenges posed by the age. For women, he created a Commission on the Status of Women, whose work resulted in part in the Equal Pay Act of 1963. He was also adept at attracting to his administration an intelligent, highly talented group of people who seemed to share his sense of optimism and opportunity. He was soon to make commitments to the exploration of space, in particular the Apollo project, which ended with the first human presence on the moon, and to the Peace Corps, a creative venture, a positive result of the Cold War that is still in existence, through which Americans were sent abroad, especially to developing countries, to give assistance however they could.

In most respects, however, Kennedy's worldview was shaped by the same forces that had determined the United States's foreign policy throughout the postwar period. He believed firmly in the theory of containment that had led to the war in Korea under Truman and the less serious action against Lebanon under Eisenhower in 1958. Shortly after taking office, Kennedy agreed to a C.I.A.-led guerrilla-style attack on Cuba that was supposed to result in the overthrow of the government of Fidel Castro, which had become increasingly anti-American—and pro-Soviet—since the overthrow of Castro's dictatorial predecessor Batista in 1959. The result—known as the Bay of Pigs invasion (April 1961)—was a major fiasco. The projected internal support for the guerrillas never materialized, and Kennedy had to take the blame for a significant failure.

Nonetheless, his policy and that of his administration remained strongly anticommunist. This commitment showed itself in August 1961, when the Soviets began construction of the wall which was to separate the Eastern and Western sectors of Berlin for nearly 30 years. Kennedy recognized the right of the Soviets to protect their own borders, but made it clear with a token force that the United States would resist any encroachment upon the Western sector of Berlin. In October 1962, Kennedy faced his worst foreign policy crisis when missile sites were detected in Cuba, only some 90 miles from mainland United States. Nine tactical missiles equipped with nuclear warheads were nearly operational. In a war of nerves with the Soviets, who were sending by ship equipment vital to the final deployment of these missiles, the United States came closer to nuclear war than at any other time in history. In general, public opinion supported Kennedy's actions, which were consistent with previous Cold War strategy in United States foreign policy. More than that, his actions were more restrained than many of his advisers had recommended. Nonetheless, the incident had brought the world to the very brink of nuclear holocaust over a very questionable issue.

Although Vietnam was not the centerpiece of United States foreign policy as it was to become later in the 1960s, it was a matter of major concern to Kennedy. In Vietnam, Kennedy's administration supported the pro-Western regime of the dictatorial Ngo Dinh Diem and escalated the involvement of the United States there by providing "advisers"—some 10,000 by 1962—to help the Diem forces in their fight against the guerrilla forces of the communist-led National Liberation Front. These South Vietnamese guerrillas were supported by Communist North Vietnam under the political leadership of Ho Chi Minh. What Kennedy's position would have been in the long term on Vietnam is not certain, but his belief in the domino theory—that, one by one, communist governments or countries would try to take over Asia—is very clear. This led him to agree, in his last year in office, to the overthrow of the Diem government which by then, through its corruption and denial of basic human rights, had lost significant support at home. When Diem and his brother were killed in the coup, Kennedy considered it his greatest foreign policy mistake since the Bay of Pigs.

MARTIN LUTHER KING AND THE PRINCIPLE OF NONVIOLENCE

In domestic politics, Kennedy's major preoccupation was the civil rights movement. Its tactics, as determined by Martin Luther King, Jr., and his followers, involved passive resistance in the form of nonviolent demonstrations. The example for this kind of resistance came from the successful campaign for independence from British colonial rule in India led by Mahatma Gandhi. Another important source was Christian doctrine. According to King, the aim of nonviolence was to win over the opponent by example, not by force. Tactics included boycotts like the successful one in Montgomery, Alabama, beginning in December of 1955, against segregation on public buses, and the selective boycotting of merchants in Tuskegee, Alabama, to protest exclusionary practices in voter registration.

The beginning of the sixties saw the first lunch counter sit-ins at a Woolworth store in Greensboro, North Carolina. These demonstrations, conducted by black college students, soon spread throughout the South and provoked sympathetic actions in the North as well. Another result of the sit-ins was the formation in April 1960 of the Student Nonviolent Coordinating Committee (SNCC). This group affirmed in its founding statement "the philosophical or religious ideal of nonviolence" which it defined as seeking "a social order of justice permeated by love." In other words, the philosophy of SNCC at the outset was identical in most respects with that of King's organization. In fact, however, many of the student leaders were impatient with the patriarchy of the SCLC and sought independence from it. Though the two organizations were to remain linked in many ways, SNCC was clearly more appealing to young African Americans of college age. The Congress for Racial Equality (CORE) and the NAACP—historically, the first major organization of its kind—were other important groups in the civil rights movement.

In May of 1961, the movement began a campaign, under the auspices of CORE, to oppose segregation in bus terminals used in interstate transportation. Resistance to the Freedom Riders, as the people involved in the campaign (including many whites) were called, included the burning of a bus and beatings by members of the Ku Klux Klan in Alabama. Though federal support was slow to come, the Interstate Commerce Commission in September 1961 for the second time declared segregation in such facilities illegal.

Meanwhile, the major thrust of the movement—encouraged more aggressively by the Kennedy administration—became the voter registration issue. The theory was that, if blacks were granted their rights as voters, change would occur naturally through the political process rather than through protests and demonstrations. To coordinate registration activity, the Council of Federated Organizations (COFO) was formed. Actually registering black voters in the South was another matter, however.

As the movement spread, its activities became more intensified, and resistance to it increasingly violent. Nineteen sixty-three proved to be an especially dangerous year. Major demonstrations were launched in April by King and the SCLC in Birmingham, the most heavily segregated city in the South. The response of white authorities, led by the notorious police commissioner "Bull" Connor, was mass arrests (even of children) and the use of police dogs and fire hoses for crowd control. In May, King's supposed motel headquarters and his brother's home were bombed, resulting in riots by blacks. In September four black girls were killed and many other people were injured in the bombing of the Sixteenth Street Baptist Church in Birmingham. Between 1955 and 1963, seven deaths occurred in connection with the movement, including the assassination, in June of 1963, of Medgar Evers, head of the Mississippi NAACP.

One positive result of the Birmingham campaign was the intense media coverage of the March on Washington in August 1963. Supported by a large group of civil rights organizations, churches, and unions, this event brought hundreds of thousands of people to a gathering on the mall in front of the Lincoln Memorial. The purpose was to influence congressional passage of Kennedy's promising new civil rights legislation. It was here that Dr. King delivered his famous "I have a dream" speech. His dream of racial unity—of a brotherhood in which African Americans at last achieved equality with white America—was not borne out by the Birmingham church bombing of the following month, nor by other events soon to follow. But King's preeminence as the formulator of the civil rights movement's goals and his place nationally as its leader were never clearer than at that moment.

The support of the Kennedy administration for the movement till 1963 had been at best equivocal. On the one hand, Kennedy and his brother Robert, who, as attorney general, was the government official most responsible for the protection of civil rights, were not unsympathetic to the civil rights cause. At the same time, John worried about the political complications for his administration. His brother encountered significant resistance within the Justice Department from the Federal Bureau of Investigation, then headed by J. Edgar Hoover. Hoover—like his agency, a national institution—was virulently anticommunist and thoroughly convinced, like many conservatives and most segregationists, that the civil rights movement was backed by the Communist party. Since the FBI had major responsibility for dealing with violations of civil rights as guaranteed by federal law, Hoover's attitude, when coupled with his strong political connections in Congress, limited the attorney general's actions in many important ways. Hoover went so far as to arrange an extensive surveillance of Dr. King's private life, and amassed hundreds of pages of documentation, most of it irrelevant to any matter of federal law. Nearly all attempts of Bobby Kennedy to limit Hoover's power failed, and, as time went on, the attorney general seemed, at least outwardly, to cool markedly toward the civil rights cause. Civil rights leaders felt that the Kennedy administration proceeded too cautiously in their support, showing a reluctance to offend the politicians and electorate who were most strongly opposed to the civil rights cause.

By June 1963, however, the president pushed his new civil rights bill with a speech remarkable in the extent of its support for the black cause and for the fervor of its tone. Kennedy saw the violations of civil liberties taking place in Birmingham. He was also incensed by the naked opposition to federal authority posed by Governor George Wallace of Alabama in his attempt to keep the University of Alabama segregated. In addition, Kennedy worried that the entire situation was in danger of turning into anarchy (in Birmingham, blacks for the first time had departed from the nonviolent strategy of King in their response to police brutality). On June 12—the very evening that Medgar Evers was killed in Mississippi—Kennedy went public with his feelings on the matter in a national address, in which he said that "The heart of the question is whether all Americans are to be afforded equal rights and equal opportunities. . . ." Uncharacteristically, Kennedy stated the problem in moral, even religious, terms: "We face, therefore, a moral crisis as a country and a people. . . . A great change is at hand, and our task, our obligation, is to make that revolution, that change, peaceful and constructive for all." While his civil rights legislation would encounter significant opposition, Kennedy's personal stand on the issue had clearly changed to the point that he was willing to announce what amounted to presidential support for civil disobedience. King, who had always felt some kind of bond with Kennedy in spite of his disappointment with his lack of support, was ecstatic.

The ultimate fate of the civil rights legislation was not to be decided by Kennedy, however. In one single moment, the course of national events was to change very soon. Of all the violent acts of a violent decade, none was to be more of a shock than Kennedy's assassination, which came in November, putting his vice president, Lyndon Johnson, in the White House. With tragic finality, this event brought the Kennedy years to a close. While some of his cabinet were to remain in the new administration, most notably Robert McNamara as secretary of Defense, the new president was to bring a different perspective to the White House, and, very soon, the passage of Kennedy's civil rights bill.

THE CIVIL RIGHTS ACT OF 1964

In the wake of the Kennedy assassination, and in the hands of a man who was both a southerner and an experienced politician used to dealing with Congress, the Civil Rights Act of 1964 became the legislative cornerstone of the civil rights program that most activists had hoped to see. The Twenty-Fourth Amendment to the Constitution ratified in January 1964 abolished the poll tax, which, with the so-called literacy test, was one means of excluding blacks from voting. In addition to strengthening previous civil rights laws, the Civil Rights Act of 1964 authorized the attorney general to desegregate all public facilities, including public schools, and to bring suit for individuals whose rights were denied. Among other important provisions, it prohibited discrimination in federally assisted programs, providing for withdrawal of federal funds to enforce compliance. Furthermore, it prohibited discrimination in employment practices and established the Equal Employment Opportunity Commission. Lastly, it broadened federal responsibilities in the area of voting rights and civil rights law suits in federal courts. Johnson received the plaudits of the black community for the way he managed to push this legislation through a reluctant Congress.

However, the failure of the Democratic party, at its convention in Atlantic City in August, to seat the all-black Mississippi Freedom Democratic party in place of the white delegation from that state did not appear in the same light. Johnson, as the new head of the party, took major blame for the decision. Nonetheless, in the election that fall, Johnson would not only receive an enormous majority—61 percent of a popular vote of 70,303,305 and 486 out of 538 electoral votes—but the overwhelming support of African Americans.

Meanwhile, the civil rights organizations combined their efforts in the summer of 1964 in a voter registration campaign in Mississippi known as Freedom Summer. Hundreds of volunteers participated, including many northern white students exposed for the first time to the South. From the beginning of the civil rights movement, liberal northerners sympathetic to the cause had participated in demonstrations and marches, but in Freedom Summer there was a deliberate effort to involve northern whites, especially college students, to show southerners that it was not only blacks who supported voting rights. This effort was to have profound influence on subsequent events on northern campuses later in the 1960s.

As if to point up the dangers these students and all participants in Freedom Summer faced, three civil rights workers connected with CORE—two white, one black—were murdered by white segregationists in June. In August, their bodies were found near Philadelphia, Mississippi. The anger and sympathy this act aroused and the active involvement of the Justice Department it provoked (the only federal support for Freedom Summer) helped the civil rights cause throughout the country.

However, differences were intensifying within the movement over the issue of nonviolence. The fiery Black Muslim leader Malcolm X was the most outspoken of the critics, saying that nonviolence was a strategy of "negroes," not blacks. This was a distinction in terms that became more important as the decade went on. To many, Malcolm's viewpoint on the issue seemed reasonable considering the tactics being used by police in the South. The violence of Birmingham seemed to create a new sense that the civil rights movement could not rely on nonviolence to reach its goals. "Bloody Sunday," in March of 1965, during a march in Selma, Alabama, seemed to fulfill the worst predictions, even though the event had been supported by a federal court order. In the same year that King received the Nobel Peace Prize and the Voting Rights Act was passed by Congress, the principle of nonviolence so important to him seemed seriously threatened. In February, Malcolm X, who had broken with the Muslims the previous year, was assassinated in New York City (Muslims were responsible), and in August the first major riot in an urban ghetto erupted in the Watts district of Los Angeles.

While the next stage of the civil rights movement was clearly in question, there was no doubt by 1965 that significant progress had already been made. The movement was most successful in challenging the legality of the Jim Crow laws and the long-standing practice of segregation in the South. It faced a less definable target in the North, where segregation was not de jure, but for the most part de facto, and where the black population was not rural, but lived primarily in urban ghettos.

Its influence had already spread, by 1965, to the Free Speech Movement among students at the University of California–Berkeley and to the newly charged women's movement. It was also to have enormous influence on the movement that was to become most widespread and controversial from that year to the end of the sixties—the protest against the Vietnam War.

THE MEDIA AND THE CIVIL RIGHTS MOVEMENT

Much of the national support for the civil rights movement among non–African Americans came from the attention it received in the communications media. Many of the reporters covering the story of the civil rights movement for the national press were highly sympathetic to the cause, and photographic coverage in magazines like *Life* gave the general public an inside view of conditions in the South. As early as 1949, for instance, well before *Brown* v. *Board of Education* or the formation of the SCLC, *Life* covered a story about conditions in segregated schools in Memphis, pointing out that West Memphis spent scarcely one-fifth as much money per black student as it did for white. Stories like these, illustrated with photos showing crowded classroom conditions and potbellied stoves (the Memphis story grew out of a fire that destroyed the only school for blacks in the district), increased during the 1950s and early 1960s, raising national awareness of discrimination issues in the popular press.

Many national newspapers also provided extensive coverage of the civil rights movement and took editorial stands sympathetic to the cause of African Americans. Especially outstanding in this respect was the *New York Times*. In addition to being supportive editorially, the *Times* ran advertisements recruiting money and support for the civil rights cause. In this connection, in 1964 the *Times* won an important First Amendment case before the Supreme Court in *New York Times* v. *Sullivan*. The *Times* had been sued over an ad supposedly run by four black clergymen in support of a legal battle of Martin Luther King's. The ad contained errors of fact which an Alabama court said constituted libel against the plaintiff in the case, Police Commissioner Sullivan of Montgomery. The U.S. Supreme Court, in a unanimous decision, ruled that such errors in public debate were not libelous and that no such charge could be validated unless "actual malice" was proved—that is, deliberate malicious intent. This decision was important not only to the civil rights movement of the sixties but to free expression generally.

Television coverage was also of great importance to the civil rights movement. In the 1960s, videotaping became standard in television broadcasting. Though initially more expensive than film, videotape did not need to be processed and soon revealed other significant advantages. For television journalists, it was ultimately to prove a more flexible medium for recording newsworthy events than film. Changes in long-distance transmission also influenced the nature and extent of news coverage. Communications satellites made live coverage possible over extremely long distances.

Network nightly news broadcasts went from 15 minutes to half an hour just two months before the assassination of John Kennedy, one mark of the greater significance such broadcasts now had. The assassination itself was covered in depth from the time word was received on Friday, November 23, that Kennedy was dead until the funeral ceremony three days later. This extended coverage, unbroken by commercial interruptions, marked a new level in television coverage of special events. It also marked a new level of viewership. An estimated 93 percent of American homes with TV sets tuned in to the Kennedy funeral.

Martin Luther King was fully aware of the potential of television for the civil rights movement. Early in his career as an activist he had considered using TV to convey his message directly, but rejected the idea because then, in the fifties, so few blacks had sets. King's oratory on behalf of the civil rights cause was one of his outstanding contributions, and, as his fame grew, so did the coverage it got. The national broadcast coverage of the March on Washington in August 1963 and King's speech on that occasion were especially significant in this respect.

Civil rights leaders felt that TV coverage of demonstrations and the reactions they provoked would encourage sympathy for the movement. By 1965, an estimated 93 percent of American families had TV sets in their homes. While the nightly news never achieved ratings to equal the popularity of other programming, its coverage of violence against nonviolent demonstrators, as in the Birmingham campaign, made many whites sympathetic to a cause that before had only existed for them in name. Such coverage also gave rise, among segregationists and other critics of the movement, to claims that broadcasters were biased in their presentations.

The same principle that worked in favor of the civil rights movement in Birmingham and elsewhere would work against it when riots began in northern and western urban ghettos in 1965. These were covered by television, too, and the spectacle of violence directed against police and firefighters and wanton destruction of property alienated many non–African Americans. Such footage fed the arguments of those opposed to the movement, who said that its real goal was anarchy or the overthrow of the existing order.

To what extent was TV coverage biased in favor of the civil rights movement? Perhaps that question cannot be answered adequately without a detailed analysis of coverage throughout the entire period. Certainly neither television (nor print media) coverage was decisive. So much else enters into the forming of opinion on social issues that media influence is difficult to measure and easy to exaggerate. However, given the extent and the nature of the coverage provided the civil rights movement, it surely led many people at least to question their assumptions about civil rights and matters of race.

THE FOLK MUSIC REVIVAL AND BOB DYLAN

The music associated with the civil rights movement had a more direct message. Born of the traditional folk music of black and white America and of the labor union movement, it spoke unambiguously to its listeners and became the cornerstone of the folk music revival in American music of the late fifties and early sixties. At the vanguard of this revival was a young white musician from Duluth, Minnesota, who was to become arguably the single most important figure in popular music of the sixties.

Born Robert Allen Zimmerman in 1941, Bob Dylan (he borrowed his new name from the Welsh poet Dylan Thomas) moved to New York in early 1961 after having attended the University of Minnesota for three semesters in the late fifties. Dylan's move stemmed partly from his admiration for folk artist Woody Guthrie, by then already suffering from Huntington's chorea, a disease of the nervous system that had killed Guthrie's mother. Dylan played the coffeehouse circuit—an important venue for folk artists—and eventually came to the attention of John Hammond, an A & R (artists and repertory) man from Columbia Records, who signed Dylan to his first contract and produced his first album.

That album—called simply *Bob Dylan* (1962)—was recorded in two days and features a solo Dylan singing with his own acoustic guitar and harmonica. The songs were all traditional folk songs except for "Talking New York," about Dylan's experiences in his new home, and "Song for Woody," dedicated to his chosen mentor, both of which were written to traditional folk melodies. While this album scarcely defines Dylan's range as an artist, it does capture his style at the beginning of his professional career.

Like most folk artists, Dylan's singing voice seems quite ordinary. Slightly nasal, often off-pitch, it sounds untrained. An underlying assumption of the folk music revival was that its music was of and for the people. In other words, a singer didn't need a cultivated vocal technique. More important was conveying a sense of shared experience in which everyone and anyone could join. Hence the common feature of folk concerts in which the audience is invited to sing. While Dylan did not especially invite such participation in his performances, he would reveal in the later years of his career a more varied, though always highly individual, vocal technique.

By the time of his second album, *The Freewheelin' Bob Dylan* (1963), Dylan was writing his own music. On one number, "Corinna, Corinna," he recorded with backup musicians for the first time. The most memorable songs on the album, however, were "Blowin' in the Wind" and "Don't Think Twice, It's All Right." Both became popular hits later in 1963 when they were covered by the folk music trio of Peter, Paul, and Mary ("Blowin' in the Wind" reached #2 on the *Billboard* chart). This was the first instance of many in which other musicians popularized Dylan's music. "Blowin' in the Wind" became an anthem of the civil rights and the antiwar movements. Built on a series of questions, its refrain suggests that the answers to long-standing problems of peace and freedom are about to be heard, though the song never says precisely what they will be.

In his second album, Dylan now speaks in his own voice. More than any other singer of the time, he could feel the pulse of the new generation. He would express their inner feelings, putting them into words and music in his songs. This was music to be *listened* to. The message of the lyrics is as important as the melody or rhythm. In addition to "Blowin' in the Wind," the set contains the strongly antiwar "Masters of War" and satirical "Talkin' World War III Blues"; "Oxford Town," inspired by the recent events in the civil rights movement in Mississippi; and "Bob Dylan's Blues," "Bob Dylan's Dream," and "I Shall Be Free," all of which fall into the category of topical satire in folk or blues form. Other songs on the album are more lyrical in nature. They deal with failed love or, as in the memorable "A Hard Rain's A-Gonna Fall," a young man's aspirations in an unpredictable, perhaps doomed, world. (The "rain" may well refer to the aftermath of a nuclear blast.) The lyrical ballad, often in blues form, has been a standard element in the Dylan songbook throughout his career, sometimes with an enigmatic imagery that conceals more than it reveals. Dylan's second album went gold (selling more than half a million copies) and reached #22 on the *Billboard* chart, another sign of Dylan's growing popularity.

His third album, *The Times They Are A-Changin'* (1964) shows a similar mix of material. The title song became a signature song for Dylan and a favorite of sixties protesters from various camps. Reflecting the attitude of youth in rebellion, the lyric challenges all forms of authority, including that of parents, and then suggests that the coming changes will sweep away everything in their path.

By 1964 Dylan was playing 200 concerts a year and making regular appearances at important events such as the March on Washington, where he sang "Only a Pawn in Their Game," a ballad inspired by the slaying of Medgar Evers, from *The Times They Are A-Changin'* album. This was one of a series of topical songs from the sixties and early seventies in which Dylan commemorated martyrs of the civil rights movement and victims of social injustice.

Dylan in 1966

Dylan recorded his next album, *Another Side of Bob Dylan* (also 1964), in one evening. It marks yet another milestone in his career, for here, in "My Back Pages," Dylan signalled the end to his protest song era and the beginning of something new but as yet not completely defined. Though casually sung, with occasional mistakes on Dylan's part, these songs have in common an imagery and tone that sets them apart from much that came before. "Chimes of Freedom," a paean to the outcast and the forgotten of our world, is a protest song of sorts, but one stated in such general terms that it fails to be topical.

As Dylan put it to an interviewer just after the recording session, "Me, I don't want to write *for* people anymore. You know—

be a spokesman.... From now on, I want to write from inside me. . . ." As a musician, he was also beginning a transition that was to lead him beyond his folk music roots, as he moved from folk to rock. Nonetheless, in songs written to that date, Dylan had already managed to make the singer as songwriter the new standard for popular music, and topical issues the subject matter of those songs. His music carried the message of the civil rights movement to young white Americans. The generation that was to become most politically active during the sixties had found the singer who spoke for them.

OTHER VOICES IN THE FOLK MUSIC REVIVAL

Bob Dylan was the most important musician of the folk revival of the early 1960s, but others also played important roles, including many women. Of these, the one most closely associated with Dylan, both musically and personally, was Joan Baez.

Baez's career had already begun when Dylan broke onto the scene, and in the summer of 1963, after having recorded a number of his songs, she invited him to tour with her. They became closely associated for a period of about two years and in their private lives became lovers. With a sweet, high soprano voice, accompanying herself on a guitar, Baez sang both traditional folk and contemporary protest songs. Her increasing involvement with political issues, at a time when Dylan was moving in the other direction, contributed to their breakup, but she continued to record his music. One entire album, *Any Day Now* (1969), is all-Dylan, and other albums feature Dylan songs. Even without the association with Dylan and his music, however, Baez had a prominent place in the folk revival both for her singing and for her political commitment.

Another prominent singer in the folk protest era of the mid-sixties was Phil Ochs, whose "There but for Fortune" became a hit for Joan Baez in 1965. His album *I Ain't A'Marchin'* the following year produced the title song and "Draft Dodger Rag," both of which became anthems of the antiwar movement, though the recording was banned from radio and television. Much protest music faced similar censorship. Ochs' popularity, like that of many singers in the folk movement, was tied so closely to political causes that, with the end of the sixties, his career entered an eclipse. Then, he virtually lost the ability to sing after a savage attack while traveling in Africa in 1973. Two years later, suffering from severe depression, he hanged himself.

Many musicians associated with the folk revival were not committed to political causes to the extent that Dylan, Ochs, and Baez were. Singer Judy Collins—perhaps the best voice among the folk revival singers of the early sixties—made her recording debut in 1961, and in the later sixties went gold with several albums. While Collins's later recordings show other sides to her talent, she began squarely in the same tradition that nurtured Joan Baez, though she never showed the same degree of political commitment.

Some groups who cultivated the folk music sound aimed at a broader audience. One of the earliest and most commercially successful of these was the Kingston Trio, whose first recordings appeared toward the end of the fifties. Immensely popular with the collegiate audience, this clean-cut group saw five of their first six albums go to first place, all six of them gold.

The place of the Kingston Trio was soon taken, however, by Peter, Paul, and Mary, the most popular folk group of the sixties, who debuted in the same year as Bob Dylan. Their musicianly blend of one somewhat husky female voice and two male, with acoustic guitar backup, proved appealing to a wide range of listeners. They covered songs by Dylan and others in a series of popular albums through the end of the decade.

The folk music sound was to persist among its loyal followers, devoted both to traditional folk music and to modern music in folk idiom. Its constants were to be the acoustic guitar, rather than electric, and a performance style that often invited audience participation. Some highly successful musicians of the later sixties such as Simon and Garfunkel, Joni Mitchell, and the Mamas and the Papas were also to do music essentially in the folk idiom, though varied by individual temperament and newer developments in popular music.

Simon and Garfunkel and, later, Paul Simon on his own would extend the range of subject matter in folk music to include modern urban subjects more typical of blues. Joni Mitchell, following a similar path, would add to the folk sound the rhythms of jazz, while writing songs of a highly personal, even idiosyncratic nature. Both followed the Dylan of 1964 and afterward in writing music from "inside" rather than as social or political protest. The Mamas and the Papas had six hits that reached the Top Five in their California-style folk pop idiom within two years in 1966–67, including "California Dreamin'" and "Monday, Monday." A very popular group that was prone to disagreements, they disbanded twice between 1967 and 1973. The following year, vocalist Cass Elliot became one of the victims of the drug and alcohol excesses of the era, when she died, choking on her own vomit.

ROCK ROLLS ON: "LOUIE, LOUIE" AND THE EVIDENCE OF THE CHARTS

However important folk music became, rock 'n' roll was still the music favored by most young people in the early 1960s. It may have been dominated by bland cover artists and sexy-looking teenage idols, but rock 'n' roll of this period also produced some very good music. Despite the frequently stated generalization that nothing happened in rock from the time Elvis went into the army and the arrival of the Beatles in 1964, a mere glance at the *Billboard* charts proves quickly that rock rolled on.

Besides Elvis's hits, already noted, this period produced such rock 'n' roll or R & B classics as Dion and the Belmonts' "A Teenager in Love" and Dion's solo "The Wanderer," Wilbert Harrison's "Kansas City," the Clovers's "Love Potion No. 9," the Isley Brothers's "Shout," Chubby Checker's "The Twist" (to date the all-time best-selling single in the United States), the Shirelles' "Tonight's the Night," Del Shannon's "Runaway," U. S. Bonds's "Quarter to Three," Ray Charles's "Hit the Road, Jack," Gene Chandler's "Duke of Earl," the Four Seasons' "Big Girls Don't Cry," and the Crystals's "He's a Rebel" (actually recorded by another group, featuring singer Darlene Love, but released in the Crystals's name) and "Da Do Ron Ron" (the Crystals's own, and one of the best of the doo-wop songs). With songs like these, this could scarcely be called a dry period in American music. It was also the period (beginning in the late fifties) in which the Everly Brothers, who successfully fused white country music with rock in the rockabilly manner, had their greatest success with songs like "Bye Bye, Love" and "Cathy's Clown." The Everlys exerted an enormous influence on British groups of the early sixties.

Rock 'n' roll continued to be as controversial as it was popular. From the beginning, rock 'n' roll was thought to be subversive by conservative politicians and clergy, who saw it turning American youth from the path of consensus and conformity to eroticism or anarchy. Small wonder, then, that Elvis's pelvic movements should become so hot a topic, or that the song "Louie, Louie," suspected (by people who could never comprehend its lyrics) of being obscene, should be banned from most radio stations after its brief moment at #1 spot in January 1964.

Written and first recorded in 1956 by Richard Berry, "Louie, Louie" (pronounced *Lou-ee, Lou-eye*) was to inspire countless covers and variations, many of them inspired, but none so popular or influential as the one by the Kingsmen released in 1963. Really a song about a Jamaican sailor and his lover, the Berry original, with its cha-cha beat, became something very different in the Kingsmen's version. With its simple chord progression (*duh duh duh. duh duh*), its vocal that garbles the words to the point that most of them are incomprehensible, and a thrown-in phrase (first used in an earlier version by a group called the Wailers): "Let's give it to 'em, right now!"—the Kingsmen's "Louie, Louie" made the group instant one-hit wonders. It also became the subject, like Martin Luther King and various members of the folk music revival, of an FBI investigation, extending over a period of two years, in which even J. Edgar Hoover became involved. As recounted memorably by Dave Marsh in *Louie Louie* (1963), the FBI had no more luck understanding the lyrics than anyone else did. Nonetheless, their investigation was symptomatic of the bias against rock 'n' roll which has persisted in American culture till the present day.

By the time the FBI investigation ran aground through lack of conviction in its own case, the Kingsmen had broken up and regrouped, and the song they had recorded had begun its course toward rock 'n' roll immortality, with many other versions to follow.

BERRY GORDY, JR., AND MOTOWN RECORDS

The early sixties also saw the beginning of an important musical phenomenon in Detroit, the first fully black-owned and -operated record company, featuring all black artists. The dreamchild of songwriter Berry Gordy, Jr., a former boxer and record store owner gone bankrupt, Motown Records became the source of much major talent and music of the 1960s. It also benefited from the climate of change in race relations and the widespread popularity R & B enjoyed.

Berry Gordy's early efforts as a songwriter combined features of R & B and gospel, and this formula was to be the basis of the Motown sound, a combination of pop and gospel-based soul. Starting under a different name in 1959, the Motown label officially began in 1962 with recordings by Mary Wells (Motown's first major star), Eddie Holland, and Marvin Gaye, as well as a number of the groups that would be long associated with the company: the Temptations, the Miracles, the Marvelettes, the Contours, the Vandellas (later joined by Martha Reeves), and the Supremes, featuring one of the most important female singers of the sixties and seventies, Diana Ross.

Diana Ross and the Supremes

Motown was to become one of the great success stories of the sixties, with 42 #1 hits in the course of the decade and 75 percent of its releases reaching the charts. This would have been a respectable record for any company, but especially for one that was entirely black. Motown was more than just a recording company, however. It had its own staff composers to produce the music, staff musicians to provide the necessary backups and arrangements for the recordings made in its own studios, and its own publishing company to do the sheet music and handle the copyrights for its songs. Motown was a total musical operation.

Gordy went further, however. He groomed his artists much as the old Hollywood studios had groomed their stars, requiring them to conform to his standards of performance. His theory was that black music, especially R & B, had long remained the small change of the record industry because its lyrics and artists had not been willing to make the necessary accommodation to the prevailingly white audience of American music. By the early 1960s that audience was more sympathetic than ever to black music. It made sense to meet it halfway and hook the mainstream group—something that R & B had never quite managed to do.

In this effort, Motown benefited from the civil rights movement in various ways. With public attention focused on the rights of the African-American minority in the United States, the rights of black musicians also came under scrutiny. Old wrongs—of black musicians being underpaid and underpromoted—were being righted. Moreover, changing mores made the majority white audience more accepting of black performers generally.

However, indebted as he was to the movement, Gordy did not allow the music of Motown to reflect the struggle for civil rights in any major way. The formula was to keep it simple and tuneful, with clean lyrics and danceable rhythms. In some respects, Motown music was imitating the white imitations of black R & B. If it reflected the civil rights movement, it was as the musical equivalent of the integration with the white community sought by Martin Luther King and the SCLC, not as the equivalent of the separatism and militancy that characterized the Muslims and Malcolm X.

Eventually, social and political themes began to appear in Motown music, but never to the extent that they did in other music of the sixties. As early as 1966, the young Stevie Wonder, another Motown discovery, recorded his version of Bob Dylan's "Blowin' in the Wind" on the label (it reached #9 on the chart), and in 1970, long after the antiwar movement reached its height, Edwin Starr's antiwar song "War" reached #1 by September 1970.

Motown artists eventually included, in addition to those mentioned above, the Four Tops and the Jackson Five, the last major Motown act, discovered by Diana Ross, featuring the young Michael Jackson. Some became restive under the restrictions placed on them by Gordy, who, again like a movie mogul of the studio system, ran a very tight ship. Diana Ross was one of these, eventually moving from Motown to RCA. By then, however, in the late seventies, Motown itself had moved on to Los Angeles and into movie production, at which Gordy found less success than in the music world.

Nevertheless, Motown represents a milestone in the history of American popular music. For the first time, in a major way, African Americans asserted total economic control over their music. Although the seventies were to see some setbacks, the national music scene was more open to black musicians and more rewarding for them than ever before.

HOLLYWOOD AND AFRICAN-AMERICAN STEREOTYPES: RACE AND ETHNICITY IN POSTWAR FILMS AND THE MEDIA

The African American in Hollywood traditionally fared no better, perhaps actually worse, than his or her counterpart in the musical world. Even in the sixties, only a few black actors managed to satisfy a broad—that is to say, non–African American—audience, chiefly by avoiding any roles that might possibly offend that audience's preconceptions about appropriate behaviors. In doing so, however, they risked rejection by fellow African Americans increasingly concerned with their own sense of identity. At the same time, few Hollywood films dealt seriously with racial themes. This avoidance of a controversial and topical subject provides an analogy with Vietnam: Hollywood was unable to produce anything of any significance about American involvement there until after the war was over.

Historically, black actors were only welcomed in Hollywood in roles that conformed to stereotypes. These included characters like Uncle Remus (in the Disney film—*Song of the South*, 1946) or Stepin Fetchit, played by Lincoln T. Perry, the popular black actor of the 1930s. Stepin is comical, somewhat stupid, and totally dependent on white society for his identity and sustenance. The literary and cultural forebears of these roles and others like them were Uncle Tom (from the nineteenth-century abolitionist novel by Harriet Beecher Stowe) and Sambo (the jolly, somewhat stupid servant of folk tradition). The Uncle Tom character was loyal to his master, kindhearted, and selfless—"the ideal plantation negro," in the phrase of Malcolm X. Sambo was cut from the same cloth, but had less intelligence. Related stereotypes, also represented in screen roles, were the natty, comic urban black or "dude," a citified version of Sambo, and—especially in the silent film era, when portrayed by whites in blackface in minstrel show style—the evil Nat, who was rebellious and disloyal to the master and the system (from Nat Turner, leader of a slave rebellion).

Roles for black females were even more limited. Practically the entire range is represented in one film, the MGM adaptation of Margaret Mitchell's romantic novel of the ante- and postbellum South, *Gone With the Wind* (1939). Continuing the Uncle Remus/Uncle Tom tradition, this film shows black servants remaining loyal to their slaveholding family during the worst of times following the Civil War. Hattie McDaniel plays Mammy (the same stereotype as Aunt Jemima of pancake fame) and Butterfly McQueen is Prissy, the female equivalent to Stepin Fetchit/Sambo, a silly, high-voiced maid. Significantly, in December 1939, when this highly publicized film was premiered in Atlanta (site of some of its most memorable scenes), none of the black actors took part in the parade, reception, and three-day holiday inspired by the event.

In the postwar period, all of these stereotypes persisted in Hollywood movies and the communications media, despite occasional attempts to transcend them. As part of the migration in the early 1950s of popular radio shows to television, "Amos 'n' Andy," a long-running series about two stereotypical black men and their cohort of friends, was produced with black actors (not, as on radio, whites) in the major roles. Objections from the NAACP eventually ended the series, though reruns continued well into the 1960s. Another series, "The Beulah Show," first aired in 1950, featured renowned black actress Ethel Waters in the Mammy role of a servant to a middle-class white family. This also was withdrawn after a few years as a result of NAACP protests. Not until the 1970s did American television begin in earnest to transcend such stereotypical views of African Americans.

In Hollywood films, there were a few exceptions in the post-war period in dealing with racial or ethnic issues, though these efforts frequently muted the more controversial aspects of the topic. Mark Robson's *Home of the Brave* (1947) dealt with prejudice against blacks in the segregated armed services during the Second World War. In Elia Kazan's *Gentleman's Agreement* (1947), actor Gregory Peck portrayed a writer who pretends to be Jewish and finds out firsthand the kind of bigotry members of this ethnic group faced in American society. The same director's *Pinky* (1949) dealt delicately with the theme of miscegenation (then a crime in many states, especially in the South) with white actress Jeanne Crain in the role of a mulatto passing for white. *Intruder in the Dust* (1949), a courtroom drama based on a novel by William Faulkner, treated the problem faced by white southerners in reconciling their feelings about blacks as human beings with the regional code requiring blacks to be subservient to whites. In the film, a black man is accused of a murder he didn't commit and is threatened with lynching. The characters include a youth who is just becoming aware of the southern dilemma and his uncle, a lawyer, who is willing to defend the accused man in court on a point of law. *Intruder in the Dust* anticipated a more successful, and much more popular, treatment of the same theme to emerge some three years later.

This was Robert Mulligan's *To Kill a Mockingbird* (1962), based on the Pulitzer Prize–winning novel by Harper Lee. In this film it is a young girl named Scout, a six-year-old tomboy, who provides the principal viewpoint on events. Her widower father Atticus Finch (Gregory Peck) is an attorney ordered to represent a black man falsely accused of raping a young white woman. As in *Intruder in the Dust,* this is a story about racial relations in the South and also about the initiation of a young girl, her brother, and their best friend to the complicated morality of the adult world. In the script, these two lines intertwine in such a way that one feeds the other thematically. In defending the black man, Atticus goes beyond the limits set by his society, in which a guilty verdict, regardless of the plaintiff in the case or the evidence presented, is a foregone conclusion. Nonetheless, his defense of Tom Robinson gains Atticus the respect of the black community. It also earns him the hatred of Bob Ewell, father of the alleged rape victim. Ewell is later killed in his attempt to get revenge.

As in Faulkner, *To Kill a Mockingbird* suggests that the educated southerner has a more enlightened, morally complicated view of African Americans than do poorer whites like the Ewells. At the same time, no matter how racially enlightened, the enlightened southerners are also constrained by the code of their society. Although the impact of the story is to some extent vitiated by the fact that it takes place in Alabama in 1932, the audience of the early sixties read its message in the terms being set by the civil rights struggle in progress at the time.

THE CASE OF SIDNEY POITIER

Of all African-American actors of the 1960s, none achieved quite the success of Sidney Poitier. In a career that began in 1950, he rose to stardom in such films as the all-black *Porgy and Bess* (1959), based on the folk opera by George Gershwin, *A Raisin in the Sun* (1961), from the play by African-American writer Lorraine Hansberry, and *Lilies of the Field* (1963), for which Poitier won an Academy Award as best actor. To many, Poitier realized more fully than anyone before him the potential of the black actor in Hollywood. To others—especially the more radical black activists—he seemed a new version of Uncle Tom: gifted, versatile, but bland, a liberal's idea of what a black actor should be, an assimilationist all too eager to deny his own blackness. With singer-actors Harry Belafonte and Sammy Davis, Jr., Poitier was widely regarded by black radicals as a white man's Negro, another in the long tradition of plantation types haunting black history. These opposing views illustrate in themselves the difficulty that a black actor faced in the sixties in reaching an audience that would include whites as well as African Americans.

Two films of Poitier's, both released in 1967, deal more explicitly with racial issues than anything he had done before that date. Their euphemistic treatment of racial themes and internal contradictions reveal all too clearly the problem Hollywood still had, some 13 years into the civil rights movement, in dramatizing such issues convincingly.

In the Heat of the Night, which won the best picture award for 1967 from the Motion Picture Academy, cast Poitier as Virgil Tibbs, a black detective from the North, who, in visiting his mother in the rural South, is wrongfully accused of the death of a rich white man. When his authority is established, Virgil begins to collaborate with the white sheriff investigating the crime (Rod Steiger). In this relationship, in which the black detective is essentially playing by the rules set by southern white society, critics of the film saw yet another example of black identity being sacrificed to prevailing white standards.

Guess Who's Coming to Dinner attempts to present the issue of biracial relationships in semi-comic terms. Poitier (John Wade Prentice) is a black surgeon engaged to the daughter of a wealthy California couple (Spencer Tracy and Katharine Hepburn). This situation, novel to Hollywood films of the day, is made considerably less controversial by the generally light tone of the film and by the fact that the couple plans to live in Switzerland, not in the United States. The film takes a serious issue and reduces it to inconsequentiality at the very time such relationships were being validated and even legitimized in American society.

By the second half of the sixties, considerable progress had been made in legal protection of the civil rights of African Americans, and real progress in some aspects of the living conditions of many. Motown had shown the possibilities of black entrepreneurship—if, to some extent, by accommodating the values of black music to a white audience. Black musical artists and actors were finding a degree of acceptance, and financial reward, greater than ever before in American history. Hollywood had at least attempted, however tentatively, to deal with serious racial themes. Much remained to be accomplished, however, and the end of the sixties and beginning of the next decade would not see any significant improvements or changes in these aspects of American popular culture. In fact, a similar reluctance to face the facts of the Vietnam War during the same period suggests that Hollywood and broadcasting both had been so badly bruised by the HUAC and McCarthy investigations that they were unwilling to take the financial or moral risk that controversial subjects required.

Chapter 4

"GIVE PEACE A CHANCE": VIETNAM AND THE ANTIWAR MOVEMENT

As United States involvement in Vietnam escalated after 1964, so did protest against the undeclared war. Many people felt betrayed by Lyndon Johnson, who took a moderate stand on the issue in the election campaign of 1964. Gradually, during the next few years, the bombing raids on North Vietnam increased and more and more American ground troops were sent over by his administration. At the same time, antiwar demonstrations became larger and more violent. The climax was reached in Chicago in August of 1968 during the Democratic Party National Convention. By then, the American public was almost evenly divided, for and against, on Vietnam. As a result of the growing credibility gap over his handling of the war, Johnson had removed himself from the race. As his popularity declined and the costs of the war went up, Johnson's ambitious Great Society plan and its war on poverty suffered.

Television coverage of Vietnam and the antiwar movement was important to public opinion on both subjects. For the first time in history, TV brought images of an ongoing war into living rooms throughout the country on a daily basis. Coverage of the antiwar demonstrations, however, turned most of Middle Amer-

ica against the protesters. Ironically, this happened at the same time that the war itself became unpopular with many of the same group. American popular music reflected the same division of opinion on the war as among the American people, with protest songs (often banned from the airwaves) balanced by more patriotic ones. Hollywood would not deal honestly with the war and its effects on soldiers or civilians until the 1970s, when it was all over. Then, a series of films—culminating in Oliver Stone's brilliant Vietnam trilogy—would open up the subject.

John Kennedy was elected to the presidency by an extremely narrow margin, but his successor fared much better in 1964. After serving out Kennedy's first term, Lyndon Johnson of Texas led the Democratic ticket to an overwhelming victory against the conservative Republican candidate, Senator Barry Goldwater of Arizona.

LBJ was advantaged by a strong feeling among much of the electorate that the work of his predecessor had been left unfinished at his death and by an economy that remained extremely buoyant. A man of the people, born in distinctly unprivileged circumstances, Johnson began his political career during the Great Depression. He resembled the homespun Harry Truman more than the sophisticated John Kennedy, and voters warmed to the man and his message. Both were in marked contrast with the political naiveté and tactlessness of his opponent.

Goldwater campaigned on a platform opposed to big government and social programs, but the majority of the American people in 1964 were not strongly opposed to either. The two candidates differed also over foreign policy, with Goldwater, prone to making off-the-wall statements, sounding like the hawk he was. It now seems clear, however, that Johnson's campaign position on Vietnam was not the one he actually held.

JOHNSON, THE GREAT SOCIETY, AND VIETNAM

The major domestic theme of the Johnson campaign was the Great Society. Unlike the externally focused New Frontier of Kennedy, the Great Society was an ambitious attempt to solve numerous long-standing domestic problems with programs similar to those created by Franklin Roosevelt's New Deal in the 1930s. In a way, Johnson's plan amounted to New Deal II.

Early in 1964, Johnson had already begun what he called a "war on poverty," the goal of which was to eradicate all forms of poverty from American society. This social policy was influenced by such studies as Michael Harrington's *The Other America: Poverty in the United States* (1964), which suggested that poverty was not an aberration but a continuing fact of life for large numbers of people, both black and white. This war became the cornerstone of the administration's domestic policy. It led to the formation of the Office of Economic Opportunity (OEO) and the founding of various programs, such as Upward Bound, Head Start, and the Job Corps, designed to eliminate poverty by providing better education and jobs. So promising a public policy (and, for so many, such a great hope) was not to succeed to the degree promised by the new president and his policy makers. It was undercut by the United States' increasing involvement in the war in Southeast Asia.

The Achilles' heel of the Johnson administration and its plans for the Great Society was Vietnam. Had American involvement there not escalated so much after 1964, and had resistance to that involvement not intensified as it did, Johnson might have gone down in history as the equal of his idol Franklin Roosevelt. As it was, however, much that LBJ had hoped to bring about was lost as a result of the war, including his reputation as a great president.

The degree to which Johnson was personally responsible for what happened is open to question. If one views history as a series of inexorable economic, social, and political events in which individual leaders make little difference (the materialist view), then LBJ is as much a victim of Vietnam as the soldiers in the field. If, on the other hand, one views history as a series of events over which certain individuals have control and for which they bear responsibility, then he is culpable. Perhaps the best view is one that mixes the two approaches, but certainly, at the time, however, LBJ was seen as the villain by those who opposed the war. Quite consciously, he made a series of decisions that committed the United States more extensively to involvement in Vietnam.

It is now clear that, when Johnson presented himself as a dove during the presidential campaign, he and his advisers were already planning to escalate the war. The major event in this process occurred in August 1964, when North Vietnam was accused of attacking the destroyer *Maddox* in the waters of the Gulf of Tonkin. This incident was in fact to a large extent provoked by the United States and the South Vietnamese. When it occurred, the Johnson administration released only the information that put the North Vietnamese in the worst possible light. The result of the incident was the so-called Gulf of Tonkin Resolution, passed by an overwhelming majority in Congress. It gave the president virtually unlimited power to do whatever he deemed necessary "to repel any armed attack against the forces of the United States and to prevent further aggression" in Southeast Asia. This resolution became the legal basis for all that followed as the U.S. war effort escalated. By the end of 1965, the United States had some 200,000 troops in Vietnam and had been engaging the army of the National Liberation Front, better known as the Viet Cong, on the ground for six months. Systematic bombing of the North, begun in the spring of the year, supported that effort.

ESCALATION AND PROTEST: THE SPREAD OF THE ANTIWAR MOVEMENT

In March 1965, in response to that bombing, a "teach-in" on United States involvement in Vietnam was held at the University of Michigan in Ann Arbor. An all-night affair, this was the first of a series of similar events sponsored by various groups on college campuses throughout the country. Such teach-ins focused attention on issues raised by the war. Though they attempted to present speakers for and against, in the end they mainly increased opposition to the war.

Objections to the war were raised on several grounds and became more complicated with the passage of time. Initially, concerns were largely humanitarian, with civilian deaths—an inevitable result of the kind of saturation bombing taking place in North Vietnam—the issue. Eventually, however, other issues seized the attention of protesters, especially colonialism and race. The United States was seen as a colonial power with an interest in maintaining the economic and political status quo in Vietnam and bolstering a corrupt South Vietnamese government. In terms of the race issue, the war was seen as analogous to the civil rights cause, with whites pitted against people of color. African-American soldiers were caught in the middle. Eventually, even Martin Luther King, initially quiet on the issue, found himself compelled to declare publicly his opposition to the war.

Leadership of the antiwar movement fell to different groups, but tended to be focused on college and university campuses, where protest was accommodated more readily than elsewhere in American society. Perhaps the most important single organization in the growing antiwar movement was Students for a Democratic Society, founded in 1962 at a conference in Port Huron, Michigan. In a document which grew out of that conference, known as the Port Huron Statement, the original members of SDS expressed criticism of American society as an oppressive, antidemocratic system dominated by a social and economic elite. They set as one of their major goals the return of this country to its original ideals of participatory democracy. What SDS lacked in 1962, however, was a specific issue to galvanize it, to give it the forward thrust it needed as an organization. By 1965, that issue had appeared: the war in Vietnam.

As the war escalated, so did protest against the war and the number of active memberships in antiwar organizations like SDS. These were helped by a "purge" of white students in the civil rights movement. SNCC, which had spearheaded the assimilation of whites into the movement for Freedom Summer, asserted the need for blacks to fight their own cause ("If we are to proceed toward true liberation, we must cut ourselves off from white people. We must form our own institutions, credit unions, co-ops, political parties, write our own history.") Many students who had been active in the civil rights cause began protesting the war. Draft card burnings became common events, as well as marches and other forms of public demonstration. Peaceful protest gradually gave way to more active forms of resistance.

Meanwhile, American commitment to the war grew exponentially. By April 1966, American casualties in Vietnam exceeded those of the South Vietnamese for the first time. By the end of that year, American forces numbered some 380,000; by the end of 1967, that number increased to nearly 475,000, with steadily rising casualties. The bombing had been going on for more than two years, to no apparent effect on the military operations of the Viet Cong. Ground missions—called "pacification" in the vocabulary of the war—too often resulted in civilian deaths (by an estimated ratio of six to one). The basic military strategy was to keep South Vietnam anticommunist. To accomplish that goal, from 1965 to 1969 United States units would search out and destroy Viet Cong and North Vietnamese Army units. It was hoped that such missions, combined with the bombing raids, would make the war too costly for North Vietnam to support and weaken the Viet Cong to the point where the army of the Republic of Vietnam (South Vietnam) could handle them. Unfortunately, American soldiers on such missions too often could not tell who the enemy was and ended by alienating the very people they were supposed to help. Success was measured in body counts, and, as the killing increased, so did the acts of barbarism on both sides.

These problems notwithstanding, Washington kept insisting that things were getting better. While reporters on the scene in Vietnam were being treated to daily news briefings which they called (for the time of day they occurred) "The Five O'Clock Follies," Americans at home were hearing reports from the Pentagon and administration sources that objectives were being met and that the war was being won. Privately, LBJ anguished over the increasing casualties and the prolongation of the conflict. Publicly, he maintained that the United States was on the road to victory. At the same time, his impatience with criticism and dissent became obsessive, isolating him even from many of his own closest advisers and from the doves in the Democratic party.

For no group was the credibility gap larger than for the servicemen and women in active combat in the war zones of Vietnam. They also received the optimistic reports from Washington, but they could compare those reports—in the news magazines and newspapers they subscribed to, in the broadcasts they sometimes heard—with the reality of the war. Firsthand, they knew that there was a gigantic discrepancy between statements of optimism about the way the war was going and the events taking place daily and nightly in the field.

Changes in the Selective Service System (or the draft), enacted early in 1968, did not help to alleviate the negative feelings among young men back home. Criticism of the system had mounted with the deepening involvement in the war. Instituted in the 1940s on the principle of local control, the Selective Service System in the Vietnam era operated to the advantage of the most privileged classes in the country. Because of the exemptions available to college students, and the concentration of middle- and upper-middle-class people in certain localities, a disproportionate number of those drafted to serve in Vietnam came from poor neighborhoods, underprivileged backgrounds, and minority groups. In other words, by social class and racial delineation, the troops in Vietnam did not reflect the true proportion of white to persons of color, or of well-to-do to poor, in American society as a whole. In many respects, it was a working-class war.

Under the new regulations, deferment procedures were tightened. Graduate students who had not completed two years of study by spring 1968 would be eligible, and so would graduating college seniors beginning the same year. While these rules did not completely change the system, they introduced a new note of uncertainty for a group that up to then had been protected. This occurred as resistance to the war on college and university campuses was reaching a peak.

NINETEEN SIXTY-EIGHT

The most traumatic year of a violent decade began, ominously enough, with an unexpected attack by the North Vietnamese and Viet Cong on a wide range of targets in South Vietnam at a time when such an attack was least expected. The commander of the U.S. forces in South Vietnam, General William Westmoreland, just weeks before had stated publicly that the war was going better than it ever had. Tet, the Buddhist holiday, had just begun. Suddenly the North Vietnamese and Viet Cong were everywhere. Back home, the nightly news featured footage of American soldiers having to defend the American Embassy in Saigon.

From a military standpoint, the North Vietnamese and Viet Cong lost more soldiers in the Tet offensive than in any other single campaign of the long war. They also failed to maintain their positions against the counterattack of the U.S. and South Vietnamese forces. However, from a psychological standpoint, the offensive was extremely damaging and had to be counted a victory for the North Vietnamese and Viet Cong. It had demonstrated that, despite the presence of nearly half a million U.S. troops and an air power second to none in the world, the forces of the North Vietnamese and the National Liberation Front were able to penetrate deep into the South at will and without detection by U.S. or South Vietnamese intelligence. Clearly, as far as the Communists were concerned, the war was not over, and they were not losing.

The political cost to Johnson was great. With ratings already low on his handling of the war, Johnson's credibility gap grew larger than ever before. By now, members of his own party were openly opposing continued U.S. involvement in Vietnam. In the

New Hampshire primary just after Tet, Senator Eugene McCarthy of Minnesota, a Democrat who opposed the war, took 42 percent of the votes to the president's 49 percent. An incumbent president facing such dissidence within his own party could make only one choice. On March 31, at the very end of an address on nationwide television in which he announced a halt to the bombing of most of the North, he said that he would not run again.

With LBJ out of the race, Bobby Kennedy soon emerged as the major challenger to the candidate that the president and most of the party regulars preferred, Hubert Humphrey of Minnesota, Johnson's vice president. Humphrey's record as a liberal had been tarnished by his association with Johnson and his refusal to come out against the war. Kennedy had stayed out of the race, his critics said, until it was obvious that he had a chance to get the nomination. McCarthy of Minnesota was not a strong contender, considering the opposition he now faced.

Regardless of who would lead the party in the next election, it was clear during primary season that the Democratic party was badly split on the issue of the war. In this, it reflected feelings throughout the country. By the middle of 1968, people were almost evenly divided on whether the United States should remain involved in the war or pull out. Those who argued for the latter were not all opposed to the idea of the war, simply discouraged at the prospect of not winning it. Nonetheless, the war in Vietnam had become the least popular war in recent American history, and the link had been established between it and the Democratic leadership in Washington.

The mood of the country was not improved by the assassination of two major public figures between April and June. In April, in Memphis, where he had gone in support of a garbage workers' strike, Martin Luther King was assassinated as he stood on the balcony of the motel where he was staying. In June, in Los Angeles, just after he had won the California primary, strengthening his position as a candidate for his party's nomination, Bobby Kennedy was shot to death as he passed through a hotel kitchen after making a victory speech.

King's assassination provoked days of violent rioting by African Americans in a hundred or more cities across the country and saw machine guns installed on the steps of the nation's capital to keep order there. The loss to the civil rights movement was enormous. King's death undercut the principle of nonviolence and vindicated the more violent tactics being espoused by radical black activists. Kennedy's assassination dimmed the hopes of all those who felt his candidacy was the last hope for the Democratic party in the election of 1968. Many thought he was the only candidate of either party pledged completely to end the war in Vietnam and bring real improvements to race relations at home. Kennedy's death sealed the nomination of Hubert Humphrey as the Democratic candidate for president.

Whatever hopes Humphrey may have had of overcoming the divisions in his own party were decisively diminished by the events in Chicago in August. Antiwar demonstrators flocked to the city for the Democratic convention, planning on peaceful demonstrations to support their cause, but, through a combination of circumstances, they soon found themselves in the middle of the most violent antiwar events thus far in the decade.

Blame for what happened fell on both sides. The Chicago police were aggressively provocative throughout the demonstrations. They were encouraged to use whatever tactics suited them and clearly had not been trained to deal with large-scale demonstrations of the kind they faced. At the same time, demonstrators who disagreed with nonviolent tactics encouraged others to respond to violence with violence. Some demonstrators were not bona fide members of the antiwar movement, but police or government plants whose purpose was to stir things up. Others were members of Chicago youth gangs with a long history of antagonism toward the police. The result was a bloody melee caught on camera by national television. The violence did much to assure the success of Richard Nixon, Humphrey's Republican opponent. In the fall campaign, he made one of the great comebacks in American politics. Chicago also did much to alienate the majority of viewers from the antiwar protests.

VIETNAM AND THE MEDIA: THE FIRST TV WAR

The effect of media coverage of the Vietnam War on public opinion has been the subject of much debate ever since the late 1960s. In fact, it was during the presidential campaign of 1968 that it first became a major issue, raised especially by the Republican candidates Nixon and Agnew.

Those who saw media coverage of the war as slanted or prejudicial attribute to it much of the failure of the U.S. effort. Their theory is that, if the media had been kinder to the military and less inclined to show the worst side of the war, the United States and the South Vietnamese forces would have won. Defenders of the media claim that what damaged the success of the war effort had nothing to do with the coverage; lack of clear objectives and an inability to recognize what the people of Vietnam really wanted led to the defeat.

One reason why media coverage of the war became such an important issue is that Vietnam marked the first time in history that a war in which the United States was involved was covered extensively by TV. At the time of Korea, network news was in its infancy, and coverage was limited to what could be filmed by conventional means. By the mid-sixties, however, technology had improved vastly, and network news had become an important part of the programming of the major networks. With the number of TV viewers at an all-time high, the potential for influencing opinion seemed all the greater.

However, studies of network TV coverage of Vietnam, especially in the form of the nightly news, have uncovered few signs that indicate prejudice on the part of reporters. For the most part, TV coverage was too brief or truncated to develop a consistent point of view of any kind. It also tended not to focus on the actual fighting, much of which was conducted at night or in places to which television reporters did not have ready access. Editorially, or with documentaries on the subject, television reporters did at times become critical of the war, but generally this came relatively late in the sixties, after public opinion on the subject had already been formed. What influenced public opinion more than anything else was probably the extended nature of the conflict (Vietnam was the longest war in U.S. history) and the sense, especially strong after Tet, that no progress was being made.

Virtually all reporters who covered the war in Vietnam came to see it as an immense waste of lives and money to support a South Vietnamese regime of dubious ethics and little public appeal. Although they were sometimes limited by the policies of their newspapers as to what they could report, journalists for mainstream publications played an important role in shaping public opinion on the war.

As in the coverage of the civil rights movement, newspapers like the *New York Times* treated the war in depth and raised

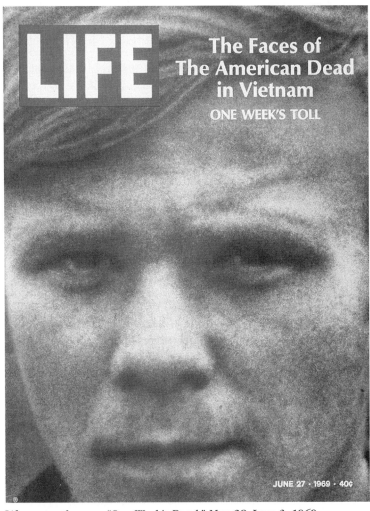

Life *covers the war: "One Week's Dead," May 28–June 3, 1969*

questions about its conduct that influenced public opinion, especially among the more educated electorate. Popular weekly magazines also helped show the nation's thinking, although their coverage of the war was generally positive until late in the 1960s. An outstanding example of a more critical stance was the issue of *Life* magazine of June 27, 1969, featuring pictures of one week's American dead in Vietnam: 242 soldiers. This 12-page series of photos— not taken by *Life* staffers—preceded by a short introduction and captioned only with names, ranks, ages, and home addresses was an eloquent statement of the futility of the war effort by one of the nation's most popular magazines.

Many magazines published the work of independent journalists, who could often write more freely than regular staffers. One of the best known of these was Michael Herr. His book *Dispatches* (1977), made up of articles commissioned by *Esquire* magazine, chronicled the war in the field in 1967 and 1968, as morale fell in the wake of Tet. It is one of the best examples of war reporting ever published.

Underground (as opposed to independent) journalists were not especially important in Vietnam, but the underground press itself was a major part of the antiwar movement. Originating from centers of campus unrest throughout the country, the underground press took an antiestablishment view and was consistently critical of the status quo, regardless of which political party represented it. In addition to reflecting a way of thinking which appealed to many young people of the late sixties, it provided a means of communicating among various groups in the antiwar movement and the counterculture. Through its pages, events like the protest in Chicago recruited participants from throughout the country.

VIETNAM AND AMERICAN MUSIC

The music of the antiwar movement was for the most part the same as that of the civil rights movement. Both belonged to the folk music revival of the early to mid-sixties. Antiwar songs written or sung by artists like Bob Dylan, Joan Baez, and Phil Ochs became important, though in some cases the songs were either traditional or not directly related to the war in Vietnam. "We Shall Overcome," which civil rights demonstrators sang to demonstrate solidarity, was adopted by the antiwar protesters, with a slight modification of its lyrics. Since the ranks of the antiwar movement initially were heavy with people who had been active in the civil rights cause, such musical carryover was understandable. Eventually, rock music also reflected antiwar themes. These emerged most strongly toward the end of the decade, but their references to Vietnam were often indirect or allusive.

One of the first songs to touch directly on Vietnam was Barry McGuire's "Eve of Destruction," released in mid-1965. Influenced by Dylan (even down to the use of a harmonica), this song, which reached the top of the chart in record time, alludes not only to nuclear destruction but also to soldiers too young to vote but not to carry a gun into conflict in the East. Part folk and part rock, "Eve of Destruction," like Dylan's "Masters of War," suggests a world under the control of sinister forces that dictate what young people must do.

Nineteen sixty-seven's "I-Feel-Like-I'm-Fixin-to-Die-Rag" by Country Joe and the Fish, the most political band to emerge from San Francisco's countercultural scene, satirized in shuffle style patriotism and the call to duty in Vietnam, where loyal soldiers were sure to die. Country Joe's "Rag" was a great favorite of soldiers in Vietnam, though, like all antiwar songs, it was banned from armed services radio.

In 1968, the Doors introduced "Universal Soldier," an antiwar song which, in concert, left lead singer Jim Morrison lying in mock death on the stage. In the same year, the Byrds' "Draft Morning" and "Wasn't Born to Follow" (both from their album *The Notorious Byrd Brothers*) supported the growing number of young men who refused to serve.

By 1969 and 1970, protest music became more commonplace, with a broad musical base. Creedence Clearwater Revival's "Fortunate Son" dealt with the vagaries of the Selective Service System. John Lennon's "Give Peace a Chance" was a chant-like plea for the peace process (begun in Paris in 1968) that turned into Lennon's first hit as a solo performer. The Jefferson Airplane's "Wooden Ships" created the image of a place of peace for two dead soldiers. The haunting "Find the Cost of Freedom," sung *a cappella* by Crosby, Stills, and Nash, commemorated a burial ground. Jimi Hendrix's "Izabella" and "Machine Gun" grew out of the war, and Edwin Stanton's "War" was the first overtly antiwar song in the history of Motown.

However, no one singer or group came to epitomize the spirit of protest against the war in the same way that Dylan, Baez, Ochs, and a few others spoke for the civil rights cause earlier in the decade. The music against the war was in many ways indistinguishable from the music that issued a general call to revolution, which could be interpreted to mean a number of different things.

At times this vagueness showed lack of commitment or, at the very least, uncertainty as to how best to express support for the antiwar movement. Such feelings were not strange considering the commercial climate in which musicians operated. Agents and producers typically did not encourage their clients to do protest music, and commercial radio stations often refused to play it. Patriotic songs like Sergeant Barry Sadler's "Ballad of the Green Berets" (1966), Dave Dudley's "Hello Vietnam" (1966), or Merle Haggard's "Okie from Muskogee" (1969)—the latter two big hits on the country chart—did not face the same problem.

Another reason for the frequent vagueness of rock lyrics about the war is that by the time the antiwar movement reached its height, so did the psychedelic movement and its music. Given that direction to rock, the lack of a large number of overt political statements on the war is more understandable. As David James points out, "All [rock music] could be functional within the rituals and other social practices of the antiwar movement, and on many levels rock music supplied the libidinal and imaginative energy of contestation. But by the same terms, the music was equally functional in social quietism and . . . the prosecution of the war itself." In other words, rock music fell on both sides of the war issue, even serving—as numerous soldiers would attest—to fuel them up for combat when "in country" in Vietnam.

In many ways, the serious exploration of the war in rock music would have to wait until after the sixties, when the war was over but not done with, to be dealt with by artists like Bruce Springsteen. In a number of songs from his albums *Nebraska* (1984) and the frequently misinterpreted *Born in the U.S.A.* (1986), Springsteen explores the emotions provoked by America's most unpopular war with a depth that most music of the sixties and early seventies cannot equal.

HOLLYWOOD AND VIETNAM

Although a considerable number of prominent Hollywood figures openly opposed American involvement in Vietnam, the American film industry was even more reluctant to deal with the issue of the war than was the music industry. In fact, it was not until the latter half of the 1970s, after the war was over, that any truly significant films about Vietnam would come from Hollywood.

By contrast, during World War II, Hollywood produced a long list of films supporting the war effort of the Western allies well before the United States formally entered the war in December 1941. By mid-1940, for example, the Motion Picture Committee Cooperating for National Defense was established to produce short features backing the defense effort. Later in the same year, studio facilities were made generally available to the armed services for making training films. Among major feature releases of the year, *Sergeant York*, which earned its star Gary Cooper an Academy Award as best actor, would celebrate the achievements of an American World War I hero fighting against the Germans. Charlie Chaplin's *The Great Dictator*, also released in 1940, was an outright satire of Hitler and the Nazis, with Chaplin himself as the Fuehrer. Other films were similarly critical of Germany, whose blitzkrieg of Europe had begun in September 1939—so critical, in fact, that by August 1940 Germany banned all films from Metro Goldwyn Mayer and Twentieth Century Fox in territories under its control.

Soon many of the best known Hollywood stars would enter military service. Rallies and premieres would be organized on the theme of buying war bonds. Camp shows and special appearances by stars at military bases here and overseas would become commonplace. Films such as *Mrs. Miniver* (1942), set in England during the Blitz, *Casablanca* (1943), set in North Africa during the German occupation of French Morocco, and *Watch on the Rhine* (1943), about the resistance to the Nazis in occupied Europe, would become artistic and commercial successes. Also in 1943, the first actual World War II combat film would premiere: *Wake Island*, set in the war in the Pacific. Many more combat films would follow, both during the war and afterward. Descendants of these combat films would also emerge in the postwar period, with their patriotic themes poured into a Cold War mold.

Two major exceptions to the general solemnity of this genre date from the early sixties: Billy Wilder's *One, Two, Three* (1961) and Stanley Kubrick's *Dr. Strangelove or: How I Learned to Stop Worrying and Love the Bomb* (1963). Neither was a combat film, but each dealt satirically with themes associated with the Cold War.

Wilder's film, set in West Berlin just before the Wall went up, is a fast-paced comedy about East-West relations in which the Coca-

Cola manager for West Berlin, MacNamara (James Cagney), tries to keep his job as his boss's daughter Scarlett (from Atlanta, the company home) falls in love with an East German Communist. As the farcical plot develops, the script crackles with satirical comments on everything from the Russians, Germans, and Americans in Berlin to the civil rights movement in the United States (MacNamara at one point remarks that he'll catch a Freedom Train to Atlanta). The comedy is all the more pointed because of Wilder's background. One of the best of Hollywood directors, Wilder's career started in German cinema of the late twenties and early thirties. A Viennese-born Jew, Wilder fled the Nazi regime and rebuilt his career in Hollywood.

Also heavy with satire on East-West relations and the Cold War was Stanley Kubrick's *Dr. Strangelove*. In fact, no other Hollywood film so thoroughly satirized American foreign policy and the military in the postwar period. It illustrates comically the ease with which nuclear destruction, barely avoided just a few months before its release in the Cuban missile crisis, could occur if power fell into the wrong hands. General Jack D. Ripper (Sterling Hayden) and the sinister, German-born Dr. Strangelove (Peter Sellers) devise a plan to initiate an irreversible nuclear attack on Russian strategic targets. In spite of the attempt of President Merkin Muffley (also played by Sellers) to convince the Russian premier that it's all a mistake, Dr. Strangelove's plan unfortunately succeeds. Though far-fetched in plot, as befits a dark comedy, the film still addresses the fundamental danger of leaving such monumental decisions as these in the hands of irrational men.

Compared with the Second World War (or Vietnam), the Korean conflict inspired relatively few films, though several were to become popular favorites and even cult classics. The first major film to come from the "Forgotten War" was *The Bridges at Toko-Ri* (1954), based on a novel by James Michener. Starring William Holden as a World War II fighter pilot called back for a dangerous bombing mission in North Korea, this film did little more than rework staple elements of previous Hollywood war movies in a new setting. The same thing can be said of *Pork Chop Hill* (1959), about an American battalion defending its position in the final days of the Korean conflict.

John Frankenheimer's cult classic *The Manchurian Candidate* (1962) is more a political thriller than a war movie, though it has a crucial flashback that takes place during the Korean War. In this tautly directed story of political intrigue and murder in the Cold War period, the son of a White House aspirant is brainwashed as a prisoner of war to become an assassin in the control of the Soviets. With an outstanding cast headed by Frank Sinatra, Angela Lansbury, and Laurence Harvey, the film captures the paranoia so pervasive during the period, even though its treatment of the effects of brainwashing now seems incredible.

Robert Altman's comedy *M*A*S*H* (1970) about a front-line medical unit in Korea, was an episodic comedy of dark vintage starring Donald Sutherland, Elliott Gould, and Robert Duvall. Part satire, part farce, part serious drama, the film commented bluntly about the brutality of war, in contrast with the many films that glorified it. Though its setting was Korea, no audience could miss the relevance of its statement to the conflict in Vietnam. As a television series starring Robert Alda, it was to become one of the most highly rated shows from 1975, when it moved to a different time slot, till it finally went off the air nearly eight years later. However, the satirical edge of the movie was dulled on TV, along with its antiwar message. Its success was due to the characters and the writing, not the light it shed on the Forgotten War. The final episode of the series, aired on February 2, 1983, still holds the all-time record for any network series at 60.2 percent on the Nielsen scale.

If Korea was neglected by Hollywood, Vietnam was postponed. With no exceptions, serious treatment of this war waited till it was over. This is all the more strange when one considers the length of time the United States was involved in Vietnam. The Korean War lasted just one month more than three years. Vietnam actively engaged the forces of the United States for ten long years, but our involvement there, in one form or another, lasted for more than two decades.

During the ten most committed years, only two American films about Vietnam were released (not counting documentaries): John Wayne's *The Green Berets* (1968) and Elia Kazan's independently produced *The Visitors* (1972). Wayne's film—shot in part, with the full cooperation of the military, at Fort Benning, Georgia—is a reworking of various conventions of the war genre, with a patriotic theme. Wayne was one of the major Hollywood stars who strongly supported U.S. involvement in Vietnam, and he made the film (with his son Michael as producer) to show his support. The film perpetuates various themes typical of westerns and war movies, in both of which Wayne achieved enormous success at the box office. In the category of combat films of World War II, three of Wayne's films are among the most popular of all time: *The Fighting Seabees* (1944), *Back to Bataan* (1945), and *Sands of Iwo Jima* (1949), in the last of which Wayne plays a Marine sergeant.

In *The Green Berets* (which uses the Barry Sadler song as its theme), Wayne is a Marine officer called back to active duty to lead a dangerous mission in Vietnam. As in westerns, there are "good Indians," in this case the South Vietnamese officers and people, and bad, the Viet Cong ("Charley" in the film) and their sympathizers. In the broadest sense, the enemy is communism and the American press, which generally opposes the war. The gradual conversion of a journalist (David Janssen) to the military's point of view is one of the major themes of the film. However, by reducing the issues of the war to such a simplistic level, *The Green Berets* (despite a few realistic scenes) has only a slight relationship to the actualities of the Vietnam experience. Much of it does not rise above the level of a government-sponsored propaganda film.

Kazan's *The Visitors* falls on the other side of the issue. Written by his son Chris and produced on a low budget, *The Visitors* tells the story of a Vietnam veteran, James Woods in his screen debut, living in the Connecticut countryside and trying to forget the war. Unfortunately, the war comes home to him, his girlfriend, and their infant son in the form of two vets (responsible for the rape of a Vietnamese woman) who terrorize the couple. Released a year after the conviction of Lieutenant William Calley of responsibility for the massacre of at least 175 Vietnamese civilians during the My Lai incident of March 1968, Kazan's film was considered too controversial for normal funding or distribution.

Indeed, controversy is the key to understanding why so little was said about Vietnam in American films until the war was over. While the broadcast and print media were covering the war thoroughly (if not always in depth) and popular music was being written about it, Hollywood remained silent. This was not simply a result of the studio system, which by then was in its demise. By the mid-sixties, many highly successful films were being produced independently of the major studios. For instance, *The Graduate* (1967) and *Easy Rider* (1969), two of the most important films of the sixties, were independent productions. With numerous major Hollywood figures against, or for, the war, why was nothing filmed?

Part of the answer lies in the lack of funding. The economic boom of the early to mid-sixties saw an escalation in the cost of

productions. If directors or producers found no way to raise sufficient money, their scripts could not be filmed. And the sources of
that funding—banks and investment companies—were not eager to
support anything that might cause major controversy.

Another part of the answer lay in the Hollywood experience
during the HUAC and McCarthy investigations of the late forties
and early fifties. Lingering fears about offending political conservatives certainly played their role in the long silence on Vietnam, especially as the conservative resurgence occurred in American politics in the mid- to late sixties. By the mid-seventies, however, with
the United States involvement finally winding down, the silence
ended, and filmmakers attempted to find a vocabulary to express
the tragedy Vietnam had become.

The first major film to capture some part of this tragedy opened
in February 1978. In *Coming Home*, set in 1968, Sally Hyde (Jane
Fonda), the wife of a Marine officer, decides to work as a volunteer
in a veterans' hospital while her husband (Bruce Dern) goes to Vietnam. A paraplegic patient, Luke Martin (Jon Voight), whom Sally
knew faintly from high school days, attracts her sympathy and interest. He is fiercely angry about his condition but unwilling to deal
with it. Sally helps him learn to cope, and, at the same time, as their
relationship develops, Luke helps Sally realize the person she really
is. By the time her husband returns, Sally and Luke have had an affair. However, Sally does not plan to leave her marriage. Nonetheless, damaged just as irreparably as Luke, Bob is unable to cope
with his injuries, which are mental, not physical. His suicide at the
end of the film releases Sally from their marriage, but leaves the audience asking how much must any individual pay for a war that
can't be won. As Luke puts it during a tense confrontation in which
Bob threatens both Luke and Sally with a loaded, bayoneted
weapon, "I'm not the enemy. Maybe the enemy's the fucking war."

Coming Home is distinguished by strong performances, especially Jon Voight's as the paraplegic Luke, but burdened by a melodramatic, indecisive ending. However, in semidocumentary style, it
conveys well, through scenes like the Fourth of July celebration
and other vignettes involving major and minor characters, the atmosphere of the time when it supposedly takes place. While this is
not new territory—Stanley Kramer's *The Men* (1950) explored it,
with Marlon Brando (in his screen debut) as a paraplegic veteran of
World War II—*Coming Home* makes it believable. A major contributing factor to its success is the musical score, based primarily

on rock music of the sixties, featuring songs by the Rolling Stones, Steppenwolf, and other popular groups.

The second major film about Vietnam was *The Deer Hunter*, released in December 1978, the story of three young steel workers from the Pittsburgh area, Michael (Robert De Niro), Steven (John Savage), and Nick (Christopher Walken), whose lives are changed permanently by what happens to them during the war.

In *The Deer Hunter*, the Vietnam experience is part of the search for masculine identity, a process of initiation in which all three young men are willing participants. As members of the working class and descendants of immigrants from Russia, they accept the draft as their fathers did in World War II. The banner at their farewell party says it well: "Serving God and Country Proudly." They leave behind various commitments to family and loved ones, fully expecting to resume their roles after Vietnam.

Before they leave, the three visit a hunting camp with some of their friends. Here the act of hunting (which gives the film its title) becomes another metaphor—the central one in the film—for the process of initiation. Accompanied by music from the Russian Orthodox liturgy, the hunt becomes a mysterious ritual of search and destroy, soon to be duplicated when they are in country in Vietnam.

There, serving in the same unit, all three are captured by the Viet Cong, who torture them and force them to participate in a deadly game of Russian roulette. Another metaphor of initiation, this game also represents the war itself, in which one's chances of survival are purely the result of chance. Each of the three reacts differently to the game, and their reactions, ranging from paralyzing fear to stoic resolution, predict their future behaviors.

These metaphors give the film thematic direction, while the story itself is grounded in closely observed realistic detail within a somewhat vague time frame. The focus here, as in *Coming Home*, is not on the war, but the effect the war had on the lives of soldiers and their loved ones. Most of the film takes place in Pittsburgh, not Southeast Asia. As it opens with the wedding of Steven and his bride and the farewell party for Michael, Steven, and Nick, it ends, on an elegiac note, with Nick's funeral and the gathering of his friends afterward. The final singing by this group of "God Bless America" provides an ironic, though not hopeful, close.

The change of attitude in Hollywood about the war can be measured by the fact that *Coming Home* and *The Deer Hunter* dominated the Academy Award presentations the year following their release. Among the top awards, *The Deer Hunter* was named best picture, Christopher Walken received the best supporting actor award, and Michael Cimino the award for best direction. Jon Voight and Jane Fonda of *Coming Home* received the awards for best actor and actress. Fonda's award was especially notable because of the controversy she inspired in the Vietnam period with her antiwar stance, a position that gained her the unflattering nickname "Hanoi Jane." By 1979, despite a national conservative trend, the political climate in Hollywood had shifted in a decidedly more liberal direction on the issue of Vietnam. By then, it was possible for actors and directors to express their viewpoints more openly within their medium.

The third major Vietnam film of the seventies was Francis Ford Coppola's *Apocalypse Now* (1979). It was not only the most expensive movie to be made about Vietnam, it also became legendary for the problems that occurred during its shooting on location in the Philippine Islands. Coppola had made his name as a director with *The Godfather* (1972) and *The Godfather: Part II* (1974), two artistically successful reworkings of the genre of the gangster film that were extremely popular with audiences. He had proposed making a film about Vietnam in the late sixties, but could not get funding to do it. Originally to be shot in a period of six weeks, *Apocalypse Now* would end up taking 16 months and run far over budget. At one point a typhoon destroyed sets, causing a delay of several months. The helicopters used in the film were donated by Ferdinand Marcos, dictatorial president of the Philippines, but were borrowed back frequently for raids on rebels against the government. Marlon Brando, who had turned in a brilliant performance in the first *Godfather* film as Don Corleone, threatened to withdraw from his role in *Apocalypse Now* but eventually turned up drunk and overweight without having read either the script or the book it was based on. Arguments lasted for days over small bits of dialogue, and eventually large portions of the script were ad-libbed. Martin Sheen had a heart attack during the filming, and Coppola twice threatened suicide. A number of scenes were filmed and then cut, and Coppola ended up pouring his own money into the production when it ran over budget. With problems like these, one would expect the result to be an uneven film, and that is decidedly the case with *Apocalypse Now*.

On the one hand, it captures brilliantly certain aspects of combat in Vietnam and the traumatic stress experienced as a syndrome by many Vietnam veterans (already dramatized in *Coming Home* and *The Deer Hunter*). On the other hand, it is burdened with a plot based on a classic novel by Joseph Conrad and a surrealistic editing and cinematography technique which, particularly toward the end, tends to take over the film.

The novel in question is *Heart of Darkness* (1902), a quest tale in which the narrator, Marlowe, goes into the heart of the African jungle in search of a man named Kurtz. This work, with its overtones of colonialism and race, provides the structure for *Apocalypse Now* but little of its substance. In Coppola's film, Marlowe becomes Captain Benjamin Willard (Martin Sheen), sent on a mission to kill the renegade Colonel Walter Kurtz (Marlon Brando). Kurtz is a superior West Point graduate once thought likely to rise to the top of the military hierarchy. He has established his own kingdom in Cambodia, where he rules as king to the Montagnards, a group of aboriginal people from the mountains of South Vietnam. He has dissociated himself from the Special Forces (which he joined at 38) and his country. Willard has a similar detachment from reality. For him, as for Kurtz, the war has become all that is real. As he puts it at the beginning of the film, set in Saigon, "When I was here, I wanted to be there. When I was there [in country] all I could think was getting back into the jungle." As a detached, emotionless observer, Willard is the ideal person to send on a mission of assassination. He travels upriver, toward the Cambodian border, in the company of a group of young soldiers. On the way, they encounter various obstacles, real and imagined, in their progress into the heart of Kurtz's darkness.

Coppola's way of rendering these experiences is dreamlike and hallucinatory, in keeping with Willard's (and Kurtz's) vision of the war as something unreal and out of anyone's control. (The same imagery enters into *The Deer Hunter*'s Vietnam sequences, especially those in Saigon, but doesn't pervade the whole film.) It also fits with the drugs and alcohol used so freely by Willard and the soldiers on the boat.

Their journey is increasingly nightmarish. It begins with the helicopter attack by a unit headed by Lieutenant Colonel Kilgore (Robert Duvall) ("I love the smell of napalm in the morning") and continues with an attack by a tiger, the senseless slaughter of a boatload of Vietnamese people, a USO show that features go-go dancers and ends in a riot, artillery attacks on Willard's boat that leave two men dead, and a commanderless outpost of soldiers on drugs defending a bridge in the middle of nowhere. It ends with the entrance of Willard and his two remaining companions into the dream kingdom of death where Kurtz reigns. Coppola's film suggests that the war was not only horrible (Kurtz's last words are "The horror, the horror") but also dehumanizing, reducing its participants to a primeval level in order to survive.

Except for its final, rather murky section in Kurtz's domain, *Apocalypse Now* is unequalled among Vietnam films of the 1970s for its realism and emotional intensity. Not until the first of Oliver Stone's Vietnam trilogy, seven years later, is combat experience in Vietnam represented so vividly on the screen.

THE VIETNAM TRILOGY OF OLIVER STONE

Stone's trilogy presents three different perspectives on the Vietnam experience. *Platoon* (1986) is a combat film told from the viewpoint of one soldier. Based on the experiences of Stone himself, it focuses on the search and destroy missions of the Bravo Company of the 25th Infantry, operating near the Cambodian border in late 1967 and early 1968. *Born on the Fourth of July* (1989) is based on actual events in the life of its protagonist, Ron Kovic, a Marine sergeant whose wounds leave him a paraplegic like Luke Martin in *Coming Home*. The film shows his gradual transformation from hawk to dove, from someone who tells his younger brother to love his country or leave it, to a leading member of a group of veterans against the war. The final film in the trilogy, *Heaven and Earth* (1993), looks at the Vietnam experience from the viewpoint of a young Vietnamese woman who survives hardship and suffering during and after the period of the war. Like the previous films in the trilogy, this one is based on the life experiences of its protagonist, Le Ly. Together, these films represent the most serious attempt by any one director to deal with the meaning of Vietnam in the language of popular film.

Platoon begins on an elegiac note with the arrival in Vietnam, where the entire movie is set, of a new group of grunts about to go into the field. The background music—the slow, sad strains of Samuel Barber's eloquent "Adagio for Strings"—supports the mood of sadness that hangs over the airport scene. Soldiers on their way out shout discouraging remarks to the new recruits. Body bags are being loaded onto a plane. In this way begins one of the most vivid recreations of war experience ever filmed.

The narrator of the film is Chris Taylor (Charlie Sheen), a young college dropout who has volunteered for Vietnam because he believes that the rich and privileged classes should not be exempted from serving there. Though he is labeled a crusader by another soldier later in the film, Chris is better described as someone who lacked direction in his life and hoped to find it through the military. He is not a gung-ho patriotic type like Ron Kovic in *Born on the Fourth of July*, but at the same time he shares with him the need to prove himself in some way by military service.

The slow opening of the film soon gives way to a series of suspenseful scenes of search and destroy missions, as Chris learns what warfare in Vietnam is really like. The Bravo Company is divided into two units, each headed by a different sergeant. Barnes (Tom Berenger) is the hawk of hawks, a tough soldier so hardened by his experience that he has neither compassion nor even good judgment. Elias (Willem Dafoe) is the humane leader, concerned not only for the welfare of his men but also for the Vietnamese people. The conflict between these two provides the focus of the film's plot, as well as a means for Stone to deal with the major moral issues that the war presents.

These are summed up particularly in one memorable sequence, in which Barnes's unit attacks a village suspected of being a Viet Cong stronghold. As the emotions of Barnes and most of his men fly out of control, innocent people are killed. When Sergeant Elias interrupts the carnage, he and Barnes end up in a fight that symbolizes their essential differences and also the paralyzing, unresolvable dilemma of the United States in Vietnam: What were we doing there, and why did so much of it, despite the best of intentions, turn out so badly?

The fight is broken up by the Bravo's commanding officer, an inexperienced young lieutenant (Mark Moses) who becomes increasingly cynical as the film proceeds. He orders the shooting to stop, but also has the village torched. What can't be solved can be burned out of memory. As the villagers march away from their smoking huts, some soldiers carrying their children, everyone, including the Americans, seems to have left all hope behind.

That feeling is not changed by the rest of the story of Bravo Company. When they are ambushed in the field, Barnes takes advantage of the opportunity to frag Elias (shoot him in the middle of

William Dafoe as the abandoned Sgt. Elias in Oliver Stone's Platoon *(1986)*

battle). Elias, not dead, is killed by VC soldiers as he tries to catch up with the helicopter carrying his men away. Later in the film, Chris, by then almost as hardened to what he is doing as Barnes, frags Barnes after the latter attempts to kill him.

Marked by fast editing and graphic images of firefights and other aspects of ground fighting in Vietnam, *Platoon* is a powerful indictment of war and its effect on the men involved in it. "The first casualty of war," the advertisements for the film read, "is innocence." The special quality of *Platoon* is how it manages to convey the message that, in Vietnam, the enemy lay within.

The theme of the nature of the enemy is taken up in the second film in Stone's Vietnam trilogy. *Born on the Fourth of July* traces the experiences of Ron Kovic (Tom Cruise), a paraplegic Vietnam veteran, born to a middle-class Roman Catholic family from Long Island. Ron's childhood and youth conform to the postwar stereotypes of the new, suburban middle class, and Ron's values mirror those of his parents, devout, hard-working, patriotic people who believe their country is always right.

As a Marine in Vietnam, Ron finds that the war is not the exercise in freedom he expects it to be. Like Chris in *Platoon*, he is faced with a situation in which civilians are slaughtered (in this case mistakenly), and then he accidentally kills one of his own company. These incidents raise moral questions that his commanding officer obviously wants to avoid.

But the real test of Ron's convictions comes when he is severely wounded and finds that he will never walk again. The emotions of Luke Martin in *Coming Home* are repeated in Ron's behavior: frustration, despair, and anger. Coming home proves no solution for Ron, as his sense of futility and hopelessness are only aggravated by a conflict of values with his parents. Increasingly, he sees that American society has no place for the Vietnam veteran. A monster of its own creation, the veteran is of use only as a symbol of the very thing Ron soon rejects, flag-waving patriotism. By the end of the film, after a futile, hedonistic interlude in Mexico, Ron has become spokesman for his group of veterans against the war.

As a chronicle of American life from the early 1960s to 1976 (the film ends as Ron is about to address the Democratic National Convention), the film has occasional minor anachronisms, but captures the spirit of opposition to the war as it grew on the home front. With a central character who was himself part of that war, it becomes an even more potent statement of the problems confronting Vietnam veterans and of what the antiwar movement stood for in principle, if not always in fact.

Heaven and Earth (1993), the last of Stone's trilogy, tells the story of Vietnam from yet another perspective—that of the Vietnamese people, caught between the forces of the Viet Cong and those of the South Vietnamese army and their American allies. If the enemy in *Platoon* lies inside each grunt, and the enemy in *Born on the Fourth of July* is a false set of values imposed by American society, the enemy here is any ideology that constricts human freedom. In the story of Le Ly (Hiep Thi Le) and her American husband (Tommy Lee Jones), Stone fashions a condemnation of the political systems that destroy individuals while promising them hope. Though it lacks the intensity of its two predecessors in the trilogy, *Heaven and Earth* takes Stone's theme to a new level. Neither *Platoon* nor *Born on the Fourth of July* manages to make the Vietnamese people more than stereotypes of one sort or another; *Heaven and Earth* gives them hearts and minds. In this respect, it is the most realistic account of the war by any American filmmaker. By the end of the film, as Le Ly returns to Vietnam in 1988 to visit her aged mother (Joan Chen), the trilogy comes full circle. As *Platoon* begins with the arrival of Chris Taylor in 'Nam, *Heaven and Earth* ends with the return of someone dispossessed of her country by war and circumstance. As an aged seer puts it to Le Ly at one point in the film, "Different skin, same suffering." In war there are no victorious armies. "Victories," Le Ly says at the end of the film, "are won in the heart."

Combat experience is the focus of three other Vietnam films of note. Although none of them says anything particularly new about the Vietnam experience, they are all serious, well-directed films featuring good performances. Stanley Kubrick's *Full Metal Jacket* (1987), coauthored by journalist Michael Herr, takes place on Parris Island and in Vietnam during the Tet offensive ("We are here to help the Vietnamese," an American officer says, "because inside every gook there is an American trying to get out"). John Irvin's *Hamburger Hill* (1987) deals with one of the bloodiest battles of the Vietnam War. Finally, Brian DePalma's *Casualties of War* (1989) describes what happens to members of a platoon headed by a ruthless sergeant when they violate a Vietnamese woman.

What all of these films have in common is the theme of loss and dehumanization, with the tragedy of the war falling on both sides. Many show techniques of filmmaking derived from European filmmakers, rather than from the Hollywood studio tradition. Oliver Stone's films, in particular, show the influence of Jean-Luc Godard, a major French director of the sixties noted especially for his use of hand-held cameras and for the vivid pacing of his films. All of these Vietnam films show the liberating effects on language and situation of the changes that took place in U.S. obscenity law in the sixties. Most also make use of popular music—folk, rock, or pop—contemporaneous with the time period of the film.

Yet, as statements in popular film about the war in Vietnam, they tell only one part of the story. Another set of films—born not of pity, but of anger—tells a different one. As Americans were divided in their opinion on the war, so filmmakers of the seventies and eighties were divided between those like Coppola and Stone, who saw the war as hopeless or tragic, and others who saw the war continuing on a different front. Though less notable for their direction or acting than the films discussed previously, these films have been extremely popular with the American public. This series began in 1971 with *Dirty Harry*, the first of Clint Eastwood's five films about the San Francisco detective who takes matters into his own hands in dealing with lawbreakers. The series continued in 1974 with the first of Charles Bronson's five *Death Wish* films, about a man who seeks vengeance for the murder of his wife and the rape of his daughter. *Good Guys Wear Black* (1978) featured martial arts expert Chuck Norris as a Vietnam veteran who discovers that his battalion's final suicide mission was a CIA setup. This was the first of several films in which Norris played a wronged Vietnam vet out to settle the score.

First Blood (1982), with Sylvester Stallone, began the Rambo series, with Stallone as another Vietnam veteran who carries the war from Asia to the homefront. As an ex–Green Beret taunted and harassed in a northwestern town, Rambo wages his own guerrilla war from the mountains, in the Hollywood tradition of the outlaw of virtue. By the second film in the series, *Rambo: First Blood Part II* (1985), the hero of the title is back in Vietnam on a special mission to liberate P.O.W.s and this time, as he puts it hopefully, to win the war. All of these films have in common a warrior myth central to the paramilitary ethos that has been a pervasive feature of American life since the end of the Vietnam War. As James William Gibson argues persuasively in his book *Warrior Dreams* (1994), this ethos suggests that justice and vengeance are the same, that conventional institutions of the law are inadequate, and that individuals must become their own enforcers. In short, in response to the defeat of the United States in Vietnam, a whole culture of violence has developed to give vent to the feelings of anger and outrage this historic event occasioned. By and large, the films that reflect this culture have in common a conservative or reactionary ideology and an emphasis on action at the expense of thought or reason. If the group of films by Coppola, Stone, and others have in common a view of the Vietnam War as tragic for all involved, in the warrior films the tragedy has become melodrama in which wrongs will be righted by swift punishment of transgressors. That such films have spawned so many imitators—most of which make no reference to their historic occasion—is a strong comment on the resonance of the nation's failure in Vietnam. Through such mythologies, the war continues to be fought and, in the minds of many, won.

Chapter 5

"I WANT TO TAKE YOU HIGHER": THE FORMING OF THE COUNTERCULTURE

At the same time U.S. involvement in Vietnam was escalating and the antiwar movement was intensifying, a new social phenomenon began in this country. With roots in beatnik culture of the 1950s and early 1960s, this development was marked by the sharpness with which its adherents differentiated themselves from mainstream American values in morality, lifestyles, and goals. Ultimately dubbed "hippie culture," this group embodied values that ran counter to those of mainstream America and that were to have a profound effect on the lives of American young people and American popular culture.

Whatever the degree of their radicalism, one thing that all students of the early sixties who became activists had in common was their idealism. The black students who formed the core membership of the Student Nonviolent Coordinating Committee, the (mostly) white students who made up the Free Speech Movement at Berkeley or who joined together to form Students for a Democratic Society—all had in common the desire to bring about meaningful, positive change. They wanted to reform the then current political, economic, and legal system to make it work more democratically for students and everyone else. However, the failure of the activists to dent what they termed the "Establishment power structure" led many of them to change their goals in the later sixties. A path that some would follow led toward increasingly radical, even anarchic, attacks on a political process they perceived to be inflexible. This was the path of the Yippies, founded by media-conscious activists Abbie Hoffman and Jerry Rubin, and of radical splinter groups like the Weatherman faction of SDS or militant black power organizations like the Black Panthers.

Another path, to which the beats of the fifties had pointed the way, led toward a rejection of political idealism and politics in general in favor of more personal goals: a self-focused, often hedonistic style of living, which reversed or significantly altered the family-focused values of the postwar baby boom generation. This was the path that led to the formation of the counterculture and its most obvious symbol, the hippie.

Although the term *counterculture* may be used broadly to describe any individual or group of the sixties that opposed mainstream American values, it is perhaps more accurate to use it in reference to the hippie subculture that developed in the mid-sixties on the West Coast. The term *hippie* (or sometimes *hippy*), as one who is hip, cool, groovy, "in," probably derives from *hipster,* a pre-sixties slang term for an urban male type who often wore his trousers low on the hips. Norman Mailer, in his essay "The White Negro" (1957), defined a hipster as a kind of existentialist, who has chosen to remove himself (or has, by circumstance, been removed) from historical consciousness. In Mailer's description, the hipster lives solely in the present. His view of the world is in many respects the same as that of members of the beat generation.

Like beatniks, the hippies of the sixties chose to drop out of society and exist in an eternal present, fortified by experiments with sex, drugs, and alternative behaviors of various kinds: communal living, open sexual relationships, natural childbirth, organic vegetarianism, exotic religions. All of these had characterized fringe groups historically in America. Unlike Mailer's hipster, however, whose behavior was typically violent, the hippies of the sixties thought of themselves as gentle, peace-loving people. Their clothing was a special mark of their membership in this society. For women: flowers in the hair, worn long and flowing, ankle-length skirts that suggested nineteenth-century styles and looked hand-sewn. For men: hair also long, often done up in a ponytail, tie-dyed

T-shirts, and tight jeans. For both sexes: facial decoration, especially on festive occasions, beads and exotic jewelry, and (if any shoes were worn) sandals as standard footwear. The image sought and usually achieved was a graphic representation of their rejection of the middle-class values that had produced so many of them. In addition, their political passivity contrasted with the activism of their peers in the antiwar and civil rights movements.

In the formation of the hippie subculture, the assassinations and general atmosphere of violence throughout the 1960s were certainly major contributing factors. If establishment authorities could freely use firehoses, police dogs, and billy clubs to "control" peaceful demonstrations, of what use was political activism? Campus authorities, though not prone to use such means to control dissidents, were slow to change despite the attempts of SDS and other groups to democratize them and give students a greater voice. To the extent that such institutions and their spokesmen seemed authoritarian and unyielding to efforts at reform, they could be readily identified with the conservative values with which many young people had grown up.

While the background of members of the counterculture was by no means uniform, a great many hippies did come from families that benefited most directly from the postwar economic boom. Their parents had perpetuated the ideal of the nuclear family in suburban developments that, by the early sixties, dotted the American landscape from coast to coast. The lifestyle of the counterculture became in many ways a reversal of the homogeneous, prevailingly middle-class standards of such developments, sometimes, in fact, almost a parody of them.

Nothing from the sixties documents this aspect of hippie culture better than Tom Wolfe's brilliant piece of pop journalism, *The Electric Kool-Aid Acid Test* (1968), about Ken Kesey and the Merry Pranksters, a crazy proto-hippie community formed in California in 1964. Kesey—author of the popular novel *One Flew Over the Cuckoo's Nest*—became the father figure among an odd collection of characters who lived communally in the redwoods region of northern California and traveled together in a modified, luridly painted old school bus. Their escapades and drug experiments, especially with acid, set the stage for much that would follow later in the sixties. The rejection of established authority and mores on the part of hippies was, to a great extent, a rejection of the values of their parents. In so doing, however, hippies created families and codes of behavior of their own.

DRUG CULTURE AND COMMUNAL LIFE

Central to the hippie experience were drugs, in particular marijuana and LSD. If marijuana was the social drug of the hippies, lysergic acid diethylamide (LSD) was the supposed means of achieving a new sense of the inner workings of one's mind, a greater connection with others, and, ultimately, with the universe itself. This experience was reflected in the word "psychedelic," coined from the Greek *psyche*, or mind, and *delos*, meaning clear or visible. For some, LSD seemed to provide insights that nothing else could give. For others, particularly when the drug was laced with amphetamines or "speed," the acid trip became destructive, with hallucinatory flashbacks that drove some to psychotic episodes and even to suicide. Nonetheless, the acid trip was celebrated widely in poetry and music, giving birth to a sound especially associated with the San Francisco area known as acid rock.

Closely linked to the acid trip was the hippie enthusiasm for Eastern religions and philosophy. The sixties saw the ecumenical movement in the Roman Catholic church, which liberalized the liturgy and made other changes in policies dating back centuries. In fact, most traditional religious faiths made an increasing commitment to some form of change, sharpened by the opposition of a growing number of clerics of all faiths to the Vietnam War. For most of the young people who formed the population of hippie communities, however, traditional religion, like most institutions associated with the world of their parents, had lost much of its meaning. In its place, many began to explore such things as transcendental meditation under the guidance of gurus, self-appointed religious leaders who needed followers as much as their followers needed to believe in something or someone. Throughout urban hippie communities, among the coffee shops, small boutiques, and other gathering places, sprang up sites of meditation and worship for the followers of new religions, or old ones newly interpreted.

Even more important than the new religions were the social and economic changes encouraged by the hippie community. Instead of a monogamous relationship, sealed by a church marriage and state law, the hippies of the counterculture preferred more open relationships, with self-designed rules and rituals. In place of the suburban ideal of homes replete with the latest appliances and gadgetry, the hippies returned to the practices of earlier times, as, for instance, in food preparation and storage, using foodstuffs which were organically grown and canned or dried at home. Instead of obstetrically monitored childbirth in sanitized surroundings, the ideal became natural childbirth, in the home, with a midwife attending. And in place of structured education, at any level, the counterculture urged self-study, contemplation, and renewed awareness of nature. Most important of all was the communal quality of hippie life. Inspired by a romanticized view of the extended family and also by economic convenience, many hippies chose to live together in groups. These were far removed in most respects from the concept of the nuclear family unit that became the fifties ideal.

The communes first formed in the cities. The most famous address in hippiedom got its name from the corner of Haight and Ashbury streets in an old, run-down area of San Francisco, across the bay from Berkeley. Beginning in 1965, the Haight, as locals called the neighborhood, became the favored residence of society's dropouts, influenced by the gospel of Timothy Leary, the ex-Harvard professor who urged experimentation with LSD and told his youthful audiences to "turn on, tune in, drop out." The Haight area was full of old Victorian homes that in many American cities had survived only as rooming houses or apartments. These dwellings facilitated the formation of large, heterogeneous groups sharing the living space and associated expenses. Units of this kind were soon imitated in other cities where hippie communities sprang up. For food and clothing, they could turn to collective stores opened by fellow members of the counterculture. Free medical clinics were frequently available. Hostility on the part of city officials in San Francisco, however, bolstered by the outlawing of LSD in California by 1966, eventually led many of the Haight community to emigrate to the country, where they established themselves in communes on old farms and similar places. This movement to the country soon spread among other hippie communities nationwide.

The rural commune, by the late sixties, attracted scores of young people—and many older ones—to what they perceived as a new social order. In the country, they could reject the materialism of urban America and, at the same time, reconnect with nature and themselves. Furthermore, the rural communes had the potential, though seldom realized, of becoming completely self-sufficient. In fact, however, much of the food and other supplies came through food stamps, part-time jobs, or checks from home. When these sometimes short-lived communities had clear political objectives, they were known as collectives.

Communal existence also encouraged the development of new trends in sexual behavior. The birth control pill, generally available after 1960 to women who could afford it, was a significant factor in this behavior, as was experimentation with drugs that intensified the sexual experience. But communal living, which enhanced the opportunity for multiple partners in a frequently changing environment where many people came and went, was itself an important factor. If a greater sense of sexual freedom was a positive result of this experimentation, there was a negative side as well. Unwanted children were born because many hippies did not use the pill (at any rate, the pill was not 100% effective). In the communal sexual environment, many women came to feel they were being used sexually by males who felt free to behave irresponsibly. That recognition contributed significantly to the development of the women's liberation movement in the sixties, especially since it came at roughly the same time to women who were activists in the civil rights and antiwar movements.

Despite these problems, the social experiments of the counterculture became one of the most enduring legacies of the decade. For many young people, these experiments redefined the terms of their sexual experience. For many others, they led to a reexamination of the purpose and structure of family life. Many, in their own love relationships, would ultimately reaffirm the values of their parents' generation by marrying and settling into a middle-class existence. Others would take paths that their parents might have dreamed about, but would never have chosen.

The height of the early hippie movement was reached in the Haight during the summer of 1967, the so-called "Summer of Love," which drew thousands of young people to San Francisco and the full-scale attention of the media to the newly developing alternative life styles of the California scene. In a decade already notable for teach-ins and sit-ins, the Summer of Love—which would yield countless "be-ins" and "love-ins"—ranks high for focusing public attention on the changing values of young people in America.

In the same summer that urban riots would again begin erupting in black ghettos in major cities across the country and the

Allen Ginsberg feels the beat as the Grateful Dead perform at the first Be-In, San Francisco, 1967

Vietnam Summer Project would culminate in the March on the Pentagon of some 50,000 antiwar protesters, thousands of young people converged on San Francisco to celebrate the new freedom of the hippie culture. That summer in the Haight became one long party, and the media treatment made it clear that not all young people were political activists or antiwar radicals. However, for most Americans tuning in on their television sets, this was a moot distinction. What middle America saw on the evening news was yet one more proof that their sons and daughters had left their control. Like the more radical fringe of the antiwar movement, they seemed to be as irresponsible in what they did as in what they said. In addition, drugs appeared to be the chief means for them to achieve their personal nirvanas.

The reaction of middle America to the spectacle of nakedness, marijuana smoking, and public sex was predictable: The popular print and broadcast media, focusing for the most part on the more sensational aspects of the event, helped to create a climate of repression and sanctions against the hippie community. What it did not seem to do was to divert a significant segment of American youth—estimates would vary from 10 to 20 percent—from the path that was leading them away from their parents' values.

The underground press—so large a factor in the antiwar movement—played an equally important part in the Summer of Love and subsequent events in San Francisco. Dozens of small presses in the Haight and its environs published newsletters and journals that promulgated the philosophy of "flower power" and "truth through drugs" circulating on the street. Liberated from various editorial and commercial constraints, the underground press could print whatever flouted conventional standards of behavior or systems of belief. Above ground, one of the most important publications to come out of the counterculture was the magazine *Rolling Stone*, founded by a Berkeley dropout named Jann Wenner in the same year as the Summer of Love. With John Lennon as the subject of its first cover, *Rolling Stone* quickly became the bible of rock music and the new youth culture.

THE MUSIC OF THE COUNTERCULTURE: DYLAN AND FOLK ROCK, ACID ROCK AND THE SAN FRANCISCO SCENE

Nothing caught the spirit or tone of countercultural life better than its music. For the young people who formed the counterculture, rock would take the place of folk music as the central musical expression. However, it differed markedly from what developed in America in the 1950s. By the mid-1960s, rock music had entered a new phase.

Dylan—the single most important figure in American music of the period—pointed the way in his gradual shift, with the albums

Bringing It All Back Home (1965), *Highway 61 Revisited* (1965), and *Blonde on Blonde* (1966), from the folk style which had made him famous to a rock style which incorporated certain elements of folk along with other musical styles. As part of the process, Dylan shifted from acoustic guitar (the instrument of folk musicians) to electric, and from performing solo to working regularly with a backup group. Although initially his new music alienated his earlier audience, eventually he won most of them back.

In the process of changing his musical style, Dylan broadened his subject matter. While many of his earlier songs focused on the social and political concerns of the civil rights movement, his songs of the mid- to late sixties reflect a greater emphasis on personal experience, expressed in lyrical, often surrealistic, terms and dense poetic imagery. Two of these songs—"Mr. Tambourine Man" and "Like a Rolling Stone"—would become anthems of the counterculture as well as major hits for Dylan.

The first appeared in the *Bringing It All Back Home* album, recorded by the 23-year-old Dylan shortly before his successful solo English tour in the spring of the same year. Part of the appeal of "Mr. Tambourine Man" is the mysteriousness of its imagery: We are never exactly clear about the identity of the central figure of the song, nor what precisely he represents. Often taken as a drug song, "Mr. Tambourine Man," like many of the best lyrics of this period of Dylan's work, does not yield its meaning easily. Ambiguous, with a haunting melody, it has a resonance that makes it rank with the best Dylan—and the sixties—was to produce. As with previous Dylan songs that became popular, however, it was not Dylan's version, but that of the Byrds which hit the chart.

Another notable cut from the same album is "Subterranean Homesick Blues." A satirical song in blues-rock style somewhat in the manner of Chuck Berry, this number has street-sharp lyrics full of puns and internal rhymes. It became known later as the source for the name of the Weatherman faction of SDS, from a line in the song which announces that you don't need one to tell the way the wind is blowing. Released as a single, "Subterranean Homesick Blues" announced clearly, early in 1965, the direction in which Dylan was heading. Two other songs from this album have remained prominent in the Dylan songbook—"Maggie's Farm," one of several songs of this period which seem to be farewells to folk music, and the haunting "It's All Over Now, Baby Blue," one of Dylan's best lyrics.

Highway 61 Revisited begins with what is perhaps Dylan's greatest composition and, most certainly, if anything so qualifies, his signature song. "Like a Rolling Stone" broke new ground both for Dylan and for American popular music. It brought Dylan the singer to the upper reaches of the chart (#2 by late August 1965), establishing firmly his ascendancy in the hierarchy of popular music. It also confirmed the new direction Dylan was taking in his music, with its rock sound and backup band, featuring the guitar and organ combination Dylan, along with many other late sixties rock musicians, was to use time and again. Nominally addressed to a young woman named only "Miss Lonely," its lyric spoke differently to each listener. At the same time, it managed to sum up the feelings of a whole generation headed in directions they weren't sure about, but certain, all the same, that they could never go home again. Probably inspired by Hank Williams's "Lost Highway" (the first line of which refers to a rolling stone), it stands in some respects with the whole subgenre of rock songs about the road, where Dylan had already spent so much of his young life.

As a single, "Like a Rolling Stone" was released in two different forms. In one, its six minutes were divided between two sides; in the other, it was limited to one side to facilitate airplay. Its full-length version broke with the standard practice of limiting popular singles to not more than three minutes (usually less) to make their point. Its success with listeners, coupled with the hit status of other Dylan songs in cover versions, established beyond dispute Dylan's importance in the sixties musical scene.

Other notable songs from the *Highway 61 Revisited* album included the title song and "Desolation Row," both of which featured the surreal imagery by now a common characteristic of Dylan's lyrics. "Positively Fourth Street"—a single released after the album—satirized the folk music scene after its rejection of Dylan had become all too plain. This song also achieved hit status in this year of Dylan's greatest popularity.

Blonde on Blonde, the last of the three albums marking Dylan's progress from folk to rock musician, begins with "Rainy Day Women #12 & 35," a raucous, barrelhouse-style drug song with repeated references to being stoned, and includes the haunting "Visions of Johanna," which, though extremely private in meaning, also seems to be drug-inspired. To some extent, the unifying element of this album is the way it provides views of women in different musical contexts, from the lyrical "Johanna" to the brazen

"Rainy Day Women" to the stereotypical "Just Like a Woman." From this album, "Stuck Inside of Mobile with the Memphis Blues Again" also became popular. As in the case of "Like a Rolling Stone," it ran well over the customary time limit (more than seven minutes in length).

Dylan's first public performance with electric guitar took place in the same year as the ground-breaking *Bringing It All Back Home* and *Highway 61* albums, when he was booed at the Newport Folk Festival. The controversy (and boos) were to recur throughout the coming year as Dylan toured this country and England playing his new music. In these performances, Dylan would typically begin with an acoustic and harmonica set, then move into the newer arrangements. In the summer of 1966, a serious motorcycle accident was to put him out of the concert scene, if not the limelight, for an extended period of time.

Dylan's new musical style—which created the tag "folk rock"—was to influence an important group whose first album covered one of his major songs. The Byrds, formed by Roger McGuinn, included, with only one exception, musicians (like the young David Crosby) with folk backgrounds. They also showed, in their debut album of 1965, *Mr. Tambourine Man*, the influence of the Beatles, the importance of whose music Dylan had already recognized. The Byrds went electric, featuring a 12-string Rickenbacker that reproduced the jingle-jangle sound Dylan had written about in "Mr. Tambourine Man." The group propelled to hit status not only Dylan's song (one of many Dylan covers they were to do) but also, from their second album (1966), the biblical "Turn! Turn! Turn!," adapted from the Book of Ecclesiastes by folk icon Pete Seeger. Their third album, *Fifth Dimension* (1967), produced the hit single "Eight Miles High," which was widely banned because of its drug import. In their fusion of folk and rock elements, the Byrds epitomized the musical style of folk rock that was to prove so significant from 1965 to 1968.

Another important folk rock group was Buffalo Springfield. With a membership roll that included Stephen Stills and Neil Young, Buffalo Springfield produced some significant music in its short career, including Stills' "For What It's Worth," about generational conflict and other aspects of the so-called Movement, and Young's grandiose, studio-mixed "Broken Arrow." Plagued by arguments and instability, however, Buffalo Springfield folded as a group by the time its second album came out. In 1968, Stills was to join with David Crosby (of the Byrds) and Graham Nash (of the English group the Hollies, second only to the Beatles in popularity in Britain) to form the trio Crosby, Stills, and Nash. One of the most influential groups of the late sixties, noted for its strong lyrics and harmonizing, this trio would soon add Neil Young, who wrote some of its most memorable songs.

As the counterculture began to take shape in the Haight in 1966 and 1967, an acid-based, psychedelic musical style gained momentum there and, with it, clubs, ballrooms, and theaters, like the Fillmore and the Avalon, which served as prime venues for the new music. Song lyrics tended toward the surrealistic, but the music behind or around them, featuring guitar solos that arched far out into space, was clearly rock. Psychedelic rock eschewed traditional blues structure in favor of a freer musical form, yet, like all rock music, it retained the spirit of the blues. Searching for an aural equivalent to the acid experience, psychedelic musicians found models in Indian *ragas* and other exotic forms rather than in the traditional sources of rock 'n' roll. Among the best-known groups to emerge from the psychedelic San Francisco scene of this period were the Grateful Dead and Jefferson Airplane.

The Dead, one of the longest-running groups in the history of rock (and the longest of the psychedelic groups), formed in 1965. It was headed by Jerry Garcia, who, as early as 1961, had been active musically on the West Coast in folk groups and jugbands. Early on, the Dead defined their purpose musically: to make their concerts an experience as mind-bending as a trip on the drug of their choice. Hence the name Garcia bore in the early years of the group, Captain Trip, and also the sobriquet of their fans—Deadheads. (In sixties slang, a "head" was a drug user, especially of acid.) The group lived together, communal-style, in the Haight-Ashbury district and became as famous for their lifestyle (which carried on the ideals of the hippie culture) as they did for their music, which they performed in hours-long concerts in which they and their audience were equally high. Frequently, they planned acid "events" with Ken Kesey's Merry Pranksters, and, like Kesey's group, they cultivated contacts with the Hell's Angels, the outlaw band of motorcyclists. The Dead's later music—such songs as "Casey Jones" and "Truckin'" —was modeled on country music. Concise and well structured, it achieved considerable popularity on the air. In the end, however, the Dead were known best for their concerts, not their recordings. They were also known for their problems with alcohol and drugs.

The death of Jerry Garcia in 1995, the result of lifelong addiction to hard drugs, appears to have ended the career of the Dead as one of the most successful touring groups of all time.

Formed in 1965, the Jefferson Airplane was the first of the major San Francisco rock groups to feature a woman as a lead singer. Fusing in their music various elements of rock, folk, and country, they were also the first to sign a contract with a major recording company (RCA). In 1966, their initial female lead, Signe Anderson, was replaced by ex-model Grace Slick, whose singing style made the group even more popular. That style emerged strongly in their hit singles of 1967, the hard-edged "Somebody to Love" and the drug-inspired, frequently banned "White Rabbit," both of which Slick had brought to the Airplane from her previous group, the Great Society. These songs were part of Slick's first album with the Airplane, *Surrealistic Pillow* (1967). However, in keeping with the ideal of communality which permeated the Haight and the Summer of Love (bumper stickers on that occasion announced that "Jefferson Airplane Loves You"), lead vocals or guitar did not belong to one person, but were passed around, and many numbers featured unison singing. And, like the Dead, the Airplane shared a house in the Haight. By the time the group recorded the highly political *Volunteers* album of 1969, they had been given total artistic control in their contract to RCA, with the result that the line "Up against the wall, motherfuckers" (a phrase taken from the Black Power movement) was kept in the chorus of "We Can Be Together," a paean to activism and the counterculture. The title song of the album—which the Airplane was to sing at Woodstock—was a call to revolution aimed at the new youth culture.

Other San Francisco groups of note included Country Joe and the Fish (the most consistently political of the psychedelic bands), the Quicksilver Messenger Service, Moby Grape, the Steve Miller Band, Santana, and Big Brother and the Holding Company, now best known for its connection with another major female singer of the sixties, Janis Joplin.

Born in Texas, Joplin emigrated to California in 1965, along with many of her generation. The following June, after a brief return to Texas, she joined Big Brother, and then, in June 1967, she made her show-stopping appearance (at the same time as the American debut of an electrifying guitarist named Jimi Hendrix) at the Monterey Pop Festival, the first major outdoor rock concert of the decade. Joplin's singing style mixed elements of R & B and soul, the African-American musical style brought to prominence in the sixties by singers like Aretha Franklin. Joplin's stage persona suggested both the defiance of a woman liberated from convention and the vulnerability that such liberation entailed. In the blues tradition, the emotions she sang about were hers, and the cost was evident in her musical expression and style of living. Southern Comfort straight from the bottle kept her going, but alcohol and drugs eventually brought her down, making her one of the casualties of the counterculture of the sixties.

In music broadcasting, the longer cuts now common to psychedelic rock first made their way to radio in San Francisco in 1967. Tom Donahue, a former Top Forty deejay, began playing 20- to 40-minute cuts from acid rock albums on FM station KSAN, in what came to be termed "free form" radio. The practice soon spread to stations throughout the country, especially in major cities and college towns.

THE FIRST BRITISH INVASION: THE BEATLES AND *SGT. PEPPER'S LONELY HEARTS CLUB BAND*

All of these developments notwithstanding, as the counterculture was about to break out in its Summer of Love, the biggest music event was undoubtedly the *Sgt. Pepper* album of the Beatles, issued in June 1967. Since their first tour of the United States in 1964, the Beatles had been consistently the most popular group of its kind in the history of music. Like the Rolling Stones, the Beatles had borrowed a musical style from America and, when they brought it back, what they played and sang helped to carry American popular music from the era of fifties rock 'n' roll (and early sixties folk music) into a new age. If Elvis Presley opened up this territory for white middle-class American youth, the Beatles discovered unlimited riches there, though their stage manners were considerably less provocative than his. Yet nothing that the Beatles did would ever have happened if American rock 'n' roll had not become so overwhelmingly popular in the United Kingdom at the same time as in the United States.

By the end of 1955 and beginning of 1956, the top-selling record in the U.K. was Bill Haley and the Comets's "Rock Around the Clock." This was one sign of the gradual penetration of the British market rock 'n' roll was to achieve. Elvis Presley became popular there almost at the same time as in the United States, and so did other major rock 'n' roll artists of the fifties and early sixties, like Chuck Berry and Buddy Holly and Jerry Lee Lewis and the Everly Brothers. Original black R & B numbers that were sometimes ignored in this country were popular in England. In one of the great reverse shots in music history, the popularity of this music, part of the internationalization of the rock 'n' roll revolution, was to result in the next major development in the history of popular music in the United States, the British Invasion.

The Beatles began in Liverpool in 1957 when John Lennon first met Paul McCartney at a church social. By the following year, they were joined by George Harrison, whose guitar work had the American rockabilly sound then becoming so popular in England. They changed their name from the Quarrymen (the original name of John Lennon's group) to Johnny and the Moondogs and then later—inspired by Buddy Holly's Crickets—to the Silver Beatles, then simply the Beatles. The spelling with an *a* is a tribute to the term "Merseybeat," a label generally applied to Liverpool rock bands. (The river Mersey runs through the city of Liverpool into Liverpool Bay, which, ironically enough, was the chief departure point for immigrants to the United States in the 19th and early 20th centuries.) The final name of the group also reflects the cultural pull of the beat generation, which by then, in the late fifties, was a phenomenon known worldwide.

In 1959, the boys from Liverpool were joined by Stu Sutcliffe, later to drop out to become an artist, and in 1960 by drummer Pete Best, later replaced, for unknown reasons, by Ringo Starr. They performed in Liverpool and also in Hamburg, a German city noted throughout Europe for its musical and social underground. The original look of the Beatles was heavily influenced by the "bad boy" image popularized by James Dean in *Rebel Without a Cause* and Marlon Brando and company in *The Wild One*, complete with black leather jackets and jeans. Their music was blues-based and R & B-influenced, much of it covers of American music they had heard on records or radio. When they began to compose their own music, for which Paul McCartney and John Lennon were chiefly responsible, it had a quality of innocence and simplicity that marked many early rock lyrics, from those of the fifties white groups to Motown.

The United Kingdom was experiencing a social revolution during the postwar period, analogous to changes taking place in American society. The class lines that had marked English society so strongly in the past were giving way to a new order. With unemployment high (Liverpool, once a major industrial city, became a pocket of poverty during the postwar British recession), and young people seeing fewer opportunities, the rules began to change. What young Brits saw happening among American youth, as reflected in the popular arts and media, simply added fuel to the fire. No longer was it necessary for someone to disguise the accent he or she was born with: The Beatles when they spoke sounded like the working class background they all shared, though when they sang they echoed the sound of the best American groups.

Just as Elvis took material not his own and made it his through interpretive artistry, so the Beatles created a style in their own compositions and performances based in black American music and rockabilly. Ultimately, however, the sound they created and the music that went with it became unique to them. And no other group of the sixties was to work in so many different musical styles, nor have such wide-ranging influence.

That influence was not only musical. It extended to the very look of the Beatles, who, under the shrewd management of Brian Epstein, presented themselves to their public by the early sixties with the so-called "mod" look: look-alike collarless coats, matching pants, and long, neatly cropped hair. This new look was to be imitated by virtually every other young musical group formed at the time (for instance, the Byrds and even, yes, the Rolling Stones) and by all American (not to mention British) youth. The period of long hair and tight pants was in.

Nineteen sixty-three saw the Beatles craze begin in England, as "Please Please Me" became a popular success. By the following year, the mania had spread to this country. Without any notable chart success the previous year, "I Want to Hold Your Hand" reached #1 by February, when the Beatles, on their first frantic American tour, made an appearance on "The Ed Sullivan Show." By April—with a rapidity which exceeded even the growth of Elvis's reputation—Beatles songs, on various labels, were at first, second, seventh, eleventh, and twelfth places on the Billboard chart (#1: "Can't Buy Me Love," at the same time first on the British chart; #2: "Twist and Shout," their cover of the Isley Brothers' version of the year before; #7: "She Loves You"; #11: "I Want to Hold Your Hand"; #12: "Please Please Me"). Their first U. S. album—*Meet the Beatles* (for Capitol)—was the best-selling LP in history to that date.

To many musicians already important on the American scene, the Beatles seemed to be just another group put together to appeal to teenagers—"bubblegum music" in the jargon of the trade. But Bob Dylan, who met them for the first time in 1964, saw them differently. "They were doing things nobody was doing," he recalled in 1971. "It seemed to me a definite line was being drawn. This was something that had never happened before." The Beatles were to have their influence on Dylan, and, even more so, Dylan on them: Their effect on each other was to prove one of the most interesting cases of cross-fertilization to occur in the history of popular music of the decade. The Beatles were but the first in a wave of British groups to achieve popularity and influence in the sixties. The Kinks, the Animals, the Rolling Stones, the Who, Cream, Led Zeppelin—all of these and more were to contribute decisively to the course that American music took from that time on.

With *Rubber Soul* (1965), the Beatles' early style had reached its peak, and songs like "Norwegian Wood," featuring the sitar, the classical stringed instrument of India, and "Nowhere Man" (#7 by March 1966) showed them moving in new directions. The songs about love and friendship—"Girl" and "In My Life"—provided a new take on both subjects. As Greil Marcus puts it, "this was a new kind of love: contingent, scary and vital in a way that countenanced ambiguities and doubts earlier songs had skimmed right over." Unlike previous albums, sometimes recorded very quickly, *Rubber Soul* was conceived as an album, not merely a collection of singles. This was an important development in the evolving history of the Fabulous Four, pointing the way to what was to come.

With *Revolver* (1966), the Beatles' music became even closer to its times in subject matter, showing the influence (to cite only one example) of LSD guru Timothy Leary as well as the mind-expanding experiences of the Beatles themselves. Introduced to marijuana by Bob Dylan in 1964 during their first American tour, the Beatles soon moved on, with so many of their generation, to LSD. They also indulged in transcendental meditation, in keeping with the fad for Eastern religions. Their music now began to reflect the shifts in values many in their American audience were undergoing. With *Sgt. Pepper*, the transformation—soon to consume the Beatles as a group—was complete.

Few albums in rock history have caused the anticipation and stir this one did, and few have sold so many copies in so short a time. It remained at #1 position on the album chart for 15 weeks and eventually sold more than 8 million copies. On a grander scale than anything that preceded it, this album was *produced*. It was a studio effort concocted over a period of months and shrouded in the utmost secrecy. Even the album cover, a collage of famous faces from history and popular culture (including the Beatles themselves) was given ultra-careful attention. The entire project was the subject of intense media hype. The result, while quite different in many ways from the earlier Beatles music, seemed well worth the wait. Before and after its release, it was the only thing that anyone interested in the new pop music was talking about.

As an album, *Sgt. Pepper* has a unity analogous to that which a poet might give to a volume of verse, or a painter to an exhibition of recent work. One of the unifying elements of the lyrics is their emphasis, almost throughout, on loneliness, or the fear of separation. The songs either want to bring someone into a larger circle ("With a Little Help From My Friends," "Within You Without You") or solace someone for being outside ("Getting Better," "Fixing a Hole," "When I'm Sixty-four"). Many—indeed, most—of the songs contain allusions (some easy to read) to drugs and the drug experience. "Lucy in the Sky with Diamonds" describes hallucinatory drug experience (the title itself is an obvious acronym for LSD), "Fixing a Hole" shooting up with heroin, and "Being for the Benefit of Mr. Kite" an invitation to a drug party. ("With a Little Help" plays on the word "high," a major code word in sixties lyrics for the drug experience.) Allusions to sexual experiences also abound, but not in the innocent vein of the earlier Beatles songs. "She's Leaving Home" describes a daughter leaving home to have an abortion, "Lovely Rita" a chance sexual encounter with a meter maid, and "Good Morning, Good Morning" the frustrations of married life. The more complex lyrics—"A Day in the Life" and, especially, "Lucy in the Sky"—owe a debt to Dylan, whose way with language John Lennon in particular had begun to emulate, though they also reflect Lennon's lifelong admiration for wordsmiths like Lewis Carroll, author of *Alice in Wonderland.*

Musically, the songs depend upon effects that could be achieved only in the studio. The Beatles were not alone among sixties musical groups in their use of such effects. Motown, for instance, relied heavily on them. Phil Spector's "Wall of Sound"—an overdubbing technique in which the sounds of five or six guitars, three or four pianos, and a bank of percussion were added to a studio recording to create, in Spector's words, a dense, "Wagnerian approach"—resulted in 20 consecutive hits for Spector and his tuneshop in the early to mid-1960s and became a regular feature of much pop music afterwards. For the Beatles, the choice of such effects in *Sgt. Pepper* had special resonance. Having given up concert performances in 1966, the studio became the only means of realizing their musical intentions. *Sgt. Pepper* has its own "Wall of Sound," with dubbed-in orchestral effects, including brass, along with various human and animal noises.

Today, these effects do not seem quite so special as they did in 1967. Many of the songs lack the impact they had then, and many listeners are struck either by similarities to earlier Beatles music or by the lack of spontaneity that came from the way the album was produced. In addition, many feel that the album shows the Beatles following hip trends (drugs, Eastern religions, and so on), not, as earlier in the sixties, setting them. Nonetheless, *Sgt. Pepper* was the major contribution of the Beatles to psychedelia. In February of the same year they had released as a single their first psychedelic song, the haunting "Strawberry Fields Forever." Several other singles followed *Sgt. Pepper* before the next album. These included "Hello Goodbye" in late 1967 and McCartney's "Hey Jude" and Lennon's "Revolution" in August 1968. The latter two, issued back to back, made up the best-selling single in the Beatles' career (6 million copies).

However, as the Beatles began expanding in cosmic, or cataclysmic, directions, they fell apart as a group. Increasingly, the work of McCartney and Lennon, though jointly credited, was done separately. Significantly, their next album, the so-called White album of 1968, consisted mostly of solo vocals and, for many listeners, neither *Abbey Road* (1969) nor *Let It Be* (1970), their final album, quite recaptured the magic of their earliest years, despite the popularity of songs like the title song of the latter and, ironically, "Come Together." Before the end of the decade, the Beatles had begun to move along separate musical and personal tracks, exacerbated by a failed business venture with their own record label. By the beginning of the 1970s, all had recorded solo albums. The Beatles, the single most important group in the history of rock music, were by then defunct, though they were to remain both popular and influential for decades to come.

THE ROLLING STONES AND THE WHO

The second most important group to emerge from the British Invasion was in the end to become the longest playing. Distinguished from the Beatles in style and substance, the Rolling Stones, formed in 1962, had established themselves firmly in the contemporary musical scene by 1966. Though the makeup of the original group was to change with the death of rhythm guitarist Brian Jones in 1969 and the eventual departure of bassist Bill Wyman in 1992, their spirit would remain the same. The Stones, from the very first, had epitomized rebellion and cool eroticism in a way that was to make their music speak directly to the alienated youth culture of the late sixties and seventies. In this respect, they reached the ears and hearts of the political and social radicals more emphatically than the Beatles did. Although their backgrounds were chiefly middle class, they cultivated the bad boy look which the Beatles had given up under Brian Epstein's management.

Their slow numbers carried on the blues tradition as surely as the work of any other group of the period, especially the Chicago blues epitomized by the work of African-American musicians like Bo Diddley and Muddy Waters, whose song "Rolling Stone" gave the group their name. Songs by the Stones like "Time Is on My Side" (1964) and "Heart of Stone" (1965) appropriated the blues form and reinvigorated it at the same time. Their faster numbers, though often restrained in rhythm and musical style by comparison with groups like The Who, were still more daring than many of their contemporaries. "(I Can't Get No) Satisfaction" (1965) became a theme song of the sexual revolution, and "Get off of My Cloud" (1965) as concise a statement of the generational schism as anything written in the sixties.

By 1968, reflecting the same pressures the Beatles had begun to feel a few years earlier, their music took on a political edge that set it apart from much that they had done earlier in the decade. *Beggars Banquet* featured "Street Fighting Man," which became an anthem of radical activists in that violent year, particularly in Chicago. The lengthy, discursive "Sympathy for the Devil" in the same album was as close to a philosophical and artistic statement as the Stones were ever to come, with its topical references and special meanings for the young and the hip. In some ways it was the Stones's answer to *Sgt. Pepper*. In 1968, the Stones also collaborated with radical French film director Jean-Luc Godard in a film called *Sympathy for the Devil* in which scenes of the group rehearsing the song are interspersed with interviews with militant activists and revolutionaries. Though some of the Stones's work of the late sixties was less popular than their earlier recordings, their audience remained generally loyal, even after the disastrous debacle of their Altamont concert of

December 1969, discussed later in this chapter. With the Beatles and Bob Dylan, they contributed much to the new directions of American music in the latter half of the decade. The spice and irony of their lead singer, Mick Jagger, combined with the driving, Chuck Berry–influenced guitar work of Keith Richards to create a sound, and an attitude, no other group provided so well.

The third most popular British group from the first invasion, formed in 1964, was responsible for another major theme song of the sixties, "My Generation." With its live-for-the-moment theme, it summed up the feelings of the young people that became The Who's fanatically enthusiastic audience. For them, 30 was not transitional but terminal, and no song better summed up the generation gap that emerged so strongly during the sixties than "My Generation."

The music of The Who—for which guitarist Pete Townshend and drummer Keith Moon were mainly responsible, with shouting vocals by lead singer Roger Daltrey—was on the whole harder-edged and less subtle than that of the Rolling Stones or the Beatles. This was the hard rock of the sixties, the beginning of the heavy metal sound that would dominate rock in the decades to come. With their crashing chords and driving rhythms, The Who also anticipated the punk rock of the seventies. Townshend's trademark "windmill" strumming and leaps into the air were skills that rock 'n' roll guitarists after him felt obliged to use on the stage.

For many people, however, the Who became best known for another side of their talent: the rock "opera" *Tommy*, completed in 1969 and filmed in 1972 by director Ken Russell, with a cast including Tina Turner, Elton John, and Roger Daltrey as Tommy. With its story line of a young boy rendered deaf and dumb after seeing his father kill his mother's lover, *Tommy* is a parable of the alienation felt by so many young people in the sixties. It is also an outgrowth of composer Townshend's predilection for philosophical statements. Considering the emphasis of The Who on *performance* (every concert was an act of theater, usually climaxed by the trademark smashing of guitars), the move to another form of theater—less dynamic perhaps, but more conceptual—was very fitting.

OTHER GROUPS, OTHER NOTES

Less important musically than any of the groups discussed so far, The Doors, formed in Los Angeles in 1965, gained prominence in

1967 with their hit single "Light My Fire." The main point of attraction for The Doors was their charismatic lead singer, Jim Morrison. Morrison's good looks, as well as his stage manner and surreal lyrics, summed up so much of sixties eroticism: an adolescent, narcissistic, self-absorbed, but very sexy mixture which turned audiences on. In reality, Morrison was a hopeless alcoholic with a fierce drug habit and little in the way of self-control. Now the object of a cult (perpetuated by Oliver Stone's 1991 film, *The Doors*), in his lifetime Morrison lost a good deal of his following because of his erratic stage behavior and increasingly morbid, arcane lyrics. He would die of a heart attack in Paris in 1971. As much as Janis Joplin or Jimi Hendrix, he was a victim of the excesses of the sixties.

Another musician born on the West Coast, Hendrix holds a special place in the music of the decade. Born in Seattle, Hendrix first became known in England for his extraordinary prowess on the electric guitar. With Eric Clapton, Pete Townshend, Keith Richards, and Jeff Beck, he was considered one of the masters of the instrument in the sixties. In addition, his flamboyant stage and personal style were in many ways the essence of hippiedom. In his debut at the Monterey Pop festival in the summer of 1967, he climaxed his set by burning his guitar on stage.

Known for his lengthy, labyrinthine solos, remembered for his rendition of "The Star-Spangled Banner" at Woodstock early in the morning hours in August 1969, Hendrix was a major creative artist whose career would undoubtedly have continued at the top of American music but for a drug habit that brought him down in 1970. Less than a month before Janis Joplin's death, Hendrix died as a result of inhaling his own vomit after an overdose of barbiturate. His music, like The Who's, Cream's, and Jeff Beck's, had great influence on the heavy metal of the following decade.

Hendrix's first group, the Jimi Hendrix Experience, was a racially integrated rock band, something rarely seen in American popular music until the 1960s. (The year before his death, however, Hendrix, under pressure from black radicals, formed an all-black group.) Sly and the Family Stone, another West Coast product of the same period from San Francisco, joined black and white, male and female, race and gender, into a cohesive whole.

Sly's hit of 1968, "Dance to the Music," like the equally popular "I Want to Take You Higher" of 1969, set the tone for the group's music, a highly original and exhilarating blend of R & B, soul, and rock, which was to have a major influence on disco music of the next decade. Always somewhat erratic as a performer, with monumental ups and downs, Sly later produced music that had militant political overtones which made it less popular with audiences. Ultimately, he was to fade from the prominence he held at the end of the sixties, but his music was to have a permanent place in the history of rock 'n' roll.

The Velvet Underground was another group important to the subsequent direction of rock music. Formed in 1965, the Underground became associated late in the same year with one of the leading pop artists and cult figures of the sixties, Andy Warhol. With Lou Reed as singer, composer, and lead guitar, John Cale on bass (also piano and electric viola), Maureen Tucker on drums, and Nico, a Warhol protégé, as another singer (labeled a "chanteuse"), the Underground, with Warhol's support, became known for a music that in many ways anticipates both punk rock and heavy metal of the coming decade. In such songs as "Heroin" and "All Tomorrow's Parties," Reed painted an uncompromising picture of life on the edge that appealed to Warhol and the circle surrounding him, much noted for sexual and drug experimentation. Never popular in the sixties, and defunct by the seventies, the Underground is important for how it suggested what was to come. As a solo performer, Reed was to continue in music to the present day.

MAJOR THEMES

Rock music of the later sixties directly reflects the social and political events of the period. The key words were often *freedom, love,* and *togetherness,* but the emotions were just as often violent and anarchic. The lyrics explored the possibilities of togetherness, mind expansion, cosmic consciousness, and revolution. They could also be erotic or sensual, and sometimes just pure nonsense. The "pop explosion" (in Greil Marcus's words) which began with the Beatles and Bob Dylan continued its "cultural upheaval" as the sixties moved toward their close.

Jefferson Airplane in 1966 enjoined everybody to get together in love, smiling at one another, while making it clear, in Grace Slick's intense vocal of the following year, "Somebody to Love," that it wasn't going to be easy. In *Sgt. Pepper*, the Beatles suggested that "All You Need Is Love," but, by their next to last album (1968), they were imploring desperately for everybody to "Come Together" one last time. It was becoming clear that the glue which had bound together the counterculture—and the Beatles themselves—was no longer holding.

Drugs were to take you to the cosmic center—a "Journey to the Center of Your Mind" in the title of the Amboy Dukes' song of 1968—and everywhere you were enjoined to reach higher and *be* higher: in Bob Dylan's hedonistic "Rainy Day Women #12 & 35," with its refrain about getting stoned, in Van Morrison's "And It Stoned Me," in the Byrds' "Eight Miles High," the Doors' "Light My Fire," which plays with the word "higher," and Sly's "I Want to Take You Higher." The music of the counterculture was turning people inward, outward, even inside out, all on a note of middle-class rebellion, as in Jefferson Airplane's "White Rabbit," where the kids have gotten their habit from mother, who gave them too many pills as they were growing up. The negative side of the drug culture was also to emerge memorably toward the end of the decade in songs like Steppenwolf's "The Pusher," with its refrain condemning those who dealt in drugs, and in the raw destructiveness of the habit described in the Velvet Underground's "Heroin."

The violence of a decade dominated by the Vietnam War and Third World revolution entered music with such songs as the Stones' "Street Fighting Man," with its image of the urban guerrilla, and the Beatles' "Revolution," with its implication that radical political action gets us nowhere. In another context, Janis Joplin, in her posthumously issued "Me and Bobby McGee," suggested, existentially, that freedom and nothingness could be equated, while songs like Crosby, Stills, Nash, and Young's "Find the Cost of Freedom" and John Lennon's "Give Peace a Chance" suggested that war, whether in the name of revolution or containment, came at too high a cost.

Instrumentally, rock music became more varied, with the omnipresent electric guitar augmented by such stringed instruments as the sitar and by synthesizers and studio mixing. The sitar was popularized in the 1960s by visitors like Indian classical musician Ravi Shankar, who concertized widely. Part of its appeal derived from the vogue for Eastern religion and philosophy. From country music came the slide (or steel) guitar, used by Dylan and others. The Who used synthesizers as an integral part of their music, while mixing became a more complex art with albums like *Sgt. Pepper*, in which nonmusical elements were incorporated into the fabric of composition. Given such developments, it is no accident that the year *Sgt.*

Pepper was issued marked the first appearance in the United States of a group called Pink Floyd, forever noted for the production qualities of their music, as well as for bridging pop, acid rock, and hard rock.

Rock acquired a more aggressive sound by the end of the sixties and, increasingly, its lyrics came closer to the language of the Movement and of the street. The euphemisms and code words of fifties rock music—perhaps more evident in white than in black rock 'n' roll, but present in both—began to give way to the general freedom of speech characteristic of all of the arts in the later sixties. Groups like the Fugs (a proto-punk, antiestablishment band noted for its verbal excesses) carried it to its logical extreme, but all cutting edge rock music reflected the same trend. The social and political stance of the later sixties required a new sound and a new set of lyrics to convey the meaning of the cultural experience. Nowhere is that experience communicated better than in its music.

MOVIES AND THE COUNTERCULTURE

If Dylan, the Beatles, and other popular musicians led the way to what seemed at the time a new consciousness, movies lagged behind. By the last few years of the decade, however, a significant number of films, often not from the major studios, addressed themselves to the issues of greatest meaning to the college-age youth who by then comprised a major part of the moviegoing public. In doing so, they frequently rejected the standards, moral and aesthetic, associated with the old studio system.

One of the most popular of the new films made an important statement on a problem that grew steadily worse throughout the 1960s. At the beginning of Mike Nichols' film *The Graduate* (1967), Benjamin, played by the young Dustin Hoffman, is asked by his father what he wants his future to be. "Different," he says, not explaining what he means. This small exchange sets the tone for a film that effectively and memorably dramatizes the problem of the generation gap.

A comedy of 1960s manners, *The Graduate* operates on several levels. The theme of the generation gap is set early at the party scene at the beginning of the film, when Benjamin is forced to relate to all of his parents' friends at once, with no one his own age present. Their questions about what he plans to do are typical of parents of the baby boomer period, with their orientation toward careers and material success. One of his parents' friends tells Ben the future is to be found in one word—plastics. "Exactly how do you mean?" Ben asks. "There's a great future in plastics. Think about it," he replies mysteriously. Ben seems much less certain about what his future might be and much less concerned than his parents and their friends with material success.

Ben's affair with Mrs. Robinson (Anne Bancroft), the wife of his father's business partner, puts the theme of the generation gap on a different plane. Part of his reluctance to enter into the affair stems from the natural fear anyone his age might feel at a relationship with someone older and well known to his family. From the first, Mrs. Robinson obviously wants to remain in control of the relationship. Consistently, she addresses him as "Benjamin" (as he calls her "*Mrs.* Robinson") and keeps her distance every way but sexually.

Another element in Ben's reaction to Mrs. Robinson's advances is that he sees them as inappropriate to a wife and mother. "For God's sake," he says to her just before they first have sex, "can you imagine my parents if they saw me in this room right now?"

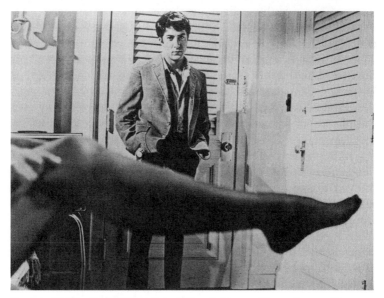

Benjamin (Dustin Hoffman) and Mrs. Robinson (Anne Bancroft) about to begin their affair in Mike Nichols' The Graduate *(1967)*

Traditional family values of the fifties and early sixties did not condone extramarital sex on the part of women (though it closed its eyes to the same activity on the part of men). Mrs. Robinson, a frustrated, bored, alcoholic suburban wife of considerable affluence but little sense of personal identity, steps outside the bounds of expected behavior as far as Ben is concerned. In doing so, in a sense she is rebelling against the pointlessness of her life, but the form of the rebellion (she has obviously had many affairs) is just as pointless and joyless.

By joining in with her plan to have an affair, Ben to some extent is transcending the traditional values of his class and social world, but he is also screwing the generation that's screwed him. His attitude in entering into sexual relations is "I'll show her," an attitude encouraged by her taunt of inadequacy on their first sexual occasion. With such feelings on both sides, it is small wonder that their relationship doesn't last. In one desperate attempt to lift it to a different level, Ben, tired of being her boy toy, demands conversation, not sex. At this point in the film he learns that Mrs. Robinson and her husband had to get married (their daughter Elaine was conceived in the back seat of a car) and that they lead totally separate lives. Mrs. Robinson's college major, art, is now something she professes to know nothing about, another sign of her spiritual emptiness. In being drawn to Elaine (Katharine Ross), Ben is asserting the primacy of his, and their, generation, over the values, sick or at best lame, of their parents. Although at first he tries to discourage Elaine because of her mother's warnings about seeing her, he can't ignore his feelings nor all he and Elaine have in common. Though Ben tells her repeatedly that he wants to marry her, it is clear by the end of the film that marriage is less the issue than separation from the older generation and what it stands for.

In being drawn to Ben, Elaine asserts the same values, but for her there is an added degree of difficulty, both in being a woman (having less freedom of choice) and in being engaged to Carl (Brian Avery), who reflects the values of her parents' generation. Elaine's fiancé is summed up by his affiliation with a fraternity that epitomizes the worst of the Greek system, portrayed in the film as both sexist and chauvinistic. In breaking with Carl, Elaine is separating especially from her mother, whose life is so empty and unfulfilling in marriage to a man with qualities similar to Carl's. Ben, sensitive and himself separating from the value system of their parents' generation, is something else. With him, Elaine has found herself. Their relationship—beginning outside of, and *after*, her marriage to Carl (their vows are said before Ben cries out to her in the church)— will set its own terms, not have them set by the world in which they grew up. The final bit of dialogue in the film sums it all up, when Elaine's mother tells her it's too late and Elaine replies pointedly, "Not for me."

With excellent acting and direction, *The Graduate* became phenomenally popular with the college-age movie audience when it was released in 1967. The stylish score by Paul Simon (who performs the music with Art Garfunkel) includes such popular songs as "Mrs. Robinson," "Scarborough Fair," and "The Sound of Silence." However, although the film deals successfully with an important theme of the sixties—the generation gap—it does so only from the standpoint of the upper middle class. In these terms, Mrs. Robinson, the tragic figure in the film, is virtually a textbook example of the problems of affluent, educated women limned by Betty Friedan in her seminal book *The Feminine Mystique* of 1963. The scenes filmed on the Berkeley campus of the University of California are also strangely empty of the fomentation taking place there in the mid-sixties. It took another film, with another sort of musical score, to give a truer voice to the counterculture.

Easy Rider (1969), directed by Dennis Hopper, was that film. Starring Hopper and Peter Fonda, with Jack Nicholson in an important supporting role, and written by Hopper, Fonda, and novelist Terry Southern, *Easy Rider* presented a picture of the counterculture from within. Less a realistic story than a fable, an attempt to create a set of symbols for what the counterculture meant, the film is a late 1960s odyssey through America and a description of what, in the view of many, it had become. That the film now seems dated (in a way that, for the most part, *The Graduate* does not) has mostly to do with how we now view countercultural ideals (as well as with the superior direction of Mike Nichols). Nonetheless, it remains the quintessential expression of the counterculture in popular films of the sixties.

Easy Rider is a trip film in two senses of the word. First, it recounts the journey across country, on their motorcycles, of Captain America (Fonda) and his sidekick Billy (Hopper). Second, it shows its main characters tripping on acid—and smoking marijuana—with no attempt to comment on the activity. Drugs are an accepted part of the life of these characters, like drinking water or breathing air. Indeed, the money for their trip to Mardi Gras in New Orleans comes from a drug deal consummated in the first few minutes of the film. Not long after the journey begins, Captain America and Billy, sidetracked by a tire problem, stop at a ranch where they are invited to join the rancher and his family for lunch. This gives rise to America's admiring comment, "It's not every man that can live off the land, you know. Do your own thing on your own time—you should be proud." This is a statement of principle for America and for the counterculture he represents.

Along the way they pick up a hitchhiker who takes them to a commune where the theme of living off the land takes on new meaning. Clearly, that is what the hippies who live there are trying to do. In addition to various touches of the communal lifestyle—smoking dope, suggestions of casual sex, and a nude swimming scene—there is also a "gorilla theater" performance, including an exhibition of tai chi from one of the commune dwellers. (The name of the theater is a misspelling of "guerrilla" and a reference to a form of theater common among radical political activists.) The most memorable scene in this section of the film occurs at the communal dining table, with a slow pan across the faces of the commune dwellers as one of their number utters a prayer of thanksgiving. This has a touch of authenticity and seems exactly right for the moment it describes in the late sixties counterculture.

Eventually, America and Billy end up in jail after they are arrested in a small town for joining a July Fourth parade without a permit. It is at this point in the film that a new character appears and, with him, a new sense of pace. The pastoral quality of the opening sequences, with their panoramic view of the American West traversed by motorcycle, gives way, with George Hanson (Jack Nicholson), to an increasingly more intense melodrama, culminating in the deaths of the protagonists in the final sequence of the film.

On the way, the film indicts various segments of mainstream culture in the late sixties United States, but especially that of small town, southern or border state America. It is "southern justice" that prevails at the end of the film, with Captain America and Billy taken down by vigilante gunfire simply for what they represent, not for anything they have done. In the final analysis, it is the counterculture that the "rednecks" are shooting at, not the characters themselves.

Emulating the technique of experimental films of the sixties, *Easy Rider* attempts to duplicate the drug experience. Just as acid rock suggested in music what it was like to trip, *Easy Rider* tries to find a visual language for the same thing. In a long sequence shot in a New Orleans graveyard toward the end of the film, the protagonists and two women they pick up get high on LSD. In this scene, wild camera angles and rapid editing imitate the hallucinatory effects of the drug, as the four characters have sex or indulge in extreme behaviors.

Although the characters of *Easy Rider* are not developed in great depth, the film does convey well various countercultural themes, especially the "them versus us" attitude which so many young people held. The choice of Peter Fonda for the role of Captain America contributed much to that theme. The star of numerous "B" films about motorcycle and juvenile gangs, Fonda brought to his role an immediately recognizable quality of rebellion.

Easy Rider was an independent production. Filmed on a low budget, it was first recognized in Europe (winning a prize at the Cannes Film Festival), then met with great popular success in the United States. Like *The Graduate*, it benefited, in its spoken and visual language, from the new freedom for American filmmakers and writers after changes in the obscenity laws in the late sixties.

Long before, Hollywood had created the Motion Picture Production Code, which went into effect in 1934 under the direction of Will Hays. The Hays office was a self-regulatory agency of the film industry that censored movie scripts before filming began. Objectionable language or situations were expunged, and sometimes whole scripts were thrown out. Any sexual explicitness or language regarded as lewd or suggestive was taboo. As the studio system declined during the postwar period, however, so did the authority of the Production Code. Frequently flouted by newly independent producers and directors, it succumbed to the times in 1968. It would be replaced by a rating system intended to warn viewers what to expect in new films. *Easy Rider* helped to push the new freedom of the late sixties to the limit, both in language and in content.

In addition, the musical score of the film is a virtual anthology of late sixties rock music. It includes Steppenwolf ("Born to Be Wild" and "The Pusher"), The Band ("The Weight"), and work by other popular groups. The music is especially prominent (like the Simon and Garfunkel songs of *The Graduate*) during transitional scenes, supporting their visual symbolism.

The violence that marks the ending of *Easy Rider* became the distinguishing hallmark of a number of important films of the sixties, as it became a symbol, for many, of the major events of the decade. No film embodies this element of the period better than Arthur Penn's *Bonnie and Clyde* (1967).

Set in Depression-era Texas, this romanticization of the exploits of a pair of bank robbers falls partly into the same genre as earlier Hollywood gangster epics in which audience sympathy for the outlaw (as in many westerns) is clearly solicited. However, the exploitation of violence in *Bonnie and Clyde* reflects new standards of permissibility in the Hollywood of the late 1960s, as the sympathetic portrayal of the bank robbers themselves represents an extension of the same countercultural myth that informs the portrait of Captain America and Billy in *Easy Rider*. In *Bonnie and Clyde*, the forces of authority are flawed and the sympathy of the audience is directed to the criminals. Clyde explains the desire to be an outlaw in terms reminiscent of Benjamin's comment on his future in *The Graduate*: "Because you're different," he tells Bonnie, "that's why! You know you're like me. You want different things . . . . something better than bein' a waitress."

Though Bonnie and Clyde are not precisely victims, their empathy with a victimized group—the farmers who have lost their houses and land to the banks—makes them modern Robin Hoods, robbing the rich to avenge the poor. The real villains of the film are those institutions of society that are supposed to be most responsive to its citizens. As the police and their representatives gradually close in, their connection with the farmers' oppressors becomes increasingly plain. For the counterculture of the sixties, the same symbolism prevailed. In the same vein, *Butch Cassidy and the Sundance Kid* (1969), another film popular with the youth culture, romanticized the exploits of bank robbers who knew they would eventually be taken by the law.

The casting of *Bonnie and Clyde* supports its romanticizing tendency. Warren Beatty and Faye Dunaway in the title roles are too beautiful to be confused with the real-life gun-toting duo of the Depression period. However, the violence of the film, which brought it special attention when first released, is quite another thing. As in another film of this period marked by the same quality, Sam Peckinpah's *The Wild Bunch* (1969), the blood and thunder of the action sequences of *Bonnie and Clyde* represent a new level of realism for such material in American film. The slow motion finale, when Bonnie and Clyde are ambushed by federal agents in their parked car along a country road, like the final sequence of *The Wild Bunch*, has an unmistakably orgasmic quality to it.

The musical score of *Bonnie and Clyde* reinforces its period and milieu with the bluegrass sounds of Flatt and Scruggs, a popular duo in this genre of music during the late sixties. Their combination of country vocal style with banjo and guitar accompaniment suits the Depression-era setting well. In the same vein, the cinematography (by Burnett Guffey) occasionally owes much to the great American photographers of the Depression years, like Dorothea Lange and Walker Evans. Director Arthur Penn's next film, *Alice's Restaurant* (1969), is yet another fable of the counterculture, with a cast headed by Arlo Guthrie, son of folk musician Woody Guthrie, and featuring a guest appearance by Pete Seeger.

If a new standard of depicting violence was set by *Bonnie and Clyde*, another film, released in 1968, set a different sort of standard of imaginative realism. As the counterculture sought through LSD to unite itself with the cosmos, Hollywood was finding new ways to depict the world of outer space. Stanley Kubrick's *2001: A Space Odyssey* did for science fiction films what *Bonnie and Clyde* and *The Wild Bunch* did for screen violence: It lifted its genre into a new dimension. At the same time, Kubrick's film provided a trenchant comment on the problems of the space age.

Landing the first men on the moon became one of John Kennedy's primary goals, enunciated early in his presidency, in his first State of the Union address. While Kennedy did not live to see the realization of his goal, the development of the National Aeronautics and Space Administration (NASA) and the Apollo mission culminated in the moon landing of August 1969, and the famous comment of Neil Armstrong, "One small step for man, one gigantic leap for mankind." However, the dream of conquering space was shadowed by the same fears that had developed in the fifties and early sixties over nuclear armament. In admitting the infinite into our lives, are we also admitting chaos? This is the question raised by *2001*. Rather than controlling the immense technology of space, Kubrick's film suggests, with its sinister computer Hal, that technology is controlling us.

Despite the seriousness of this theme in the film, and the ironies of a musical score that uses a heroic theme from the classical repertory, Richard Strauss's Nietzschean *Thus Spake Zarathustra*, the technical innovations of *2001* were not to be surpassed in sci-fi movies until well into the following decade, with George Lucas's first film in the *Star Wars* trilogy (1977).

In the same year that *2001* was released, and only slightly more than one month after America reached the moon, NBC cancelled a science fiction series that also raised serious questions in its scripts, *Star Trek*. The object of cult devotion when its reruns began in the seventies, this program—which was to spawn followers named "Trekkies" and to inspire a whole series of motion pictures based on its story line—had little success during its initial television run of three years.

To some extent, major feature films of the late sixties like *Easy Rider* reflected an important development of the decade: the increasing number of independently produced, experimental avant-garde films. In major cities and on college and university campuses, a new audience had emerged, interested in film as an art form and dedicated to the idea of seeing something other than Hollywood products. A significant number of independent filmmakers began to produce work for this audience during the decade of the sixties.

One of the most famous of the experimental filmmakers was pop artist Andy Warhol, who directed a number of films, shot primarily at the studio of his Factory in Manhattan, that deliberately flouted Hollywood conventions. These included *Sleep* (some six hours of someone doing just that) and *Empire State Building* (seven hours of the building, in which nothing happens on the screen except a change of light and shadow). In addition, many of the Warhol productions, for instance *Blowjob*, threatened to cross over the line into another burgeoning genre of the late sixties, pornography.

The changes in the obscenity law not only freed serious film writers and directors from the shackles of the Hollywood code; it also made possible the development of a flourishing, above-the-counter market in pornography. Films which only a few years before would have been relegated to stag parties at men's clubs and fraternities were now given public screenings. Like many of the trends of the counterculture and other aspects of the late sixties scene, freedom in this case often gave way to license, and the call for censorship, always to be heard in the film industry, became louder than ever.

If the counterculture of the late sixties led to films of dubious worth, it also created a genre which had barely existed before. As part of the developing concert scene in the musical world, the concert film or "rockumentary" became an increasingly popular form. As both entertainment and documentary record, such films have become an important part of the cultural legacy of the sixties.

Elvis Presley had proved, in a series of Hollywood movies not marked by any great acting talent, that an American rock 'n' roll star could draw in the youth audience. At about the same time, in the mid-1950s, deejay Alan Freed hosted a number of low-budget concert films that promoted the growing taste for rock 'n' roll. Soon after they achieved popularity, the Beatles showed the drawing power of a rock group in inventive films like *A Hard Day's Night* (1964) and *Help!* (1965) (both directed by Richard Lester) and *Yellow Submarine* (1968), the first animated film featuring rock music. With the release of D. A. Pennebaker's *Monterey Pop* in 1969, the new genre of the concert film—in this case a record of the important Monterey Pop Festival of 1967—reached for the same audience.

Two seminal films of 1970 established the popularity of the genre beyond dispute, and, together, managed to commemorate the high and low points of the late sixties concert scene: *Gimme Shelter*, a documentary based on the controversial Altamont concert of the Rolling Stones in December 1969, and Michael Wadleigh's *Woodstock*, the documentary of the most famous rock festival of the decade, in August of the same year. The latter particularly established the importance of the genre as a record of events of potential historic importance as well as artistic worth. Like other sixties rockumentaries, it adapted the techniques of experimental film—for instance the use of simultaneous images—to prove that such documentaries could be more than just a literal record of events.

WOODSTOCK AND ALTAMONT: MYTH AND REALITY

The documentary of the Woodstock festival was but one aspect of the intensive and sometimes misleading media coverage that festival received. With the exception of the Summer of Love, no other single event epitomized the spirit of the counterculture so fully, and no other event embodied more clearly most of its contradictions. An expression of countercultural values, it became known through the coverage it received by television and the press. Like other major events of the decade, it was in many ways a product of the mass media. And, as with all media events, the truth of Woodstock lies somewhere between the reporting and the reality.

The Woodstock story is probably the best known of all those associated with the sixties counterculture and musical scene: how a group of young promoters decided to hold a three-day festival of music and art in upstate New York in August 1969, celebrating the countercultural ideals of peace and love; how the event was relocated because of local objections; how the promoters vastly underestimated the numbers who would arrive (the total was between 450,000 and 500,000); how the three days there—even with the multiproblems of insufficient food and sanitation facilities, extreme wet weather and subsequent mud, and considerable drug abuse (hundreds of the attendees suffered bad reactions to LSD and other drugs)—remained dedicated to the original goals; how almost everyone who participated, either as part of the performing groups or as part of the audience, found their lives indelibly marked by the event, in which the violence of the late sixties had little part (though violence almost reached the stage in the confrontation between Abbie Hoffman and Pete Townshend of The Who, who denied Hoffman the right to interrupt their performance). Violence also provided much of the inspiration for the event, for Woodstock was first and foremost a protest concert organized to express opposition to the Vietnam War. The violence of that war and all it had come to symbolize about the U.S. government was the reason for the overarching Woodstock theme of peace and love.

More important historically, however, was what the concert suggested about fundamental changes in lifestyles. At least three things were made clear by what transpired there: one, that large numbers of young middle-class Americans (most of them not hippies) did not agree with their parents' notions of appropriate sexual behavior; second, that the music of this generation (if any doubted) was rock 'n' roll; and third, that drugs, in one form or another, were to be part of this generation's experience.

No matter how one looks at Woodstock, there is no denying that what occurred there was to be replicated, and expanded on, in the decade to come. In its hedonism, its emphasis on personal satisfaction, and its assertion of the autonomy of the values of youth culture, the Woodstock myth was to define the seventies for a large segment of American young people. It also indicated that the period of open, active rebellion against mainstream values was coming to a close. The rebellion of the seventies was to be more personal and internal, with rock concerts becoming, for many, the closest they would get to "peaceful demonstration." In addition, the values of the counterculture would be propagated by the commercial mass media. Television, radio, record companies, book publishers, concert promoters—all of these had helped to create and disseminate countercultural values and would continue doing so in the seventies and eighties.

How volatile the mix would be, however, remained open to question, especially after the concert given by the Rolling Stones at Altamont, California, in December. It was made infamous by the presence, as security guards, of members of the motorcycle gang Hell's Angels. At this concert, which was attended by some 300,000 people, drugs—especially marijuana and LSD—were just as pervasive as at Woodstock, but here the violent side of the sixties predominated. The Hell's Angels members treated the audience to beatings and personal defilement and clubbed members of the musical group Jefferson Airplane as they approached the stage for their part of the performance. One person died at the hands of the motorcycle gang (and three more from other causes), while scores of people in the audience, stoned out of their minds, looked on. If Woodstock represented the up side of the counterculture movement, the one great final instance of total be-in, then the Altamont concert was the down, the worst aspect of the sixties showing itself in the grossest possible way.

THE COUNTERCULTURE AT THE END OF THE DECADE

By the close of the sixties, the counterculture, like the antiwar movement, turned in on itself, as though burned out by the effort it had taken to get that far. Its violent and destructive side had left ruined lives and fried brains in its wake—and many children who were to be raised in foster homes because their parents had not been willing, or able, to take full responsibility for them. If the drug culture which Timothy Leary espoused had opened cosmic doors and inspired some of the best music of the decade, it had also helped to produce someone like Charles Manson.

Manson had been in San Francisco during the Summer of Love in 1967. Thinking himself to be a reincarnation of Satan and Christ combined and using LSD as a means of mind control over his followers, Manson preached a doctrine of hatred, claiming that a race war between blacks and whites was about to begin. Using the code word "helter skelter" (from the Beatles' song of that name, in which he claimed to find hidden messages), Manson led his followers—young, aimless drifters—to Los Angeles, where they set up a commune in an old movie ranch set and planned the series of murders that made them infamous.

In August 1969—the same month as Woodstock—they murdered actress Sharon Tate, wife of film director Roman Polanski, and a group of friends at the Polanski home in Beverly Hills. Ms. Tate was hanged and stabbed to death, her full-term fetus of eight and a half months dying with her. Almost immediately afterwards, the cult killed two members of the wealthy La Bianca family in another expensive Los Angeles suburb. Manson, who directed but did not participate in the actual murders, told his followers they were necessary acts to prepare the way for the coming race war.

A confession by one member of the group led to the arrest of Manson and those of his followers who were involved in the murders. The trial that resulted, like the trial of the so-called Chicago Seven after the events of the Democratic Convention of 1968, was one of the most celebrated of the decade. A media circus, it dragged on for nearly a year, marked by one bizarre event after another, until Manson was given a life sentence. He remains in prison to this day, never having expressed any remorse over anything he did. The Manson trial was important to the public perception of the counterculture, since he and his followers were regarded by many as typical hippies.

On the positive side of the countercultural experience, there were many who, in escaping, if only for a time, from middle-class life, had found a new sense of themselves and were inspired to move beyond the causes of the sixties to new goals—for personal liberation, for a life free of the limitations of gender or sexual differentiation, or for a new and more positive sense of ethnic identity. In addition, there were countless numbers of people whose lives were to be influenced indirectly by the countercultural experience, who, by the very fact that so many had chosen to do so much, found open to them choices that their parents didn't even think about making.

Chapter 6

___

BACK TO THE FUTURE: THE CONSERVATIVE RESURGENCE

The conservative resurgence in American politics and social life at the end of the sixties occurred partly because of a growing skepticism on the part of many people about the changes the decade had brought. Coupled with these doubts were the feeling that things had gone too far and the belief that the groups who were protesting the loudest were already sufficiently privileged by the system. Conservative values, never far from the center at any time during the sixties, reasserted themselves by 1968, to lead ultimately, 12 years later, to the election of Ronald Reagan, whose presidency would be marked by what many regarded as regressive social policies.

Young people, the touchstone group for radicalism in the sixties, reflected the conservative resurgence as much as any other segment of American society. A major survey by Lewis Harris and Associates for *Life* magazine, for the issue of January 8, 1971, revealed a notable affinity between the opinions of the young and those of their parents. This survey—of a cross section of some 26 million Americans aged 15 to 21—portrayed a group that differed only slightly on most subjects from their parents. By mixing together the opinions of high school and college students, the survey undoubtedly skewed its results toward the conservative side, because the younger respondents, still living at home, would tend to reflect their parents' values. Nonetheless, though they held more liberal or skeptical viewpoints on various issues, college students, asserted the text, did not seem headed for a revolution.

Eighty-one percent of respondents found their upbringing neither too permissive nor too strict, but just right, and 73 percent agreed with their parents' values and ideals. However, as one symptom of generational conflicts typical of the sixties, one out of three had trouble communicating with their parents. At the same time, three quarters saw this problem as mutual, not one-sided. Even more significantly, nearly two thirds of parents, in the opinion of those surveyed, approved of their children's values and ideals. An overwhelming majority of 90 percent of the young people surveyed considered their lives to be happy thus far.

In terms of ideals, only 61 percent believed in the quintessentially American notion that hard work leads to success and wealth, and 66 percent claimed that success and wealth were goals worth striving for. (Among college students, only the barest majority subscribed to this view, compared with 70 percent of high school students.) Heroes included Robert F. Kennedy, Bill Cosby, Neil Armstrong, and John Wayne. Least admired were Fidel Castro, Eldridge Cleaver, George Wallace, and Ho Chi Minh. The nonheroes are notable for their deviance from the center, whether toward the right (Wallace, the segregationist governor of Alabama) or the left (Castro, Cleaver of the Black Panthers organization, Ho Chi Minh). The list of heroes suggests that liberal views were admired if presented in pragmatic, middle-of-the-road terms (Kennedy, Cosby), while the ideals of scientific progress and a strong defense against enemies still prevailed (Armstrong, Wayne). The presence of Kennedy and Wayne on the same list may also suggest the ambivalence many young people felt toward the Vietnam War, which was still going on. In the 1968 primaries, Kennedy was clearly in favor of negotiated settlement. However, because the survey was done more than two years after his death, it may simply reflect memory more than history. Wayne typically ranked high in such lists, even decades after his death.

A plurality of 39 percent of those interviewed professed their politics to be middle of the road, with one quarter declaring themselves conservative, slightly more than one quarter liberal, and only 5 percent radical. Forty percent were unsure how they would vote in the next election, though 35 percent planned to vote Democratic. (By the Twenty-Sixth Amendment, ratified July 1, 1971, any citizen "eighteen years of age or older" would be able to vote in the coming presidential election. The phrasing of the survey question—stressing voting intentions in the next election—suggests that ratification of this amendment was anticipated.)

Asked about confidence in the ability of the government to solve the problems of the 1970s, only 54 percent expressed any confidence at all. Fully 90 percent favored laws penalizing air and water polluters (on April 22, 1970, the first Earth Day drew millions of participants nationwide, including many schoolchildren), 69 percent an all-volunteer army (a continuing reaction to the draft problems of the Vietnam era), and 58 percent affirmative action policies for minorities. However, 60 percent opposed a guaranteed annual income (an issue that would die in the seventies), and 66 percent opposed achieving racial balance through busing (a solution especially disliked in white northern suburbs).

In the social sphere, the results were mixed, but also leaned toward the middle. Sixty-nine percent felt that liberalized attitudes and new forms of worship made going to church more relevant, and 82 percent were certain they could marry someone of a different religion without upsetting their parents. (Endogamous marriages—by religion, race, or social class—would decline markedly after the sixties.) Even among Roman Catholics, family planning was considered important. Seventy-one percent of Catholics felt it was important to limit the number of children, compared with 77 percent overall. On the other hand, nearly three quarters of those surveyed opposed putting children in day care centers while their mothers worked.

On the issue of drugs, the overwhelming majority showed familiarity, at least through friends, with marijuana, speed, and LSD. However, they were not asked whether they had personally used these drugs. At the same time, 63 percent opposed legalizing marijuana (only 53% of college students agreed).

On sexual behavior, those surveyed thought that sex was being overemphasized in defining happiness in life (63%), thought that sex education should be taught in schools (77%), disagreed with separate behavior standards for girls (71%), split on abortion (46% in favor, 45% against, 8% unsure), considered sexual relations completely all right only if marriage was in the offing (approximately 63%), and approved of divorce if couples were unhappy (62% overall, 57% of Catholics).

The survey of reading and viewing habits showed oddly mixed results. While the Bible was the book which influenced lives more than any other (by three to one), the movie that best reflected young people's outlook on life (by two to one) was *Easy Rider*, the countercultural classic.

One survey, in one national magazine, does not tell the whole tale of a generation, nor of generational differences. The desire to heal those differences, exacerbated by war and racial conflicts, was clearly an important goal of many in the early 1970s. Divisiveness in American society had peaked by the end of the previous decade with the split over the war and related issues. Clearly, some way had to be found to bring people together again. Discussions of value differences occurred regularly in the popular press and in the relatively new genre of the television "talk show." In addition, the popular media had been put under intense pressure by the Nixon administration for their liberal leanings and alleged encouragement of dissent. It is not surprising, then, that magazines like *Life* should look for ways to bridge the widening gaps in American society.

That theme is carried out in a major article by editor Thomas Griffith, "Putting it back together," in the same issue as the Harris survey results. The author's conclusion: that generational diffences must be worked out in a civil manner and that political leaders must find ways to encourage such expression. The same hope was being expressed at the same time in American popular culture. Significantly enough, the winner of Grammy awards in three different categories in 1970 (best record, best song, *and* best album) was Simon and Garfunkel's plea for unity, "Bridge over Troubled Water."

THE NIXON YEARS

The election of Richard Nixon in 1968 by a narrow margin had done nothing to heal the breach between generations. In a campaign marked by polarizing rhetoric aimed at the so-called middle American, Nixon carried on a trend already discerned in American politics in the election of Ronald Reagan as governor of California in 1966 and in the strong third party bid by George Wallace in the 1968 presidential campaign. Nixon and his running mate Agnew blamed the behavior of the young on the Democrats. Nixon's

"Southern Strategy"—a calculated effort to play on racial fears and claim southern votes from the Democrats, who also were held responsible for failure to resolve the dilemma of Vietnam and for promoting desegregation too rapidly at home—was the opening wedge in what would eventually become a major realignment of voting patterns in the southern states. Wallace's strong showing in the South in 1968 diluted this strategy somewhat, but, in the long term, it was to prove highly successful for Nixon and the Republican party.

The presidency that followed the "law and order" campaign prolonged and intensified the war in Vietnam in the name of seeking "peace with honor" and regularly ignored the Constitution by attempting to curtail civil liberties and by drastically exceeding or distorting the constitutional powers of the executive branch. At the same time, however, the Nixon administration—partly because of a Democratic Congress—was frequently to follow a more liberal path in domestic policy, especially in areas like affirmative action and the environment. In foreign policy other than that related to Vietnam, Nixon also proved more flexible than many had expected by constructing, with his national security adviser, Henry Kissinger, the policy of détente with both Moscow and Peking.

Nixon's law and order appeal during the 1968 campaign was particularly successful with white working-class voters, "hard hats" as they later termed themselves, who were reacting against the excessive liberality they perceived in higher education and various aspects of youth culture. This group responded with a mixture of fear and loathing to the spectacle of the antiwar demonstrations in Chicago, the annual summer riots in the urban ghettos, and the general position taken by students and intellectuals on social and political issues. Among members of this group, opposition to the war focused on America's failure to win, not on moral questions about whether the nation should be in Vietnam or not. In addition, hard hats often saw the movement for greater civil rights among African Americans and other minority groups as a usurping of white power, which was frequently defined in purely masculine terms. These sentiments contributed to the general divisiveness characteristic of American society in the late sixties and early seventies.

The increased bombing of North Vietnam approved by Nixon did nothing to decrease opposition to the war among students and intellectuals, though by this point the peace movement counted many other types of people, old and young, in its ranks. Even the collapse of SDS, which split into warring fragments in 1969, did not diminish the growth of the opposition. The widespread demonstrations that followed Nixon's announcement of the invasion of Cambodia in April 1970—climaxed by the incident at Kent State in which four young people (two protesters and two spectators) were killed by National Guardsmen—only fed the antipathy felt by working-class Americans to such forms of protest. Shortly after this incident, a clash between hard hats and war protesters in New York, later condoned by Nixon, marked the first major confrontation between civilian groups over the war (and also established the term "hard hat" in common usage). The Black Panther party, formed in California in the late sixties with the avowed goal of creating a separate black nation, provoked similar feelings, even though the Panthers' insistence on the Second Amendment right to bear arms matched a favorite belief of the political right.

Nixon's reelection in 1972 by a large majority (he took 62 percent of the popular vote and 520 electoral votes against Democratic Senator George McGovern) signaled in part the success of his conservative strategy. The promised peace in Vietnam was formally settled by the agreement signed in Paris in January 1973, and two months later the last U.S. combat troops were withdrawn. Public reaction to the peace treaty, however, was not strongly positive. In addition, Nixon faced economic problems resulting from an Arab-Israeli war and subsequent Arab oil embargo that began in the same year. The recession this event provoked underscored weaknesses in the American economy that had been ignored for decades.

None of this might have had any long-term negative effects on the Nixon presidency, but for the slow uncovering of the administration's vast array of illegal activities. These disclosures began with the investigation of an illegal break-in at Democratic party headquarters at Washington's Watergate Hotel during the 1972 campaign. Many of those who voted for Nixon were dismayed by this affair and the revelations that led to Nixon's resignation from office in August 1974, the first president to relinquish the office. Nixon's cavalier disregard of the Constitution and the obvious paranoia surrounding him in his last months in office only deepened the distrust many felt for the government. The credibility gap that began with Vietnam became even wider with Nixon's divisive politics, the Watergate affair, and the downfall of the Nixon presidency.

NIXON AND THE MEDIA

The history of Nixon and the media was rocky almost from the beginning of his political career. His penchant for secrecy and his long-standing distrust of "liberal" journalism made any kind of rapprochement unlikely.

Although he had been saved in 1956 by the so-called "Checkers" speech on national television, his campaign for the presidency in 1960 was damaged by his debates with John Kennedy. An even lower point in Nixon's relationship with the media was to come in 1962, when he lost to the liberal Democrat Pat Brown in a campaign for the governorship of California. Nixon was sure that his problems in this campaign came in large measure from bad press. In conceding his loss, he squarely attacked the media, telling assembled reporters that they wouldn't have him to "kick around" any longer. In his 1968 campaign for the presidency, he and his running mate, Governor Spiro Agnew of Maryland, lambasted the "liberal media," blaming them for misreporting the war and for their sympathy for protesters. Considering this background, Nixon's actions in connection with the Pentagon Papers case, a milestone in First Amendment history, seem more understandable, if no less inexcusable.

In 1967, LBJ's secretary of Defense, Robert McNamara authorized a project to assemble as many extant documents related to U.S. involvement in Vietnam as could be found. The resulting collection, totalling some 7,000 pages, included virtually everything of significance except for highly classified White House and State Department files. Not completed until 1969, after McNamara himself had left government service, these classified documents, known as the "Pentagon Papers," became the centerpiece of a major imbroglio between the Nixon administration and the *New York Times*.

In June 1971, Daniel Ellsberg, a consultant to the National Security Council appointed by Henry Kissinger, Nixon's chief expert on foreign affairs, leaked the Pentagon Papers to the *New York Times*. Ellsberg was motivated by his personal opposition to the war and his lack of sympathy for the military policies of the Nixon administration. (McNamara himself had come to see the war as a mistake before he left his appointment as secretary of Defense, but he didn't act on his belief in any public way.) When Nixon's attorney general sought to suppress the publication of the papers, the *Times* demurred. The court case that followed led to a major Supreme Court decision in *New York Times* v. *United States* and *United States* v. *New York Times* (1971), in which the Court (6–3) ruled that publication did not violate national security and, furthermore, that attempts to block publication constituted a violation of the freedom of the press guaranteed by the First Amendment.

Infuriated by this decision, Nixon moved ahead with plans to form a secret group, to be known as the Plumbers, to delve into the files of Ellsberg's psychiatrist. He had already approved a plan, known as the "Huston Plan" (for an adviser, Tom Huston), to create an enemies list and had proposed secret surveillance of people he thought were against him. The Huston Plan was a coordinated program that sought to destroy antiwar groups through a wide variety of illegal activities, including wiretaps and infiltration. The Plumbers were established to stop leaks to the press about the Nixon administration's Vietnam policy, including the "secret" and illegal air war in Laos and Cambodia. Altogether, these activities, initiated and condoned by Nixon himself, constituted the most serious undermining of the Constitution and American democracy that had ever occurred at this level. That they should have emanated from the "law and order" president made them even more offensive.

Members of the so-called Committee to Re-elect the President (CREEP) and of the Plumbers group were responsible for the break-in at the Democratic party headquarters in the Watergate Hotel. Watergate was to prove the last, and by far the most damaging, of Nixon's conflicts with the media. Nixon's chief enemy in the case was his own arrogance, and his great mistake was the decision to tough it out rather than push the blame onto his advisers early in the evolving story. However, the Watergate case also owed a great deal to the tenacity of one newspaper, the *Washington Post*, and two reporters, Carl Bernstein and Robert Woodward. Their efforts in following that story at its beginning and not allowing it to die contributed significantly to the outcome of the episode and made journalism history.

Investigative reporting was not new to the 1970s. The history of journalism is filled with instances of reporters tracking stories, sometimes at the risk of their own lives, in the interest of truth and justice. However, the Watergate story had elements of suspense, intrigue, and dark comedy that made it unusually compelling. The mysterious aspect of what unfolded was underscored by the fact that Bernstein and Woodward's chief source—called Deep Throat, after a celebrated pornographic film of the period—remains unknown to this day. Their book about the case and the film based on it, *All the President's Men* (1976), somewhat exaggerate the importance of the press to the Watergate revelations. Much of what happened resulted from congressional or judicial investigation—and from pure politics. But, undeniably, Bernstein and Woodward and their newspaper deserve credit for having broken an important story and pursued it until Congress and the judiciary took up their investigations.

MAINSTREAM MEDIA AFTER A DECADE OF CHANGE

For the most part, however, the print and broadcast media of the sixties and seventies, as throughout much of American history, supported the status quo. Nixon, for example, had the endorsement of the overwhelming majority of American newspapers during the 1972 campaign. This was one reason he did so well. The media conservatism this demonstrated, despite allegations of liberal bias lodged by the Nixon administration, reflected the general attitude of the majority of Americans after the turmoil of the previous decade. It can also be seen in the television programming of the period.

With few exceptions, the top-rated television shows of the 1960s followed formulas set in the 1950s: comedy and variety shows that depended on the drawing power of stars like Lucille Ball, Jack Benny, Perry Como, and Arthur Godfrey; situation comedies; western and crime shows; and game and quiz programs. Variety shows sometimes served to introduce new talent and new music to the general viewing audience—as Ed Sullivan did with Elvis, the Beatles, and other musicians of the sixties. "Rowan and Martin's Laugh-In" (#1 for two seasons, from fall 1968 to spring 1970) varied the variety formula considerably with an array of new comedic talent and signature blackouts. "The Bill Cosby Show" (#11 in the season October 1969-April 1970) represented a significant breakthrough for an African-American performer. Cosby, in time, would become a popular culture institution, but, on the whole, very little prime-time programming of the sixties was in any sense innovative.

In the seventies, "All in the Family" and "Sanford and Son"—both from Norman Lear and Bud Yorkin of Tandem Productions—broke new ground. "All in the Family," the most popular comedy show of the early 1970s, spotlighted the character of Archie Bunker, a "lovable bigot," whose conservative, often reactionary, ideas on social and political issues were the focal point of the show and a cause for the despair of his wife, daughter, and son-in-law. Compared with "I Love Lucy," the most popular comedy show of the fifties, "All in the Family" was outrageous in content. It crossed the line between what people thought and what they said. "Lucy" did its own groundbreaking, especially in the pregnancy Lucille Ball was allowed to reveal and experience as a character early in the series. However, neither it nor its successor, "The Lucy Show," was in any sense about *ideas*. Archie Bunker was a spokesman for white male backlash and bigotry, debunking notions later to be labeled as "politically correct." He was also usually depicted as a victim of his own rhetoric, a man forced to recognize that, whether he liked it or not, the times were changing, even in his own family. The daring departure of "All in the Family" was to make Archie's prejudices the stuff of comedy. The fact that many people shared his ideas, or at any rate an appreciation of their free expression, guaranteed a run in first place which lasted for five successive seasons (from October 1971 till April 1976).

The second show from Lear and Yorkin was "Sanford and Son," a comedy series about an African-American junk dealer and his son. It featured black comedy star Red Foxx in the title role. Unlike "The Cosby Show," which made its leading characters representative of the aspiring black middle class, "Sanford and Son" developed its comedy from the unregenerate lower-class viewpoint of its main character. It was the first popular television situation comedy in which black characters spoke freely about their blackness—and with a gutsiness that was Foxx's trademark. From 1971 to 1976 it was almost as popular as "All in the Family," taking second or third place in the ratings for five seasons.

Other Tandem Productions included "Maude," about a liberated middle-aged woman, and "The Jeffersons," about African-American neighbors of Archie Bunker's who move into a largely middle-class white neighborhood. These shows, and others that soon appeared to imitate them, showed that the barriers on subject matter that had operated in television during its first two decades were coming down. As in Hollywood, where the new films were showing greater freedom of speech and subject matter, so these television series reflected the many changes American society was undergoing in the early 1970s.

Later in the decade, other shows courted popularity by harking back to supposedly better times, reflecting the longing of many Americans to escape from war, domestic turmoil, and economic decline. "Happy Days"—which supplanted "All in the Family" in the first place spot in 1976-77—was one such. Its nostalgic view of the fifties was part of a fifties revival that occurred in American popular culture in the seventies. "Laverne & Shirley," a close second to "Happy Days" in 1976-77, was also set in the fifties. Focusing on two best friends and roommates from working-class Milwaukee, it moved to first place during two successive seasons (1977-78, 1978-79). Yet another sign of the fifties revival was the tune music began to play.

MUSIC AND THE CONSERVATIVE RESURGENCE

One act which performed at the Woodstock Festival looked backward in time, to the decade just past when all things, music included, seemed so much simpler than they did by 1969. That act was called Sha Na Na, founded the year before by a group of Columbia University students who admired fifties rock 'n' roll. Their appearance on the Woodstock stage led to their later success as a performing group and anticipated the major fifties revival that was about to occur in American music. In October, along with Bill Haley and the Comets and Chuck Berry, they were part of Richard Nader's "1950s Rock 'n' Roll Revival," the first major "oldies" show, held at Madison Square Garden in New York. The same year marked the return of Elvis Presley to serious recording and concertizing following a comeback television special in December of 1968.

Most of Elvis's time earlier in the sixties had been spent making movies that were financially successful but musically mediocre. The comeback special produced his first hit single since "Crying in the Chapel" (#3 in 1965, though actually recorded in 1960). "If I Can Dream" reached twelfth place in 1968. A soundtrack album from the same special reached the eighth spot on the album chart. In July 1969, Elvis began a series of concerts in Las Vegas. These not only netted him a considerable financial return but also initiated more hit recordings, including "Suspicious Minds," his first #1 hit since early in 1962. Elvis, the greatest rock 'n' roll star of the fifties, had returned. Other stars—for instance, Dion and the Belmonts—would soon follow with reunion shows heavy with fifties nostalgia.

The opening of the hit Broadway musical *Grease* in 1972 was another signal that the fifties were back. With a musical score in fifties-style rock 'n' roll and a high school setting from the same period, it became one of the most popular shows in Broadway history. The same year, significantly enough, marked the closing, after a run of four years, of one of the leading musicals of the late sixties, *Hair*. Labeled a "tribal love rock musical," *Hair* epitomized countercultural values, including an antiwar message. It was also one of the first productions on the New York stage to feature full frontal nudity. *Grease*, by contrast, kept its cast members fully clothed but expressed some of the new artistic freedoms in its dialogue and lyrics. In the film version starring John Travolta and Olivia Newton-John (1978), the group Sha Na Na both performed and contributed lyrics.

One interpretation of the fifties craze of the early seventies was proffered by Chicago deejay Dick Biondi. In a *Life* magazine article of June 16, 1972, the cover of which announced the "Wacky Revival" of the fifties, he was quoted as saying: "I get the feeling . . . that through this music some of the kids are finding a backdoor way of getting together with their parents."

While this may have been true, an analysis of the hit charts of the sixties reveals that, in many ways, fifties music had never receded completely from general popularity. Motown saw hit after hit in a musical style that followed familiar fifties patterns of R & B. Groups other than Motown's—like Little Anthony and the Imperials, the Righteous Brothers, Frankie Valli and the Four Seasons, and the Temptations (to name only four)—had major hit singles in traditional R & B styles at the same time the Beatles and other British groups were gaining a big audience. The musical styles of these American groups were either formed by, or were in some way imitative of, styles of the fifties and before. Like Motown, their appeal crossed racial lines, while the attraction of the British groups, like most of the popular American rock groups of the sixties, was primarily to whites. At the same time, singers like Frank Sinatra (without argument the most influential male pop singer in the history of American music) and Barbra Streisand would produce hits that equalled or exceeded the best chart positions that the newer musicians on the scene achieved. In fact, Streisand is, to date, the all-time best-selling female artist with the most platinum albums of any recording artist. In all, she has sold more than 50 million albums in the United States and additional millions abroad. She is also a singer whose repertoire, overall, has been limited to Tin Pan Alley (that is, commercially conceived pop songs in recognizable categories) and Broadway melodies.

By the late 1960s, rock music had also begun to look back and by the mid-seventies it splintered into so many different styles that it is impossible to identify a dominant one. Dylan's career provides an illustration. After his motorcycle accident of 1966, Dylan retired from public view until 1968. He spent most of the intervening time at his farm near Woodstock, New York. There, with the Canadian-American group The Band, he experimented with music with a folk-country base. This led to a widely pirated series of tapes later released under the title *The Basement Tapes* (1975). This collection features songs written by Dylan and by The Band and sung by both. With its mixture of qualities, this music presents a different sort of complexity from the one associated with Dylan earlier in the sixties. The Band—then known as the Hawks—had toured with Dylan in England in 1965-66, as his music was evolving into rock. Their music was folk-based like his, but was the kind to later earn the rubric "roots rock," a style which emphasizes the basic elements of rock music—country, gospel, R & B. The songs on *The Basement Tapes* combine these elements, along with a rich dose of blues, in an evocative mixture. They have none of the touches of the exotic and surreal that characterize acid rock or *Sgt. Pepper*.

Dylan's first recording venture after his accident would come in 1968, with the album *John Wesley Harding*. With the exception of the haunting and enigmatic "All Along the Watchtower" (later recorded so memorably by Jimi Hendrix), Dylan's music in this set lacks the intensity of the great studio albums he made earlier in the decade, *Highway 61 Revisited* and *Blonde on Blonde*. It was a pause to look back, not a leap forward. At the same time, it helped Dylan to define the change that had come over him and his music during the Woodstock interlude. Even his voice sounds fresher and more open here than in the previous albums. "I'll Be Your Baby Tonight," featuring Dylan on piano, is in the country style to characterize his next major release. Significantly, for his return to the concert stage early in 1968, Dylan performed with The Band at a memorial concert for his first musical mentor, Woody Guthrie.

Dylan's next album represented another move in the same direction, though with a sound that was more commercial. *Nashville Skyline* (1969) reached first place on the album chart for rock music. It owes much to the musical style associated with the city in Tennessee long considered the home of country and western music. Songs like "Lay Lady Lay" (#7 in 1969) and "To Be Alone with You" convey this sound best. The instrumental backup includes steel guitar, a staple of country music also used in several cuts from *John Wesley Harding*. One song, "Girl from the North Country"—first recorded by Dylan for his second album—features a duet with country singer Johnny Cash. The Byrds, whose Dylan covers had launched their career, followed a similar country trail in their albums *The Notorious Byrd Brothers* (1968) and *Sweetheart of the Rodeo* (later in the same year). Both were recorded in Nashville. The latter in some respects anticipated, and perhaps influenced, Dylan's *Nashville Skyline*.

After several more albums, including the poorly received *Self-Portrait* of 1970 and the more popular *New Morning* of the same year, Dylan would go on tour with The Band in 1974, introducing his public to a more declamatory style of singing suited to the larger venues in which they performed (*Before the Flood*, 1974). The Band backed Dylan in the vibrant *Planet Waves* (1975), but his strongest album of the seventies was *Blood on the Tracks* (also 1975). This album featured the first appearance of three major songs in the Dylan repertory: "Tangled Up in Blue," "Shelter from the Storm," and "Idiot Wind." The last of these in particular seems to sum up the central message of the album—uncertainty, abandonment, and rejection of all the easy answers which a few years before might have seemed valid. On a personal level, these songs reflect the painful period of separation and divorce that Dylan was going through. At least for the moment, the artist who began as a central figure in the musical protest scene had become a private citizen, shaping the world, as best he could, to his own personal vision.

However, with the unpredictability that has characterized Dylan's entire career, *Desire*, released in 1976, began with an eight-and-a-half-minute protest song. "Hurricane" tells of the arrest and conviction for murder of middleweight boxing contender Rubin "Hurricane" Carter. In its subject matter, the song recalls the Dylan of the early sixties. An important part of a concerted effort to have Carter's case reconsidered, the song helped to bring about the judicial review that ended by freeing him after nine years in prison. Few protest songs have had such direct and positive effects.

However, most of the songs in this eclectic album are about women, mythical ("Isis") or real ("Sara," Dylan's wife). Among the musical forces involved, the violin of Scarlett Rivera introduces a sound new to Dylan's music. Backup vocals are by Ronee Blakly, the Barbara Jean of Robert Altman's film *Nashville* (discussed in the next chapter). Folk singer Emmylou Harris wrote the harmony. Lyricist Jacques Levy, director of the Broadway production of Kenneth Tynan's sensational sexual romp, *Oh, Calcutta!*, cowrote all but two of the songs with Dylan.

The Band would continue as a group for only a short while after the *Before the Flood* tour of 1974. Originally formed in 1967, they had made several seminal contributions to rock musical history. These included their debut album, *Music from Big Pink* (1968) ("Big Pink" was the house near Woodstock in which the celebrated *Basement Tapes* were recorded), and *The Band* (1969), a paean to southern country life that was closely linked in spirit to the commune movement. *Moondog Matinee* (1975) was a tribute to Alan Freed and fifties rock 'n' roll. The group's final concert in San Francisco on Thanksgiving Day 1976 was the basis of an outstanding rockumentary directed by Martin Scorcese, *The Last Waltz* (1978), in which Dylan, Van Morrison, Joni Mitchell, Neil Young, and other prominent musicians of the sixties generation appear.

At the same time as The Band was working with Dylan and the Byrds were moving toward a country style, a West Coast band, working in a modified rockabilly style, achieved great popularity, especially in the years 1967–70. This was Creedence Clearwater Revival, featuring vocalist John Fogerty. Formed in California in 1959, CCR did not put out its first recording till 1968. With a combination of original music and covers, they had seven hit singles in the late sixties, including "Bad Moon Rising" and "Down on the Corner" (second and third place on the chart in 1969). In the same year, they appeared at Woodstock. Their musical style aligned them with groups like The Band and with southern rock, but, unlike the latter, their political message was distinctly liberal.

Southern rock, which would peak in popularity in the early seventies, grew out of a combination of country, gospel, blues, and R & B. The first significant group associated with the style was the Allman Brothers Band, formed in 1968 in Macon, Georgia. Their first album—*The Allman Brothers Band* (1969) (issued on

Capricorn, a regional label from the South)—had no commercial success but marked a milestone in rock history. It was a return to basics by a group of skilled musicians, including Duane Allman and Dickey Betts, lead guitars, and Duane's brother Gregg, lead vocalist. For the first time since rockabilly had died out in the early sixties, a significant white rock musical style had emerged. By the time of *At Fillmore East* (1971), a memorable concert album, the group had reached its peak. Sadly, the death of Duane Allman in a motorcycle crash in September of that year, followed by the death of bassist Berry Oakley in a similar accident in the fall of 1972, spelled the end of the group's initial chemistry, though not of its commercial potential.

Among a number of bands influenced by the Allmans, the best and most successful was Lynyrd Skynyrd, formed in Florida in 1966 but without a debut recording until 1973. In the mid- to late seventies, Lynyrd Skynyrd (named for a high school gym teacher, Leonard Skinner, who detested boys with long hair) became increasingly popular. Their first album, *Pronounced Leh-Nerd Skin-Nerd* (1973), featured "Free Bird," a tribute to the late Duane Allman. It achieved considerable airplay and eventually became a signature song for the group, who were noted for their heavy metal, three-guitar hooks. Their second album, appropriately titled *Second Helping* (1974), included one of their most popular songs, "Sweet Home Alabama." It was an answer to Neil Young's devastating critique of southern racism, "Southern Man." Lynyrd Skynyrd's song defends the South against the kind of negative judgment Young makes. Referring to him by name, it asserts, somewhat sentimentally, the validity of life as lived in Dixie—including, by inference, segregation. Within the next few years, the group became steadily more popular, especially in their concert performances. Continuing the tragic tradition begun by the Allman Brothers, however, three members of the group, including lead singer Ronnie Van Zant, died in a plane crash in 1977.

Other groups would take up the country sound, either in its southern or its Nashville form, and make it part of their commercial success. The Eagles, for example, formed in Los Angeles in 1971, became one of the most popular groups in rock history with a style strongly infused, at least initially, with country. However, none of these groups would have the energy, focus, or plain down-home quality that characterized the work of the Allmans and Lynyrd Skynyrd. With a message (like much of country and western music) that was basically conservative, southern rock stood apart from the music that preceded it in the sixties, while at the same time it sustained all the basic features of the rock music style.

In the seventies, rock music, like the political left, began to fragment. The Beatles broke up, with Paul McCartney and John Lennon (now with Yoko Ono) pursuing successful solo careers. Dylan went into a new, less certain phase, resulting ultimately in his brief conversion in 1979 to born-again Christianity. Southern rock asserted the vitality of white country roots in its music, but would not survive the decade in its purest form. Heavy metal, epitomized by groups like Led Zeppelin and Grand Funk Railroad and Aerosmith, would dominate the concert and recording scene through the eighties, along with newer trends like disco, "glam rock," "shock rock," and—most notable of all—punk. Only the last of these, discussed in more detail in a later chapter, would have the political significance of much of the major rock music of the sixties. However, its message would not be one of optimism, but of nihilism, anger, or despair.

MOVIES AND THE MIDDLE OF THE ROAD

By the end of the sixties and the beginning of the next decade, television and music both, in their own ways, reflected the pull to the right. In American movies, something similar can be discerned, though it was clearly counterbalanced by other factors. On the one hand, movies in the seventies were to have a new frankness in language and sexual content. In addition, they were willing and able, at last, to deal more honestly with American involvement in Vietnam as well as other difficult subject matter. On the other hand, the seventies would also see the growing popularity of "warrior myth" heroes like Rambo (Sylvester Stallone) and Dirty Harry (Clint Eastwood), along with the usual plethora of formula comedies and action films, all of which achieved considerable popularity.

At the very beginning of the decade, *Joe* (1970), a low budget, independent production, provided an answer to the previous year's countercultural hit, *Easy Rider*. A crude allegory of the schism between the generations, *Joe* introduced, in its title character (Peter Boyle), a spokesman for the working class, hard hat segment of the electorate. An unfunny Archie Bunker (a character he predates by at least a year), Joe hates liberals (all "queers"), hippies, and "niggers"

(who are taking white men's jobs) and treats his wife like the prover-
bial doormat. When Bill Compton (Dennis Patrick), an upper-middle-
class ad man, reveals to Joe that he has inadvertently killed his daughter's drug-dealing, hippie boyfriend, the two men form a strange,
uneasy alliance. Increasingly, Compton's behavior is controlled by
his foul-mouthed, lesser-educated companion. Eventually, in search
of his missing daughter (Susan Sarandon, in her screen debut), who
has learned what her father has done, Compton and his strange ally
Joe explore hippie haunts in Greenwich Village, smoke marijuana,
and have sex with two young women. At the climax of the film, in re-
taliation for the theft of their wallets, they attack a commune with
weapons from Joe's collection and kill the young people they find
there. In the final shot of the film, Compton kills his own daughter.

While the plot descends to melodrama and coincidence, the scenes
between Compton and Joe explore the links between the classes at
the height of the generation gap. Neither they nor the younger
characters in the film are very appealing. They all share a common
suspicion of each other and a willingness to exploit any differences
to their own advantage (there is even a hint of past incest in the relationship between Compton and his daughter). Joe's assessment of
the youth culture (using a term he has just learned from Compton
and his wife) sums up the attitude of Compton as well: "They're all

Joe (Peter Boyle) complaining about the "culture" in the film Joe *(1970)*

screwed up, so they're screwin' up the culture." While *Joe* has numerous false notes, its ending—every bit as bleak in its own way as that of *Easy Rider*—suggests that there will be no easy solutions to the generational rift.

The vigilante justice that climaxes *Joe*, as Joe and Compton raise their rifles in the commune, provides the whole theme of the Dirty Harry films of Clint Eastwood, beginning with the entry of that name released in 1971. The first of five films in which Eastwood plays the same character (the last—*The Dead Pool*—would come out in 1988), *Dirty Harry*'s trailer set the tone: "You don't assign him to murder cases. You just turn him loose."

Building on the character he developed in westerns in the 1960s, Eastwood as Harry is the antiestablishment cop who bypasses regular procedures in pursuit of his concept of justice. Specifically, the enemy in *Dirty Harry* is not so much the killer "Scorpio" as the liberal establishment that protects him at the expense of his victims and those who try to enforce the law. "Where does it say that you have the right to kick down doors, torture suspects, deny medical attention and legal counsel? Where have you been?" the district attorney asks Harry at one point in the film "Does Escobedo ring a bell? Miranda? [references to cases in which the Supreme Court upheld the rights of suspected criminals] Why, surely you've heard of the Fourth Amendment? What I'm saying is, that man had rights." To which Harry replies sarcastically: "Well, I'm all broken up over that man's rights."

Much political rhetoric was spilled over the issue of defendants' rights in the late sixties, most notably during the 1968 Nixon campaign. The sentiment against such rights, as defined by the courts, is a major theme of this and other films of the Harry series. From the opening shot—a list of names of officers of the San Francisco police department killed in line of duty—to the last—Harry contemplating his badge before throwing it away—*Dirty Harry* plays to the conservative, hard hat view of the criminal justice system. Its emphasis on vigilante justice also connects it to the Rambo series of Sylvester Stallone and other "warrior" films which, in effect, extended the action in Vietnam to the home front.

An equally acerbic, though artistically more exciting, attack on the liberal establishment came in the same year as *Dirty Harry*: Stanley Kubrick's *A Clockwork Orange*. Based on the novel of the same title by British author Anthony Burgess, *A Clockwork Orange*, while purporting to be set in the future, in fact comments on the British welfare state of the postwar period. Detailing the "adventures of a young man whose principal interests are rape, ultra-violence and Beethoven," the film indicts social workers, penologists, psychologists, and politicians, all of whom abuse or subvert their responsibilities or powers for their own personal benefit. As a result, Alex (Malcolm McDowell) almost becomes an object of sympathy as he is worked over and recycled by the system. He becomes a snivelling masochist, literally licking the shoe of the man who kicks him during a public exhibition of his transformation. Alex is both criminal and victim, but, in the end, his motives, however perverse, have a purity that raises him above the crowd and makes of him a kind of hero.

Alex's world has many similarities to the urban mass society of the postwar United States. He lives in a high-rise flat with his mother and father, who obviously have no control over him. He avoids school, spends most of his time seeking violent thrills with his buddies (called "droogs"), and has neither a conscience nor a sense of guilt. His social worker grabs at his crotch and his psychologists use him for an experiment in remediation which will benefit the ministry in charge of prisons and fulfill their desire to test out their theories. His former droogs become police officers who get their revenge on him (for his sadistic treatment of them) by forcing his head under water till he almost drowns. An author, now apparently crazed, whose wife Alex and his droogs once raped, tortures him with Beethoven's "Ode to Joy" until he attempts suicide. (Beethoven for Alex has been, perversely, the source of his most violent fantasies. Now, because of his brainwashing, he can't stand to listen.) By the time Alex reverts to type at the end of the film—after a fall that presumably jolts him back to his original state—his relapse comes almost as a relief.

Burgess's novel, like George Orwell's earlier *1984*, interprets the modern reality as a totalitarian nightmare in which the individual is inevitably lost. To suggest the universality of this world, Burgess created his own dialect—a mixture of British working-class slang and Russian—which Kubrick retained, with some modifications, in the film version. Criticized for its violence, banned in England and Australia (in the United States it merely earned an "R" rating), *A Clockwork Orange* remains difficult for some viewers to endure even today.

Stanley Kubrick's work is among the most uncompromising of any American director of the sixties and seventies. Any review of filmmaking of this period must count him among the small handful of people who created a significant body of work. From the first,

Kubrick tackled subjects other directors would not be willing to touch and ignored Hollywood shibboleths in pursuing his artistic ends. He was also able to obtain, and sustain, total artistic control over most of his films. Like *Dr. Strangelove* and *2001, A Clockwork Orange* presents a distinctively original viewpoint on contemporary society and its problems. Though not limited to one particular place and time, it nonetheless comments more trenchantly on various issues than many more topical films.

The same point might be made about another film of the seventies about a specific place in the past, *Chinatown* (1974). It was directed by Polish-born Roman Polanski, whose wife's murder by the Manson sect was one of the most tragic stories of the sixties. Set in Los Angeles in the 1930s, this film noir mystery features Jack Nicholson as Jake Gittes, former policeman turned private detective, who becomes gradually involved in a case of Watergate complexity involving, incest, water rights, and a fraudulent land scheme. In *Chinatown*, the corruption stems from money and the unbridled lust for power, and Chinatown itself becomes a symbol of all that lies beyond the control of ordinary people.

This tightly plotted film, with script by Robert Towne, takes the audience through several layers of secrets and lies. Its revelations of immorality, public and private, make it devastatingly, depressingly clear that justice does not triumph when faced with people like the wealthy Noah Cross (John Huston). "Why are you doing it?" Jake asks him, referring to his scheme to divert water from farmers who need it for their fruit crops. "How much better can you eat? What can you buy that you can't already afford?" "The future, Mr. Gittes," Cross replies, "the future."

Cross is willing to destroy anyone in his path, including his daughter's husband, Hollis Mulray, Cross's former partner, who has become an honest public official ready to blow the whistle on his father-in-law's plans. Cross also destroys his own daughter, Evelyn Mulray (Faye Dunaway). Her death in Chinatown at the conclusion of the film, as she attempts to escape her father's trap, merely completes a process begun long before, when he and she had an incestuous relationship. The result was the birth of "my daughter and my sister," as Evelyn screams hysterically to Jake at another point in the film. "Let the police handle this," Jake urges her. "He *owns* the police," she cries. In the end, as Cross reaches out for his daughter's daughter, her mother dead of a policeman's bullet, the audience shares Jake's sense of helplessness in the face of such omnipotent evil.

A film which many thought well suited to the Nixon years—it was released at the height of the Watergate scandals—*Chinatown*, like *A Clockwork Orange*, suggests that the individual has little chance against the power of those who control politics and economic life. Jake Gittes, like Dirty Harry, is willing enough when necessary to operate outside the framework of the law and is already free of his badge to do so. But even he has no chance against the money and the power of a Noah Cross. As his associate Walsh says to him at the end of the film, "Forget it, Jake, it's Chinatown."

Another tale of intrigue, structured like a mystery but based on fact, captured yet another aspect of public corruption in the 1970s. Alan J. Pakula's *All the President's Men* (1976), was based on the book Carl Bernstein and Bob Woodward wrote about the Watergate case. Starring Dustin Hoffman and Robert Redford, this film, in a patient, documentary style, chronicles the development of the Watergate story from the time of the break-in to the beginning of Nixon's second term in office.

If, in *Chinatown*, corruption stems from wealth, in *All the President's Men* it results from public officials' misusing the trust placed in them by the American people. From the beginning of the film, where Nixon addresses Congress on his return from a trip to China, to the end, where he addresses the nation on the occasion of his second inauguration, this film vindicates the freedom of the press guaranteed by the First Amendment. Unfortunately, as in *Chinatown*, not all the villains in the case were punished. Thanks to the pardon he received from his successor Gerald Ford, Nixon went free.

These films and others like them raised questions about cherished dreams and assumptions of the sixties and earlier years without coming up with definite answers. Their pessimism, a characteristic of many major films of the decade, perhaps reflected the direction of events in Vietnam and in Washington, as well as the economic decline perceptible throughout the nation by the middle of the seventies. Even films like Peter Bogdanovich's *The Last Picture Show* (1971), about life in tiny Anarene, Texas, in the period just before the outbreak of the Korean War, do not wreathe small town life in a nostalgic glow. Based on the novel by Larry McMurtry, *The Last Picture Show* is about the end of one kind of life, not about the beginning of another. Movies, like other segments of the mass media of the seventies, were coming to grips with major social and economic changes and with the tensions in American culture that these changes brought about.

Chapter 7

IN FROM THE MARGINS: THE WOMEN'S MOVEMENT AND THE BEGINNING OF IDENTITY POLITICS

African Americans were not the only group to experience major changes in social, political, and legal identity in the 1960s. Women—who comprised a much larger, more diverse group— also broke new ground. The women's liberation movement, inspired in part by the civil rights movement, would bring various gender-based inequities into the limelight. These included salaries, educational and professional opportunities, and sexual freedom. Certain landmark legislation would improve women's opportunities, while the birth control pill, in combination with changing mores, would enhance women's sexual experience. Following the example of the women's movement, groups like the Gay Liberation Front (GLF) and the American Indian movement also became prominent by the end of the sixties and beginning of the seventies. Because the improvements they sought involved their personal and social identities, the term "identity politics" came into being to cover such concerns. American popular music, movies, and the media reflected the agendas of all of these groups in various ways.

During the Second World War, many women entered the work-place for the first time, taking jobs vacated by men who were serving in the armed forces. When the war ended and these men returned, many of the same women had to give up their jobs and return to social and economic roles they had played in the past. Significantly enough, the highest divorce rate in this country prior to the 1970s occurred just after the war. This was one sign of the tensions this period of transition produced.

The nuclear family ideal, with its narrowly defined roles and its emphasis on child rearing, did nothing to improve women's status. In the endless round of child-centered activities in the middle-class suburbias, mothers were cooks, chauffeurs, and cleaning women, but frequently felt little sense of personal growth. By 1950, women would make up one-third of the workforce, but their salaries were low and opportunities for advancement few. Most middle-class women could choose to become secretaries, stewardesses, nurses, or teachers, but little else. Those who went to college often focused more attention on finding a husband than on their academic subjects. They were discouraged from choosing majors in engineering or the sciences. They were actively discriminated against in their applications to professional schools. Even women who graduated from the more congenial environment of the so-called sister schools of New England experienced the same kinds of limitations.

No one captures this aspect of middle-class women's lives in the postwar period better than Betty Friedan (a Smith graduate) in her seminal book *The Feminine Mystique* (1963). For Friedan, the central problem was one of *identity*: "the core of the problem for women . . . is not sexual but a problem of identity—a stunting or evasion of growth that is perpetuated by the feminine mystique. It is my thesis that as the Victorian culture did not permit women to accept or gratify their basic sexual needs, our culture does not permit women to accept or gratify their basic need to grow and fulfill their potentialities as human beings. . . . "

Although many women felt that Friedan did not sufficiently appreciate the importance of sexual liberation, her book provided the philosophical foundation for the new women's liberation movement. The Civil Rights Act of 1964 provided its legal cornerstone. Title VII of this act banned sexual (as well as racial) discrimination in the workplace. On this foundation, along with the Equal Pay Act of 1963 and the "equal protection" clause of the Fourteenth Amendment, a redefinition of women's rights was built. To promote this goal, Friedan and a group of women who shared her concerns founded the National Organization for Women (NOW) in 1966. They formed a leadership that was well educated, relatively affluent, and predominantly middle class. NOW's primary agenda was to lobby for legislation to improve women's lives so they could live in equal partnership with men in all spheres of life—social, political, and economic. One result of its effort was Executive Order 11375, signed by Lyndon Johnson in 1967. This order added sex to the categories of discrimination that holders of federal contracts were prohibited from exercising.

The women's movement soon attracted women from the civil rights or antiwar movements who found that neither had provided much improvement in their standing. In SDS, SNCC, and other groups, women took the notes, made the coffee, tended the children, and had sex with the men (to gain entree and to maintain status). In other words, in many respects they played the same roles as women in the idealized domestic scene of the 1950s. These activists felt that a caste system operated within the movement that was just as strong as in the larger American society. A more controversial group to join the burgeoning sisterhood was lesbians. At first opposed by leaders like Friedan, lesbians secured a place in the women's movement as gay activism increased generally after the beginning of the 1970s.

By then, feminists had found new spokespersons for their cause. One of these was Kate Millett, whose book *Sexual Politics* argued, with copious footnotes and historical evidence, the cultural oppression of women in Western civilization. Another book, Germaine Greer's *The Female Eunuch*, developed a similar argument, with emphasis on women's blunted sexuality. Other books of the same year, 1970—for instance, Robin Morgan's *Sisterhood Is Powerful* and Shulamith Firestone's *The Dialectic of Sex*—added to the growing body of writing by the new feminists.

Marches and demonstrations were also part of the program of the women's liberation movement. In August 1968, at a mock Miss America pageant during the actual festival in Atlantic City, women's liberationists crowned a live sheep and declared bras, girdles, curlers, and the magazine *Ladies' Home Journal* objects of oppression. (Contrary to popular myth, however, they didn't burn bras or any other articles of apparel.) In 1970, with the fiftieth anniversary of the Nineteenth Amendment, which gave women the right to vote, such public events became even more widespread.

Madison Avenue discovers Women's Liberation

(*Life*, January 8, 1971)

The popular press, which had followed the women's movement closely from the time of its origin, took note. Kate Millett made the cover of *Time*. Above a reproduction of its 1920 cover celebrating women's suffrage, *Life* (September 4, 1970) announced:

WOMEN ARISE: The revolution that will affect everybody.

In the same year, the first mass circulation magazine of the women's movement, *Ms.*, edited by Gloria Steinem, began publication with a run of 250,000 copies. Advertising, quick to pick up on all new social trends, reflected feminist ideals in various ways.

The collective spirit of the new feminism—blending together women of different social, economic, and racial backgrounds in a common cause—was reinforced by books like *Our Bodies, Ourselves: A Book By and For Women* by the Boston Women's Health Book Collective (1971). This book and others like it emphasized the need for women to take charge of their own lives and break their historic domination by men.

WOMEN IN JOURNALISM

In no sphere of popular culture was the second-class citizenship of women clearer than in newspaper and magazine journalism. Historically, women reporters were given "soft" news: births, deaths, society news, home and garden, the so-called "women's pages." "Hard" news—the top stories in the political and economic sphere—always went to men. Mary Welsh Hemingway, last wife of author Ernest Hemingway, describes (in her autobiographical *How It Was*, 1976) the gender hierarchy during the Second World War at *Time* magazine's New York office, when she was part of the foreign staff:

In the war between men and women inside *Time*'s antiseptic jungle, the lines and ranks were strictly drawn, the pecking order inviolate. On the editorial staff were "writers" (associate or contributing editors on the masthead) and women were "researchers," and never the twain would exchange crafts.

Women like Mary Welsh Hemingway, who got to cover important events in Europe, were the exception to the general standard. The irony of such rigid caste lines only increases when one realizes that, during this period, *Time*'s stories were seldom bylined.

The same pecking order existed in broadcast journalism, both in radio and in television. Women were featured on daytime television news shows, for instance NBC's "Today," but, even there, they did not deliver the hard news. Until 1960, in fact, none of the so-called "Big Three" networks—ABC, CBS, or NBC—included a female correspondent on their staff.

The first broadcast journalist to break this shibboleth was Nancy Dickerson of CBS News. Dickerson began as a producer for news programs on CBS in the 1950s. As a reporter, she was the first woman to broadcast on TV from the floor of a national political convention. In 1963, she moved from CBS to NBC, where she hosted her own daytime news program from the nation's capital. Criticized because of her close association with various residents of the White House, Dickerson left NBC after ten years over a contract dispute. She later became a reporter for PBS (Public Television).

Another woman, still active in broadcasting as of this writing, went even further. Barbara Walters joined the NBC "Today" show in 1961 as a writer and occasional on-the-air feature reporter. Within a few years, she became co-host of the program with Hugh Downs. By 1971, in the wake of the women's movement, she was given her own show, "Not for Women Only." In 1976, she switched networks to become coanchor (with Harry Reasoner) of "The ABC Evening News" with an unprecedented $1 million per year contract. This was the first time that a woman played such a major role in network evening news. Walters stayed on as coanchor until 1979, when she became cohost of "20/20," then a new show. Especially adept at interviewing, Walters has had a distinguished career in broadcast journalism. Her tenure as coanchor of an evening news broadcast has never been matched by any other woman in the Big Three networks.

Connie Chung came closest. She was coanchor, with Dan Rather, of "The CBS Evening News" from 1993 to 1995. Other prominent women broadcast journalists, like the late Jessica Savitch of NBC or Carole Simpson of ABC, have been relegated to anchorships of weekend news reports. One major exception to this pattern—and perhaps a sign of things to come—has been the Cable News Network (CNN), which regularly features women (and minority) anchors in its news broadcasting.

As reporters in the field, women have come closer to achieving equal status with men in the major network news organizations. Journalists like Cokie Roberts (ABC) and Ann Richards (NBC) regularly cover the White House and Capitol Hill or participate in the news-oriented talk shows that are staples of Sunday daytime programming. Women commentators and reporters have also found a congenial situation in NPR (National Public Radio) and PBS. However, such women are still the exception, not the rule, in a field that remains largely dominated by men.

Traditional gender barriers also exist in print journalism, though the opportunities for women have improved. Political commentators like Elizabeth Drew appear regularly in the pages of *The New Yorker* and other major national magazines, and bylined articles by women reporters are regular features of major newspapers and news magazines. Magazines with a targeted feminist audience, like *Ms.*, print the work of women commentators and reporters almost exclusively. Political columnists like Ellen Goodman, while less common, have also made their way onto the op-ed pages of newspapers throughout the country.

WOMEN IN MUSIC

Women in popular music have experienced the same inequities as women in all other areas of American life. Not surprisingly, these have been worse for African Americans than for any other group. Only in the past several decades—in the wake of the women's liberation movement—have women, white and black, begun to equal the power and status of men in the music business.

The most innovative, risk-taking women in music before the 1960s were black singers in jazz and R & B. Jazz singer Billie Holiday refined the blues for the Depression and war years, and in the song "Strange Fruit" dealt head-on with the subject of lynching in the South. Dinah Washington became the leading blues singer of the fifties with songs like "Love for Sale," written from the viewpoint of a prostitute advertising her wares. Ruth Brown—"Miss Rhythm"—emerged as the preeminent R & B singer of the same decade, recording more than 80 sides for Atlantic Records and becoming a regular on Alan Freed's "Moondog Show." The audience for the recordings of these singers was limited, however, and their financial rewards small.

By the early sixties, the Motown artists—Mary Wells, the Shangri-Las, the Supremes—had a string of first-place hits and began reaping the benefits of their organization. Aretha Franklin, after an uncertain beginning to her recording career at Columbia, became the unchallenged "Queen" of soul music after she was signed by Atlantic Records. Her "Respect" (1967) was a strong statement of feminine autonomy in a form of music that usually celebrated the opposite. At the same time, major white female artists, influenced in varying degrees by black artists, began to form part of the rock 'n' roll scene. First and foremost among these were Janis Joplin and Grace Slick (discussed in Chapter 5).

Singers like Joan Baez and Judy Collins (discussed in Chapter 4) were important to the folk revival of the early sixties. The young Laura Nyro—writing highly individual music in a style that melded together pop, folk, and jazz— popularized a confessional mode of song writing that paralleled Joplin's self-exposing style of performance. Primarily a composer, Nyro's hit songs included "Stoned Soul Picnic" (made popular in a recording by the Fifth Dimension, 1968), "Eli's Coming" (popularized by Three Dog Night, 1969), and "Stoney End" (by Barbra Streisand, 1971).

The confessional mode also found an important representative in Canadian-born singer-songwriter Joni Mitchell, whose recording career began in 1968. With roots in folk music, later blended with rock and jazz, Mitchell's songs typically dealt with her own personal experiences in a countercultural lifestyle. Her albums *Ladies of the Canyon* (1970) and *Blue* (1971), both of which went platinum, epitomize her early musical style and contain some of her best songs.

Carole King—a singer-songwriter in a more popular vein— achieved great success in the late sixties and early seventies with hits like "It's Too Late" (#1 in 1971), part of her first place album *Tapestry*. The latter sold more than 15 million copies and stayed on the chart for more than five years. King's broad-based musical style helped to define the singer-songwriter type for the seventies.

At the same time as white women singers and composers were reaching new heights in the rock and pop categories, singers like Tammy Wynette and Loretta Lynn were broadening the subject matter of country and western music to include contemporary themes. Wynette's "DIVORCE" and "Stand by Your Man," opposing views of the same subject, were back-to-back hits on the country chart in 1968. Lynn was notable for her feminist viewpoint in songs like "One More's on the Way" (1971), an amusing critique of women's liberation by a young, married working-class woman, and "The Pill" (1972), a celebration of women's sexual independence. "The Pill" was widely banned from radio when first released.

Feminist themes—women's need for independence, for taking charge of their own lives, experiencing the same freedom as men—informed a great variety of popular music of the early seventies, as the women's liberation movement reached its peak.

Yoko Ono and her husband John Lennon (with help from Eric Clapton, Timothy Leary, and others) joined together in the Plastic Ono Band's *Live Peace in Toronto* (1969), part of the couple's ongoing commitment to the peace movement. Yoko's unique vocal style, known as the "primal screech," anticipated what would emerge later in the decade in punk and other forms of avant-garde rock. Criticized for her alleged role in the breakup of the Beatles, Ono, with John, moved on to record the feminist "Woman Is the Nigger of the World" in the album *Some Time in New York City* (1971). The same album included Ono's solo "Sisters, O Sisters."

Cher—first known as the other half of Sonny and Cher, a popular duo of the mid-sixties—also cultivated new ground in popular music subject matter with a raunchy series of hit singles including "Gypsies Tramps & Thieves" (1971), "Half-Breed" (1973), and "Dark Lady" (1974). Her material was notable for its sexual frankness and avoidance of euphemism.

However strongly the songs of Cher, Joni Mitchell, Loretta Lynn, or Laura Nyro challenged traditional concepts of women's lives, surely no song expressed the spirit of the feminist movement of the early seventies better—or with more popularity—than Australian-born Helen Reddy's "I Am Woman" (#1, 1972). One of a string of hits by Reddy, this song won her a Grammy for best pop vocal of the year. (At the award ceremony, she would make news by referring to God as "she.")

Other prominent female vocalists of the late sixties and early seventies whose music altered feminine stereotypes in various ways include Diana Ross, Tina Turner, Linda Ronstadt, and Bette Midler.

Ross's career began with Motown, but when she split with it in 1970 she went on to become one of the most popular singers of the seventies. She also carved out a brief career for herself in movies. In breaking with Berry Gordy, Jr., Ross showed an independence that was to become characteristic of many women vocalists after the sixties. Tina Turner began her career as the other half of the Ike and Tina Turner Revue. Noted for the sexual frankness of their lyrics, they achieved considerable popularity in the late sixties through performances as well as recordings. However, Tina alleged later that the relationship between them was abusive and grew worse with Ike Turner's growing dependence on alcohol and cocaine. Eventually, in 1976, she would leave him and build a career on her own, to become, like Diana Ross, a highly successful single.

Linda Ronstadt built her initial repertory out of songs by composers whose work might otherwise not have reached a mainstream pop audience. With carefully crafted arrangements and a strong singing voice, Ronstadt has had a long and successful career performing a great variety of music. Bette Midler made her first album—*The Divine Miss M* (1972)—chiefly out of hit songs of the forties and fifties that she performed in energetic arrangements by Barry Manilow. Midler had begun her career with performances in the New York bathhouses frequented by gay males. Never one to expose her innermost self to her audience, Midler assumed a variety of roles in her music and performance patter, some of which was highly risqué. Her later manifestation as a Disney movie star and singer of sentimental songs bears little resemblance to the original Miss M. Her first album and a later live album (*Live at Last*, 1977) preserve her original presence, the personification of the theatrical form of behavior known popularly as "camp."

Although women individually and collectively reached new levels in popular music during the sixties and early seventies, it was not until the later seventies that anyone would equal the impact on rock music of Janis Joplin and Grace Slick. That singer was Patti Smith, who recorded in 1974 what is perhaps the first true punk rock record on an independent single, the standard "Hey Joe," backed with "Piss Factory." She was an important part of a new chapter in rock history discussed in more detail in the next chapter.

Despite the musical innovations and feminist ideas introduced by major women artists of the sixties and seventies, however, most music of the period perpetuated well established notions of women's roles in American life. In fact, the liberation movement provoked a considerable amount of backlash. If 1972 saw Helen Reddy's "I Am Woman" go to first place on the chart in December, it also saw the Eagles' "Witchy Woman," with its stereotypical view of women as seductive vamps, reach #12 the previous month.

GENDER WARS AND COMEDIES OF MANNERS: HOLLYWOOD, THE WOMEN'S MOVEMENT, AND THE SEXUAL REVOLUTION

The same polarities could be seen even more strikingly in American film. In 1967, *The Graduate* provided a memorable portrait of a young woman (Elaine) who pointedly expresses revulsion at the idea of repeating the mistakes of her mother's life. In the same year, *Bonnie and Clyde* gave its audience a portrait of a gun moll who was not dependent on her gangster partner for her identity as a bank robber or as a person.

At the same time such liberated female characters were making their appearance in American movies, however, the Bond films were giving us Pussy Galore. Among the most popular entertainments of the sixties, this spy adventure series about British agent 007, James Bond (Sean Connery), provided its audiences with women straight out of the *Playboy* centerfold. Pussy, the femme fatale of *Goldfinger* (1964), was only one version of a recurring type. Similar feminine stereotypes abounded in popular films.

If *The Graduate* and *Bonnie and Clyde* held the promise of greater honesty in their portrayals of female characters, the overwhelming majority of Hollywood films of the late sixties and early seventies did not join in the trend. Indeed, despite the new freedom in language and situation in American popular films, the women's movement seemed to provoke views of women that were as stereotypical as ever.

Love Story (1970), based on the popular novel by Erich Segal, provides a case in point. This tale of two modern star-crossed lovers—Oliver Barrett IV (Ryan O'Neal), an upper-class Harvard pre-law major, and Jenny Cavilleri (Ali McGraw), a Radcliffe music major on a scholarship—perpetuated stereotypes by modernizing them. Though the tone and language of the film (like that of the book), is decidedly contemporary ("Love means never having to say you're sorry"), the behavior of the lovers is straight out of *Romeo and Juliet*. (Indeed, the popularity of the film may have been partly due to the highly successful film version of Shakespeare's play directed by Franco Zefferelli, released in 1968.) *Love Story* was popular with audiences of all ages because it suggested that young people were not much different from what they had always been. As a "cancer film," it also allowed its audience to identify with the suffering of a young woman (Jenny) who would die when she seemed to have everything to live for. Certainly, *Love Story* did not seriously challenge any traditional views of women or marriage, nor did many popular films of the late sixties and early seventies.

One exception is *Soldier Blue* (1970), with Candice Bergen, Peter Strauss, and Donald Pleasence. This excessively violent antiviolence film dramatizes the general ill-treatment and massacre of Native Americans during the period following the Civil War. It is also the story of the sexual awakening of Kathy Lee, also known as "Cresta," the character played by Bergen. However, because the real focus of the film is on the Native Americans' plight, the sexual awakening theme, though important, is subsidiary. Another partial exception is Alan J. Pakula's *Klute* (1971), with Jane Fonda as Bree, a would-be actress and real-life call girl, who becomes the target of a psychopathic killer. In this role, Bree's choice of profession is part compulsion and part desire to control her relationships with men. In a decidedly conventional ending, however, Bree chooses to marry Klute (Donald Sutherland), the detective who saves her life. As Sally Hyde in *Coming Home* (1978) (discussed in detail in Chapter 4), Fonda has an affair with a paraplegic Vietnam veteran, but she does not decide to leave her husband when he returns from the war. If Sally experiences a sense of sexual liberation from her affair, she makes a conventional decision about her marriage. Her husband's suicide at the end of the film, not her own volition, releases her from her marital obligation.

If Hollywood did not seem willing or able to deal directly or honestly with many issues raised by the women's movement, it did provide some fairly trenchant commentary on the changes taking place in American society as a result of the new feminism and the sexual revolution. In a series of films that fall chiefly into the genre of comedy of manners, Hollywood described an era of gender wars.

Paul Mazursky's *Bob & Carol & Ted & Alice* (1969) takes a satirical look at these changes, focusing on two trendy California couples who experiment with "open" relationships. At the beginning of the film, Bob (Robert Culp) and Carol (Natalie Wood) visit a spa where they try to come in touch with their own feelings. The sensitivity training they undertake during this visit parallels what was offered widely in the sixties at places like the Essalen Institute in California. In the film, however, the training, with its accompanying meditation periods and massage, seems bogus, and Bob and Carol are victimized by their own trendiness. This quality in their relationship is only reinforced by their permissive parenting and indulgence in casual drug use and sex. In contrast with them, their friends Ted (Elliott Gould) and Alice (Dyan Cannon) are more conservative in their behavior, though obviously much intrigued by the experiments Bob and Carol have undertaken.

In keeping with his dictum that "the truth is always beautiful" and that truth to one's feelings is most beautiful of all, Bob confesses to having a brief affair while on a trip to San Francisco. Carol responds by having her own affair, which Bob at first has trouble accepting. Eventually, however, he even tries to befriend her somewhat bewildered young lover. Alice meanwhile has begun to see a psychiatrist and realizes through her therapy that she doesn't trust Ted and, at the same time, feels an attraction toward Bob.

With all of these contradictions in the air, the four of them travel to Las Vegas for a vacation. The film leaves them as they apparently decide against any further experiment in "sexual freedom." Seen with opposite partners in the large bed of their suite, they flirt with the idea of switching partners, but soon join a symbolic throng of diverse types to the tune of Jackie DeShannon's "What the World Needs Now Is Love."

Though the ending seems a cop-out, there are scenes in *Bob & Carol & Ted & Alice* that capture the fads and foibles—and the ideals—of their era perfectly. These include the sequence at the spa that opens the film (with music from Handel's *Messiah*), a long bedroom scene between Ted and Alice when he wants sex and she doesn't, and Alice's sessions with her psychiatrist, who is never interested in pursuing anything beyond one hour.

Mike Nichols' *Carnal Knowledge* (1971) explores the insecurities felt by men in a period of changing values. The film begins at an unspecified point in the late forties or early fifties, when its protagonists Jonathan (Jack Nicholson) and Sandy (singer Art Garfunkel) are undergraduates at Amherst. It concludes some twenty years later, when, exhausted by compulsive sexual activity and countercultural experimentation, the two lead meaningless lives despite their professional success.

The story of Jonathan and Sandy unfolds tableau fashion, with segments set in different periods of time, as innocence gives way to experience and self-deceit. Jonathan sees relationships with women only in terms of sexual conquests, while Sandy, the more innocent of the two, pursues the Holy Grail of the ideal relationship. Jonathan's only marriage, to the masochistic Bobbie

(Ann-Margret), ends in failure, as does Sandy's to his first college sweetheart, Susan (Candice Bergen). With an irony that is only too obvious, Jonathan must resort by the end of the film to ritualistic sexual encounters with hookers for whatever satisfaction he can derive, while Sandy is having an affair with a flower child young enough to be his daughter.

Too nasty to be funny, too superficial to be taken altogether seriously, *Carnal Knowledge* reflects the ambivalence of its characters toward their own sexuality and toward emotional commitments. Many people felt the same uncertainties in the period when the film was written and produced. Its authors were Mike Nichols and cartoonist-turned-playwright Jules Feiffer.

Shampoo (1975) also tries to be funny and serious at the same time. Set in 1968 in the same social milieu of Los Angeles explored in *Bob & Carol & Ted & Alice* and *The Graduate*, *Shampoo* is the story of a Beverly Hills hairdresser who fixes more than the coiffures of his customers. George (Warren Beatty) is having an affair with Felicia (Lee Grant), the wife of Lester, a wealthy Hollywood fat cat (Jack Warden). At the same time, George has a steady girlfriend, Jill (Goldie Hawn), who wants to marry him. He also revives a relationship with a previous mistress, Jackie (Julie Christie), who is currently having an affair with Lester. This tangle of commitments belongs to the world of classic farce, but *Shampoo* makes of it a contemporary statement.

George's inability to make emotional commitments parallels that of Jonathan and Sandy in *Carnal Knowledge*, but the tone of *Shampoo* is much lighter and its satire on upper-middle-class mores sharper. As long as *Shampoo* remains on this level, it works very well. Scenes like those at a Republican fund-raising dinner (for the Nixon-Agnew campaign) at which Jackie performs fellatio on George under the table, or another, by a swimming pool during a party at Lester's and Felicia's house, when Lester discovers George and Jackie making love in a cabana, cast a satiric light on the lifestyle of the rich but not so famous.

Where the film works less well is when, toward the end, the audience is asked to take more seriously the plight of George, a character of much libido but little depth. The final scenes have George experiencing some kind of existential despair. For a character whose main concern has been opening his own hair salon and sleeping with a succession of women, such emotion is rather hard to believe. Nonetheless, for a satiric look at a particular class of

American society at the end of the sixties, bloated by its materialism and surfeited by its pleasures, *Shampoo* occupies a special
place among the films of this period.

Robert Altman's *Nashville* (1975), set in the capital of country
music, has a more ambitious agenda. It is a film of epic scope shot in
a semidocumentary style influenced by television. It also does not
fall into the category of comedy of manners. *Nashville* follows more
than a dozen characters through several critical days in "the home of
country music." Altman's purpose is to provide a political and personal cross-view of America at the end of the sixties in a place remote from the major centers of conflict. The city of Nashville epitomizes the phony ideals and crass realities of American society, all
dramatized within the world of a heavily commercial, yet determinedly "down-home" music. It is also one more site for the gender
wars of the period, though they are but one part of the complicated
network of stories and themes that make up the film.

The main thread of the plot involves country star Barbara Jean
(Ronee Blakley), who has just returned to Nashville after a period of
illness that required hospitalization. Barbara Jean is still suffering, not
physically but emotionally. Her fragile condition, which soon takes
her back to the hospital, is a paradigm for other forms of sickness af-
flicting the other characters in the film. All are in some way sick or incomplete. The several days' events of the story only serve to make
these problems plainer. Barbara Jean's death at the end of the film at
the hand of an assassin, despite the ministrations of her overly pro-
tective husband, underscores the pointlessness of all the characters'
lives. It also suggests that, in penetrating to the heartland, the violence of the sixties had become pervasive in American life.

Other characters prominent in the film include Linnea Reese
(Lily Tomlin) and her husband Delbert (Ned Beatty). She is involved
in the music business as a singer; he is part of the local establishment promoting the city of Nashville. Linnea has a brief affair with
Tom (Keith Carradine), a compulsively sexual young singer in town
to make a recording. Meanwhile, Bud Hamilton (Dave Peel), son of
established country star Haven Hamilton (Henry Gibson), pairs off
with L.A. Joan (Shelly Duvall), who is in Nashville to visit her uncle
(Keenan Wynn), whose wife is dying of cancer.

Also important are characters whose function has less to do
with the plot of the film than with its theme of alienation. Principal
among these is Opal (Geraldine Chaplin), an English journalist
doing a documentary on Nashville and the country music business.

Her role provides commentary and occasional perspective on the events of the story, though she too becomes involved sexually with Tom. There is a young soldier who is devoted to Barbara Jean, and there is her assassin, who carries his weapon in a violin case and takes a room in the home of L.A. Joan's uncle. In addition—though not a character—the sound truck of a conservative political candidate is seen and heard driving through the Nashville streets throughout the film. Its slogans suggest something at once sinister and irrelevant. At the end, as Barbara Jean is shot, the candidate (whom the audience never sees) is whisked away just as he is about to emerge from a limousine to make a speech at the political rally where the assassination occurs.

Nashville is flawed by Altman's penchant as a director for the spontaneous, with much of the dialogue seeming improvised. Certain characters (like actor Elliott Gould) are introduced only because they were stars at the time and seem to have little to do with the plot. Nonetheless, *Nashville* is one of the most ambitious attempts of its period to capture the changes—sexual, social, and political—brought about in American society by the 1960s. And Altman's decision to show these changes in the city that is famous for the Grand Ole Opry and country music seems especially appropriate, given the importance of that music to the late sixties and early seventies in American popular culture.

None of the films just discussed (with the exception of *Love Story*) was among the most popular of the decade (*Shampoo* did best of all at the box office). None did more than partial justice to the ideals of the women's movement. With film directorship and production firmly in masculine hands, women found little reflection in American films of the seventies of the many important changes they were experiencing in their lives. Occasionally, fantasy figures like Princess Leah in George Lucas's *Star Wars* (1977) showed a streak of independence, but American movies for the most part were unable to deal effectively with the real-life situation of one half of the population.

GAYS AND LESBIANS: OUT OF THE CLOSET AND INTO THE MAINSTREAM

Beginning with an incident of symbolic importance—the riot at the Stonewall Inn in Greenwich Village in June 1969, when gay men retaliated forcefully against a police raid—the gay rights movement soon spread to college campuses and elsewhere. Gays and lesbians became more openly defiant of societal strictures against their sexuality. In American popular culture, where gays and lesbians were typically treated as objects of humor or derision, the first serious treatment of gay life would come in film.

Historically, gay and lesbian characters remained in the closet in American movies as they did in real life. Their sexual orientation was hinted at vaguely, if at all. *These Three* (1937), the film version of Lillian Hellman's celebrated play *The Children's Hour* (1934), changed the nature of the accusation made by a malicious schoolgirl against two female teachers in her boarding school. While the play makes it clear she thinks they are in "an unnatural relationship," the movie version (written by Hellman herself) changes the plot "to make the code." A heterosexual love triangle becomes the basis of the false accusation. In a rare instance of one director having a second chance at the same material, William Wyler would direct a second version of the same story in 1962. Using Hellman's original title, the new version made the nature of the accusation much plainer, though the outcome, a suicide, remained the same.

In general, postwar American playwrights were able to deal more frankly with such subject matter than Hollywood screenwriters and directors could. Robert Anderson's play *Tea and Sympathy* (1953), about a sensitive young boarding school student accused of homosexuality, became especially problematic in its film adaptation. One problem was the intimation that he might be gay (his peers call him "Sister Boy"). Another was that the boy's emotional dilemma is resolved by an adulterous liaison with his coach's wife. Since the play presented not one but two possible violations of the screen code (against the sympathetic depiction of "sexual perversion" and of adultery), it required considerable reworking before an acceptable film could be made of it. The resulting script, directed by Vicente Minnelli, altered the original to downplay both controversial elements. Homosexuality is barely suggested. In a flash forward at the end of the film, the boy enters into a "normal" heterosexual marriage as an adult and the coach's wife suffers as a result of her transgression against her husband. It is a classic instance of the effects of the film code.

In film adaptations of the plays of Tennessee Williams—among the frankest explorations of sexual behavior in the American theater of the forties and fifties—similar changes took place. In *A*

Streetcar Named Desire (1951), Blanche Dubois's allusion to the homosexual relationship of her young husband (who commits suicide after she finds him having sex with an older male friend) is cut out. Similarly, in the film version of *Cat on a Hot Tin Roof* (1958), references to the homosexual relationship of Brick (Paul Newman) and his dead friend Skipper are omitted. As a result, the reason for the failure of his marriage to Maggie the Cat (Elizabeth Taylor) is lost.

Sometimes filmmakers found ways to suggest homoerotic attraction without referring to it specifically, as Alfred Hitchcock did in *Strangers on a Train* (1951). In this film, based on a novel by Patricia Highsmith with a script by novelist Raymond Chandler, a psychopathic murderer meets a handsome young tennis player on a train. Jokingly, Bruno (Robert Walker) and Guy (Farley Granger) agree to swap murder targets. What Guy doesn't realize is that Bruno is dead serious and will kill Guy's fiancée at an amusement park. His motive? His obvious infatuation with Guy. In a later scene in the film, Bruno is seen at a tennis match. While the rest of the crowd follows the ball from one side of the net to the other, his eyes stay fixed on his good-looking friend. The implication is hard to miss, the visual image effective.

By 1962—the year the new version of *The Children's Hour* was released—the movie production code had been changed to allow filmmakers greater freedom in treating the subject of homosexuality on the screen. With emphasis on the need for "care, discretion and restraint," the Motion Picture Association of America cautiously approved such subject matter in the fall of 1961. Director Otto Preminger forced the decision over his film version of Allen Drury's Washington novel, *Advise and Consent*, which contained a homosexual relationship. Again, as in *The Children's Hour*, a character (in this case a U.S. senator) commits suicide because of stories circulating about a past affair with a young man who has now become a hustler in New York. Homosexuality in *Advise and Consent* is a curse from which the only real escape is death.

By the mid-1960s, independent filmmakers were treating gay subjects with much greater freedom, though for a more limited audience. A milestone in this development was Andy Warhol's *My Hustler* (1965).

At his Manhattan Factory, Warhol, one of the major pop artists of the sixties, began experimenting with short black-and-white films in 1963. In general, Warhol's films, like most independent avant-garde films, eschewed Hollywood studio conventions. They had no narrative content, no big name stars, no editing, and little technical finesse. Their "stars" were amateurs, often straight from the street. Warhol's entire aesthetic as a filmmaker was predicated on amateurism. As a director, Warhol was passive—a voyeur rather than an auteur—and not interested in producing films for a general audience. Eventually, however, he was persuaded to consider entering the burgeoning market for soft-core pornography. *My Hustler*—the first commercially conceived film to deal so frankly with the subject—was his first production in this vein.

My Hustler was shot in real time (a Warhol trademark) on Labor Day weekend, 1965, at Fire Island, a beach resort popular with the New York gay community. It begins with a conversation between Ed, an aging gay male, and Genevieve, a female neighbor whom Ed calls a "fag hag." Somewhat later, they are joined by Joe, a male hustler of Ed's acquaintance. The topic of conversation is their mutual attraction to another hustler, Paul, whom Ed—as the "john," or client—has hired for the weekend. In this discussion, much homosexual slang is used, and the camera remains focused much of the time on Paul, who is lounging, half-naked, on the beach. The actors used their real names and, in fact, represented slightly fictionalized versions of themselves.

The second reel is shot in the bathroom of Ed's condo, where Paul and Joe have taken cooling-off showers and are drying themselves. In the process, Joe quizzes Paul about his hustling activity and his degree of commitment to it. Both by what he says and by physical contact—rubbing Paul's back with lotion, for instance—he makes very clear his interest in the younger man. Paul, on the other hand, pretends an innocence he probably does not have. The film ends with brief reappearances by Ed, Genevieve, and an unidentified third person, all of whom try to woo Paul away.

Despite the simplicity of the concept, the film has a considerable narrative pull. Unlike many films of Warhol's, it also has conventional, if rather static, cinematography. Novelists had dealt frankly with male hustlers and their customers—most notably perhaps John Rechy in *City of Night* (1963)—but in American films the subject was virtually untouched. To deal with it so unpejoratively was unusual indeed. In Warhol's work, *My Hustler* anticipated other, more openly gay films like *Bike Boy*, *The Loves of Ondine*, and *Lonesome Cowboys* (all from 1967-68). All of these films played in New York's Times Square porn houses.

Ed and Paul at Fire Island in Andy Warhol's My Hustler *(1965)*

Flesh (1968), produced by Warhol and directed by his collaborator Paul Morrissey, stars Joe Dallesandro, a product of the Warhol Factory (he appears in a nude wrestling scene in *The Loves of Ondine* and also in *Lonesome Cowboys*). It is the first of three films by Morrissey starring Dallesandro and dealing with male prostitution and drugs. (The other two are *Trash* [1970], and *Heat* [1972].) *Flesh* provides a much fuller look at the life of a male hustler than Warhol's *My Hustler*. Joe (Dallesandro's character) hustles for money so his wife's girlfriend can have an abortion. With full frontal male nudity (including erections), sexual encounters with various johns, and a scene in which a former girlfriend performs fellatio on Joe in the presence of two drag queens, *Flesh* comes much closer to conventional pornography than do most of Warhol's films. At the same time, it suggests even more strongly than *My Hustler* the limitations of sexual commodification. Joe's passivity is moral as well as physical: As a sexual object, he is acted upon by others, never active himself (the exception on the physical level is one brief moment with his wife early in the film). *Flesh* carried its subject one step further than any commercially released film had done previously and set the stage for the first film from a major studio to deal with the same subject.

John Schlesinger's *Midnight Cowboy* (1969), with Dustin Hoffman and Jon Voight, became the first (and so far only) film with an "X" rating to win an Academy Award as best picture of the year. The picture also won awards for best direction and screenplay. The story of Joe Buck (Jon Voight), a young hustler, and Ratso Rizzo (Dustin Hoffman), a physically disabled small-time thief, *Midnight Cowboy* graphically dramatized the harshness of New York street life and the futility of a hustler's existence.

As a hustler, Joe Buck is notably unsuccessful. Dressed in macho cowboy gear, he imagines himself making money from sexual encounters with women, but finds that he is more attractive to men. Unlike Joe in *Flesh*, however, Joe Buck is clearly unable to accept his bisexuality. Dallesandro's Joe tells a young hustler: "It's not a matter of being straight, being not straight. It's just—you do what you have to do." But Joe Buck wants so much to be straight that he ends up beating up a john and stealing his money so he can take his ailing friend Ratso to the milder climate of Miami. The real focus of the film is on the friendship between Joe and Ratso, in which sexual feelings are sublimated to the ideal of selfless bonding. For Ratso, Joe is the physical ideal he has never been able to match. For Joe, Ratso is the friend he has never had. Joe does what he has to do to try to save his life, only to find, as they arrive by bus in Florida, that his friend has died. With memorable performances by a strong cast, *Midnight Cowboy* is also of interest for the glimpse it gives, in one scene, of a Manhattan party featuring the actress Viva and other "stars" of the Warhol Film Factory, a left-handed tribute to Warhol's ground-breaking films on the same subject.

By 1970, Hollywood would deal more frankly than ever before with the lives of gay men in a film version of Mart Crowley's 1968 play, *The Boys in the Band* (1970). Eight gay men gather for a birthday party at which a young hustler is the "gift." In a series of conversations and games, they reveal their feelings about themselves and their homosexuality. With emotions ranging from acceptance to self-loathing, the characters are intended to be representative of gay society at the time the gay liberation movement was just beginning. Today the characters seem more like stereotypes, and their promiscuity, after the AIDS crisis, unwise. Nonetheless, *The Boys in the Band* introduced the general movie audience (as it did its initial stage audience) to aspects of gay life that were new to many of them. It also had a cathartic effect for a generation of gay men who were still accustomed to keeping their sexual lives closeted.

No such film from a major studio was to occur for lesbians, though lesbian relationships had been described frankly and been celebrated in novels like Rita Mae Brown's *Ruby Fruit Jungle* (1968). Hollywood did present at least one instance of a positive lesbian relationship (among many more negative ones), in the film adaptation of Jacqueline Susann's popular novel, *Once Is Not Enough* (1975). More commonly, however, lesbians were punished in one way or another for their sexual preference.

As the seventies progressed, gays were increasingly depicted on the screen as freaks of one kind or another in films like *Dog Day Afternoon* and the campy *Rocky Horror Picture Show* (both from 1975). It took two decades for a major studio to produce a film in which gay men were seen in loving, long-term relationships. *Longtime Companion* (1990) used the AIDS crisis to win a wider acceptability for its touching depiction of a marriage till death between two men.

On television, the serious treatment of gays did not go so far or so deep. The high point was the made-for-television drama *That Certain Summer* (1973), about a gay father revealing his homosexuality to his son. In the 1980s, during the Reagan years, gay characters virtually disappeared from network television.

In popular music, gay subject matter came out with the gay rights movement. Two figures were especially important to what happened: the American Lou Reed, originally with the Velvet Underground, and British-born David Bowie. Reed left the Underground at the beginning of the seventies over disputes with John Cale and other members of the group about the direction it should take. His first album after the start of his solo career was *Transformer* (1972), containing the Top Twenty hit "Walk on the Wild Side." This song was a tribute to Andy Warhol and the "stars" of his movies, many of whom were gay. With its obvious allusions to homosexuality, "Walk on the Wild Side" soon joined the long list of songs banned from radio. Shortly after the release of *Transformer*, Reed dyed his hair blond and painted his fingernails black, bowing to the trend toward "glitter"—sometimes called "glam"—rock.

The producer of *Transformer* was David Bowie, a longtime fan of the Underground and himself to become a leading exponent of androgyny in seventies rock. At the beginning of the same year that Reed's album appeared, Bowie publicly identified himself as bisexual. Shortly afterwards, he began to develop the stage persona he called Ziggy Stardust, a doomed rock star who becomes a cult icon much like The Who's Tommy. Ziggy, however, was sexually ambiguous. At a time when standard dress for rock stars was still T-shirt and jeans, Bowie's fantastic outfits and orange-colored hair introduced a whole new dimension to concert rock. With his backup band, the Spiders from Mars, Ziggy's third album, *Aladdin Sane* (1973), which reached #17 on the chart, was to prove the breakthrough for Bowie in the United States. However, in the very year of its release, Bowie, taking one of the rapid shifts of direction for which he was to become famous, disbanded the Spiders and gave up the Ziggy persona altogether.

By the end of the seventies, groups like the Village People achieved great popularity with songs like "Macho Man" (#25 [1978]) and "Y.M.C.A." (#2 [1979]), which had obvious homosexual overtones. Dressed in the manner of gay stereotypes—a biker, a construction worker, a cowboy—the group combined disco style with recognizably gay themes in a way that would have been impossible before the work of Reed and Bowie and the brief, early seventies trend to glitter rock.

THE AMERICAN INDIAN MOVEMENT AND THE NEW WESTERNS

The American Indian movement—given definition by novelists like the native American author M. Scott Momaday (*House Made of Dawn* [1966])—found its strongest expression in American popular culture of the sixties and early seventies in movie westerns and in music. Condemned to reservation badlands with appallingly high levels of alcoholism, poverty, and loss of social identity, these first Americans began to feel the stirrings of rebellion in the late 1960s.

Members of the counterculture were especially sympathetic to the Native American cause. Rural commune-dwellers imitated Native American costumes, their manner of living close to nature, and other customs. The environmental movement—begun in a sense by one book, Rachel Carson's *Silent Spring* (1962) and culminating in the massive Earth Day celebration of 1970—complemented their enthusiasm for the Native American lifestyle.

In popular music of the sixties and seventies, Buffy Sainte-Marie, a Cree Indian by birth, was chief spokesperson for Native Americans. A folk-style musician, Sainte-Marie was successful as a composer as well as a singer. Her protest song "The Universal

Soldier" achieved classic status in covers by sixties folk singer Donovan and by country pop star Glen Campbell. Her own version served as theme music to the 1970 film, *Soldier Blue*. "Now That the Buffalo's Gone" and "My Country 'Tis of Thy People You're Dying" were moving tributes to the culture of the Native American, which was obliterated by the westward push of white America. In addition to the music of Sainte-Marie, a number of other significant songs of the early seventies pay homage to the Native American. Elton John and his longtime collaborator Bernie Taupin produced "Indian Sunset" for the 1971 album *Madman Across the Water*, and Paul Revere and the Raiders, a West Coast group popular in the same period, recorded "Indian Reservation" in 1971.

In popular movies, where they were called "redskins" or simply Indians, Native Americans were traditionally portrayed one of two ways. Most frequently, they were the enemies of brave white settlers hazarding life and fortune to open up new land for farming, commerce, and something called progress. Alternatively, they were the friends of these settlers, supporting them or their representatives—the military commanders and the lawmen—in their quest for land and law and order. It was the difference between Geronimo, rebel leader of the Apaches, a historical figure, and Tonto, the mythical companion of the Lone Ranger. Though the movie audience might have a sneaking admiration for the first of these two stereotypes, they couldn't trust him the way they could the second. Tonto was the "good Indian," more loyal to whites than to his own people.

For the film image of the Native American, the most significant revisionary statement of the period was Arthur Penn's *Little Big Man* (1970), a sprawling, frequently funny, chronicle of the demise of the Plains Indians, in which the Cheyenne—whose name means "human beings"—are the heroes and General George Custer and his troops the genocidal villains.

Little Big Man is narrated by 121-year-old Jack Crabb (Dustin Hoffman), a survivor of the story's tragic events; the title comes from his Indian name. The film posits an ideal Native American world in which people are true to the land and to each other, but manage to match the superior arms and relentless aggressiveness of the white military only once. This comes, of course, at Little Big Horn, where Custer and his troops—having viciously attacked a Cheyenne village, killing innocent people, including Jack's wife—are themselves surrounded and annihilated in the crowning moment of the Plains Indians' resistance to the encroaching white civilization.

What makes *Little Big Man* so successful in dealing with its essentially serious theme is its element of humor and its strong performances. Especially notable are Chief Dan George as Old Lodge Skins, Jack's adopted grandfather, and Hoffman himself. The humanity of the Native Americans—their quality as "human beings"—defines them as characters and makes the audience care about what happens to their way of life.

Their treatment at the hands of merciless soldiers struck many in the first audience of this film as comment of another sort—on what had happened in Vietnam in such places as the village of My Lai. In addition, the Native American philosophy, as enunciated by Old Lodge Skins, resonated (unhistorically) with the ideals of the counterculture. Released the year after Woodstock, *Little Big Man*, though set in the past, suggested that countercultural values were a path to follow from the chaos of the late sixties and the hypocrisies of the Nixon years. Other films of the early seventies would touch on the same themes, but less effectively. Not until Kevin Costner's *Dances with Wolves* (1990) was Hollywood to produce a film of such scope and such deep sympathy for Native American life, though Costner's more epic concept was not endowed with the humor of *Little Big Man*.

Chapter 8

ADDING IT UP: THE SIXTIES AND AMERICAN CULTURE TODAY

This book began with the question, "Did the 1960s change our lives in any positive way?" Some readers will answer this yes, citing changes they regard as important and beneficial as a result of this tumultuous decade. Others will say no, expressing concern over fundamental values they consider to have been lost or never achieved. This chapter will consider the long-term effects of the events of the sixties on our lives today, with special emphasis on sixties legacies in music, movies, and the media.

It was popular during the 1960s to talk about "revolution" and to regard the goal of political and social activism to be not merely to modify but fundamentally change the social and political structure of this country, even the world. The peace movement raised significant questions about the United States' commitment in Vietnam and, more generally, about the entire military establishment of this country. It also helped to create the atmosphere in the U.S. Congress that resulted in the passage, in 1973, of the War Powers Act. This act in effect revoked the broad powers that the Tonkin Resolution of 1964 had given the president and required him to seek the support of Congress before making any such commitment in the future. In 1983, however, Ronald Reagan ignored this act in committing American troops to the "liberation" of Grenada. In contrast, George Bush sought congressional approval for what was labeled a United Nations action against Iraq in the Gulf War of 1991. The shadow of Vietnam fell over this vote. Congress granted its approval only because of assurances from the president that the war would be short and the fatalities few. Thus, one significant long-term effect of the sixties peace movement on the structure and operation of our massive military establishment has been to increase to some extent the accountability of those in charge. No one wants to repeat the mistakes of Vietnam. A second effect of the peace movement was the end of the draft in 1973. While it would still be necessary for all males eighteen years of age to register with the Selective Service System, they would face a period of service only in the event of an emergency.

In terms of the political process, itself, the activists of the 1960s, in their concern for the rights of the individual, had their greatest success in the civil rights movement. This movement had positive and enduring effects in the lives of millions of African Americans. The Jim Crow laws disappeared from the books, along with literacy tests and poll taxes. African Americans in the South and throughout the land found added legal protections by the end of the 1960s, and American schools were more fully integrated. Yet, in the 1990s, segregation in schools continues. Increasing numbers of white students attend suburban schools, as blacks, Latinos, and other minorities remain concentrated in the cities. People of color may not be segregated by law, but too often they are still separated from white America socially and economically. Despite significant improvements over the past three decades, racism continues to divide the people of this country.

The concern for individual rights has encouraged the spread of political and social activism among feminists, gays, and lesbians, and also among more conservative groups like the antiabortion movement. These special interest groups have used the same tactics of protest as the civil rights and antiwar movements to achieve their aims. Furthermore, many of them claim the right to disagree, even violently, with the law of the land when it conflicts with their sense of moral purpose. As was the case with special interest politics of the 1960s, however, such groups, whether left or right in their leanings, sometimes lack a holistic view. They also frequently find themselves at such extreme odds with one another that their differences—often irreconcilable—are raised to a political platform.

In the social sphere, the so-called sexual revolution has produced decisive changes. With medical technology backing, and sometimes shaping, attitudinal change, the sixties generation was undoubtedly more open and experimental in sexual expression than their parents' generation, with results that can still be felt today. Cohabitation, for instance, is now a common feature of white middle-class life, whereas in the fifties and before it was unacceptable. Attitudes toward premarital sex, teenage pregnancy, masturbation, and other aspects of human sexual behavior have also changed in major ways. At the same time, however, since the 1980s, the AIDS epidemic has introduced the need for special precautions that, for many, have inhibited free sexual expression. Moreover, conservative groups like the Christian Coalition and Promise Keepers oppose not only abortion rights for women but also same-sex relationships. So vocal has such opposition become that, in many states, it has resulted in regressive legal limitations on abortion rights and uncloseted homosexuality.

Other social changes have been equally decisive. One of these is the role of women in American society. Thanks to the liberation movement, women have more status and power than ever before. They major in what they choose at the undergraduate level and then attend professional schools in record numbers. They also play a more prominent role in the workplace. The number of households in which both husband and wife are employed has also increased dramatically since the 1960s. It is now estimated that fully two-thirds of American families have two incomes. The extent to which this has resulted in significant changes in family roles, however, is a matter of question. Much evidence suggests that, for women, it simply means that, in addition to working outside the home, they continue to have the major responsibility of running the household—cooking, cleaning, caring for the children. Furthermore, while employment has certainly given women economic advantages they once lacked, such as greater access to credit, individual retirement plans, and the like, they are still on the average paid far less than their male counterparts. Bureau of Census figures for 1967 to 1991 show an improvement in median income for women of slightly more than $3700—from $6757 per year to $10,476. However, their income at the end of that period was still nearly $10,000 less than their male counterparts.

In spite of better jobs and improved educational opportunities, women have yet to achieve the equality targeted in the Equal Rights Amendment once proposed (but not ratified by a sufficient number of states) for the U.S. Constitution.

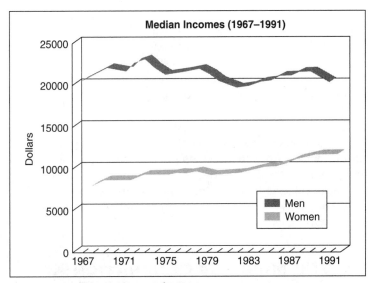

Median income by gender, 1967-1991

(Source of data: Bureau of the Census, Current Population Reports, 1992)

In the area of public policy, congressional opposition to many programs and policies initiated in the sixties and early seventies has become highly vocal since the election of 1994. The National Endowment for the Humanities and the Arts, long-standing affirmative action policies, the welfare system—all of these and more have been attacked by legislators who claim their constituents are tired of big government and its interference in their lives. This backlash began in the eighties during the presidency of Ronald Reagan, who reaped the fruit of the seeds of distrust of the national government sown in the Johnson and Nixon years.

To the extent that such criticism leads to significant revisions of policy or law, many historic trends begun 20 to 30 years ago have been reversed. One of the most notable of these revisions is the Welfare Reform Act of 1997, which passed by significant majorities in the House and the Senate and was signed into law by President Clinton, a Democrat. This law establishes limitations of time and circumstance which effect all people on public welfare, with the major decision making going to the states rather than the federal government. It is a reflection of changing attitudes toward the role of the federal government in providing for the poor and needy of our society, though poverty remains as much a problem as it was in the 1960s, affecting just as high a percentage of people. It is one more issue of the 1960s that is still not resolved.

On balance, then, the ultimate effect of the many changes begun in the 1960s has yet to be finally measured. To the extent that racism, sexism, and poverty remain a feature of American society, the idealism of the sixties has failed. If the boom economy of the 1990s also fails, poverty, without the safety of the welfare net, will only grow worse. At such a point, perhaps the solutions proposed in the sixties may take on new life. In the realm of popular culture—which from the beginning has been so vital in defining the meaning of the 1960s—the decade produced changes that are both measurable and long lasting. Especially in the popular arts and media, the focus of attention in this book, the 1960s have remained an important, unequivocal force.

THE MUSIC OF GENERATION X: FROM PUNK TO GRUNGE

R.E.M., Pearl Jam, Nirvana, Public Enemy, Phish, Hole, Rage Against the Machine, Beck—the music of the generation dubbed "X," which has matured since the beginning of the Reagan years, has deep roots in the sixties. (The phrase "generation X" connotes a lack of definition, or purpose in life, which is seen as one characteristic of this group.) Sometimes these connections are acknowledged in direct ways, sometimes in less direct ones, but, however unique the newest trends in popular music may seem, the connections are clearly there.

In fact, the music of the sixties itself remains popular with a large segment of the listening audience. In 1994-95, according to the annual ratings in *Forbes* magazine, the Beatles—who by then had not existed as a group for more than 20 years—earned more money than other musical groups, with revenues totalling $130 million. Thanks to oldies radio, specializing in the music of the fifties through the seventies, Top Forty songs of those decades are familiar to younger listeners. The element of nostalgia inherent in such programming does not in itself account for the popularity of such stations, nor does it explain the success of the many remastered, reissued CDs by sixties groups to be found in record stores and club catalogues. Groups like the Beatles and The Doors have a cult status with younger listeners that keeps their records perennially in the best-selling category.

Equally popular through concerts as well as recordings are musical groups and individual singer-composers who began in the 1960s and are still performing today. In the same year that the Beatles placed first in total revenues among all musical groups, the Rolling Stones ran them a close second. By then in their fourth decade as a working entity, the Stones earned $121 million in their *Voodoo Lounge* tour, the most successful to that date in rock history.

Among individual performers, Bob Dylan, Neil Young, Stevie Wonder, Joni Mitchell, Van Morrison, Eric Clapton, and Paul Simon remain especially important in the current musical scene. Despite occasional dry periods, they have shown a consistency in performance and creative output to put them in a special category: sixties survivors who are still significant as performing artists and composers.

From 1976 until the end of the 1980s, Dylan's albums were favorably received chiefly by the faithful. His own faith, after a conversion to born-again Christianity, provided some of the subject matter, but neither in recordings nor in performance did he generate the kind of enthusiasm he had once routinely earned from his audience. *Oh Mercy* (1989) proved that, though perhaps diminished, the talent was still there. *Good As I Been to You* (1992) and *World Gone Wrong* (1993) revisited the acoustic-backed folk songs from the beginning of his career, when Woody Guthrie was his musical hero. But the 1990s have also seen evidence of a true creative revival. Dylan's concert performances—captured brilliantly in the MTV *Unplugged* album of 1995—have shown renewed vitality with imaginative reworkings of familiar material as well as the introduction of occasional new songs. In addition, his audiences are multigenerational, with young fans among the most enthusiastic. *Time out of Mind* (1997), containing all new material, has been compared with the best songs of the seventies, especially those in the dark, divorce-influenced *Blood on the Tracks*. Now, nearing his sixth decade, Dylan's preoccupation seems to be with his own mortality.

Neil Young has continued to grow as composer and performer, since his days with Buffalo Springfield and Crosby, Stills, and Nash. Alternating between melodic, basically lyrical music like that on *Harvest* (#1, 1972) (featuring his #1 single, "Heart of Gold") and the heavier sound of *Freedom* (1989), with his favorite backup group Crazy Horse, Young has created music in a variety of styles, from (almost) pure country to garage band rock, with acoustic as well as electric guitar arrangements. His *Unplugged* album of 1993 captures the lyrical side well, and *Sleeps with Angels* (1994)—a tribute to Kurt Cobain, lead singer of Nirvana, who committed suicide in April of that year—the heavier sound. Young has great sympathy with grunge rock, a hard rock subcategory of alternative music for which Young himself has provided much inspiration and of which Nirvana was the foremost exponent. This sympathy has led in part to his collaboration with another Seattle-based group, Pearl Jam, and its lead singer Eddie Vedder in 1995's *Mirror Ball*.

Meanwhile, Stevie Wonder, who first recorded for Motown in the sixties when he was in his teens, has also followed his own direction musically and personally. Committed to various causes in the spirit of the 1960s, Wonder has varied his musical style through the succeeding decades, changing with the times. He was the first Motown artist to gain complete artistic control while under contract to that company. His career peaked in the 1970s, with hit singles like "Superstition" and "You Are the Sunshine of My Life," as well as a tour with the Rolling Stones in 1972 and a series of successful, often innovative albums. Since then, Wonder has continued to experiment in his music. His hit single "Part-Time Lover" (#1, 1985) was the first to top the charts simultaneously in pop, R & B, adult contemporary, *and* dance/disco. He has anticipated such trends as New Age and influenced artists as diverse as Jeff Beck and Bob Marley. In his use of the synthesizer and studio recording techniques, he has generated the same kind of sound (though uniquely his own) as later electronic specialists like Beck Hansen.

Joni Mitchell has followed an equally individualistic musical course, continuing to create innovative music in a variety of styles out of her own personal experiences. After a burst of activity in the 1970s, Mitchell virtually gave up concertizing in the 1980s. In that period, her albums reflected her interest in jazz as well as folk music. With the albums *Night Ride Home* (1991) and, particularly, *Turbulent Indigo* (1994) she found a critical and popular response to her new voice. Talented also as a painter and photographer (she does the art for her own albums), Mitchell has one of the longest and most successful careers of any female singer-songwriter in the music business. She has been an inspiration to such diverse contemporary artists as Morrissey of the Smiths and the Indigo Girls.

Equally individualistic, Belfast-born Van Morrison is one of the most respected and influential figures in pop music, though he has never achieved—nor perhaps desired—the kind of popularity that frequently goes with such standing. With an eclectic musical style, at times based squarely in traditional blues or R & B, at others in jazz or even mainstream pop, Morrison has charted in his long list of albums a personal progress toward spiritual understanding and his own mystical brand of born-again Christianity. None of this spiritual (and sometimes geographical) journeying has prevented him from writing the occasional hit song, as, for instance, in "Have I Told You Lately That I Love You?" originally recorded by Morrison in 1989 in his album *Avalon Sunset* and a #5 hit for Rod Stewart in 1993. From the same album, Morrison's own version of "Whenever God Shines His Light on Me" (a duet with Cliff Richard) reached the Top Twenty of the British chart, the first such single of Morrison's to do so since his early days with the group Them. More recently, his album *Too Long in Exile* (1993) paid tribute to his musical roots, with covers of songs by Ray Charles and Sonny Boy Williamson. It also included a duet version of Morrison's early hit "Gloria" with blues singer John Lee Hooker.

Like Van Morrison, Eric Clapton, though born in England, has become a permanent fixture of the American musical scene since the 1970s. One of the leading electric guitarists of the 1960s, Clapton's work with the group Cream and then, later, the Dominos helped to define the direction of heavy metal in the seventies. Clapton has recorded a considerable body of work spanning more than three decades. Recent albums, including *Unplugged* (1992) and *From the Cradle* (1994), capture the breadth of his musical achievement. "Tears in Heaven" from the first of these albums was a tribute to his son, who died as a result of a fall from the fiftieth floor of a Manhattan apartment building. It reached #2 in 1993 and won a Grammy award, as did Clapton's vocal performance and the album itself. *From the Cradle* was a tribute to Clapton's blues roots. Consisting entirely of covers of traditional blues—some, like Robert Johnson's "Crossroads," closely associated with Clapton—it reached the top of the album chart in the year of its release.

Paul Simon, originally linked with Art Garfunkel in the celebrated folk duo that broke up in 1970, has continued a solo career of great distinction. As a singer-songwriter, he has composed music that reflects many musical traditions, including rock 'n' roll, jazz, blues, reggae, and African and South American music. With the latter, he anticipated by more than a decade the trend toward so-called "world music" of the 1990s. In 1986, he produced the hit album *Graceland* (#3) and in 1990, continuing his interest in world music, *Rhythm of the Saints*, which included West African, Brazilian, and American zydeco influences. *Graceland* was widely criticized for the fact that it was recorded in South Africa, then still operating under the laws of apartheid, the South African equivalent of the Jim Crow laws of the American South. Simon defended his choice publicly, arguing that his purpose was not to exploit South African musicians, but to bring their music to the attention of the world. With such broad musical interests, Simon is a folk artist who has grown far beyond his musical beginnings. Unfortunately, his most recent major artistic venture at this writing—*The Capeman* (1998), a Broadway musical based on a street gang-related murder—was a significant failure that has led Simon to vow never to try the same thing again.

If the musical influence of the 1960s generation continues into the present in the work of musicians like those just discussed, what about the thematic content of sixties music? Protest music of that period had a definite aim: to bring to the attention of the musical audience the shortcomings and outright lies that were part of the American experience. At the same time, sixties protest music was generally optimistic. It described problems but it also suggested solutions. Like the movements it mirrored, it was idealistic. It reflected the dream as well as the reality.

Little of this spirit entered into mainstream rock 'n' roll of the 1970s. Rather, the hedonistic, live-for-the-moment attitude that was also a part of sixties music came to the fore. The world described in the music of the heavy metal bands and disco groups that would achieve great popularity in the 1970s and 1980s was largely self-focused—a feverish, somewhat desperate pursuit of pleasure without considering social or political ideas. It is sometimes very good music, but it doesn't inspire change or reflection. "Let's party" just about sums it up.

The more iconoclastic side of sixties music—heard in popular groups like The Who and The Doors and, more importantly, in proto-punk groups like the Velvet Underground and Iggy Pop and the Stooges—would find a new form by the mid-seventies in punk rock. A back-to-basics brand of music with roots in mid-sixties garage band rock, punk's basic stance was antiestablishment. However, it made little attempt to suggest any alternatives to what it attacked. With a musical style consisting of simple chords and a highly repetitive musical structure, punk would lead eventually to grunge or alternative rock in the 1990s.

Patti Smith took the solo lead in the development of punk with original songs based on her own poetry, a kind of beat verse in the spirit of Allen Ginsberg or Diane di Prima. The Ramones—formed in 1974 and generally considered the first American punk rock band—were distinctly nonliterary. With a dense buzz saw sound in their guitars and no solos, they produced deliberately provocative songs like "Beat on the Brat" and "Now I Wanna Sniff Some Glue."

Two of the best-known and most artistically successful groups associated with the American punk scene emerged in 1975: the Talking Heads (David Byrne, lead singer) and Blondie (Deborah Harry, lead singer). Both were connected by their performances at CBGB, the New York club important to the punk movement, where the Ramones and Patti Smith also appeared. Both Blondie and the Heads managed to combine the basic elements of punk style with dance rhythms (often influenced by the reggae beat of Caribbean artist Bob Marley) and rap to produce a music—sometimes termed New Wave—that had very broad appeal. The Heads would reach their greatest success in the early eighties with the album *Speaking in Tongues* (#15, 1983), featuring their highest-charting single, "Burning Down the House" (#9, 1983). Blondie hit #1 four times between 1979 and 1981 with music ranging in style from disco to rap delivered in the deadpan style that became her trademark.

Among British punk groups to achieve popularity in the United States, two in particular stand out: the Sex Pistols and the Clash. The Sex Pistols (formed in 1975) was undoubtedly the most important of the pure punk bands. With a single album, they crystallized the basic elements of the musical style. *Never Mind the Bollocks Here's the Sex Pistols* (1979) was a snarling, iconoclastic rejection of middle-class British values and also of the style of rock 'n' roll that had become standard in Britain and the United States by the end of the seventies. The Pistols were not only antiestablishment, they were antimusic, with lyrics, as in the heavily ironic "God Save the Queen," which declared there was no future in tradition-bound England. The violent, aggressive nature of the Pistols' performances, including such acts as the destruction of instruments and slam dancing, was characteristic of punk music in general. It was a physical expression of its basic emotion, anger.

The Clash, formed in 1976, had a more sophisticated political agenda and a more sophisticated sound. Unlike the Sex Pistols, they also had a definite political purpose. Their lyrics asserted the value of British working-class culture and showed support for Third World revolution. Beset by internal difficulties, including the heroin use also so destructive to the Pistols, the Clash broke up just after achieving their greatest popularity in the United States with the album *Combat Rock* (#7, 1982) and the hit single "Rock the Casbah" of the same year (#8). Their breakthrough album, *London Calling* (1980) remains, however, their most enduring contribution.

The spirit of punk—part of the musical legacy of the 1960s—found further expression in the 1980s and 1990s in college alternative and grunge rock. R.E.M., formed in 1980 in Athens, Georgia, was to become the leading and longest-lasting group from the college alternative scene. Nirvana, formed in 1987 in the state of Washington, would eventually (though for a tragically short time) dominate the burgeoning world of grunge. Finally, Eddie Vedder and Pearl Jam, while usually grouped in the alternative category, would in some ways carry on better than any other recent group the spirit of the sixties and classic rock.

"Alternative" is a loose category of rock music—influenced both by punk and heavy metal—which developed in the eighties in reaction against the clichés of mainstream groups like Bon Jovi and Mötley Crüe. Originating in smoky basement clubs and even pizza parlors in cities like Seattle, Los Angeles, Minneapolis/Saint Paul, and New York, alternative music became popular because of significant airplay on college FM stations and recordings by minor labels like Twin Tone in the Midwest and Sub Pop in Seattle. "Seattle sound," in fact, became another term for the music. Both independent record labels (called "indies") and college radio stations (important in the sixties for the spread of protest rock) played a crucial role in popularizing alternative music in the eighties and early nineties.

What links alternative to music of the sixties, besides the occasional hook or musical quote, is the social and political slant to its lyrics. While much of alternative is pessimistic and even drearily solipsistic, at times it also speaks out on issues like abortion rights, the AIDS crisis, and the environment. This tendency to take positions, sometimes unpopular ones, occasionally goes beyond the music into more public arenas, as when Pearl Jam in the midnineties decided to challenge the predominance of the Ticketmaster company in purveying increasingly expensive concert tickets. Though much of alternative has been co-opted by the musical establishment and been commercialized, a core element of rebellion—

featuring hard core, frequently obscene lyrics and a hard-edged sound—remains to set it apart from mainstream rock.

Born in the relative obscurity of college alternative, R.E.M. (referring to the "rapid eye movement" of the eyeballs in stages of sleep associated with dreaming) went on to become one of the most popular musical groups by the late eighties and early nineties. Initially, the ambiguousness and introversion of lead singer Michael Stipe's lyrics was offset by the punk and southern rock–influenced sound of the band. By 1987, reflecting the coming change of taste in rock music, R.E.M. produced *Document*, its first album to reach the Top Ten, featuring its first hit single, "The One I Love" (#9, 1987). With broadened lyrics and an eclectic sound, they would reach the #1 spot with *Out of Time* (1991), with its hit singles "Losing My Religion" (#4) and "Shiny Happy People" (#10). In the same year, the first Lollapalooza tour, replete with alternative bands, underscored the significance of the shift taking place in rock music. The harder-edged, extrovert *Monster* (1994)—following on the introspective *Automatic for the People* (#2, 1992)—would also reach first place on the album chart and prove to any who might doubt that R.E.M. could crank the volume up and still hold true to their basic musical principles.

The Seattle-based group Nirvana came to the fore in 1992 with the smashing success of their album *Nevermind*, featuring the hit single—to become a major anthem of the alternative rock movement—"Smells Like Teen Spirit" (#1). Their punk rock lyrics and snarling sound (strongly influenced by the college rock group the Pixies) carried over into their second album of new material, *In Utero* (1993). Instantly rocketing to #1 status, the album confirmed the new direction rock music had taken. The future career of the trio was cut short, however, by the suicide of lead singer Kurt Cobain, one more victim of the drug abuse that has always characterized the world of rock music. (Though he did not die of an overdose, Cobain's suicide resulted just as surely from his heroin addiction. He was subject to intense feelings of depression and self-doubt that were only made worse by drugs.) The success of Nirvana in its two years as a working entity signaled the end of heavy metal "spandex" rock of the eighties and the introduction on a wide scale of a new sensibility in the rock music world.

Pearl Jam, formed in 1990 in Seattle, jumped to instant popularity on the basis of their very first album, *Ten* (1991), which rapidly reached the second spot on the album chart. With a sound closer in many respects to Led Zeppelin than to punk rock, Pearl Jam went to first place with their next album, *Vs.* (1993). Their success is largely attributable to the charismatic quality of their intense, good-looking lead singer, Eddie Vedder. His strong sympathies with music of the sixties and seventies set him apart from many other rock stars of his generation. He and Pearl Jam guitarist Mike Mc-Cready were the only musicians associated with alternative rock to perform at the Bob Dylan thirtieth anniversary celebration in 1992 (Vedder's song choice was Dylan's "Masters of War"). He has also been involved in similar tributes to Pete Townshend and Jim Morrison. Moreover, Vedder's great admiration for Neil Young has led to Pearl Jam's recent collaboration on the album *Mirror Ball*, which tries to recreate the sound of long-playing vinyl discs of the sixties. In a tribute to the same period in recording history, Pearl Jam's smash hit third album, *Vitalogy* (1994), was released first on vinyl and then, two weeks later, as a CD.

RAP: FROM THE STREET TO THE STUDIO

At almost the same time that punk rock developed among white rock musicians in the mid-seventies, eventually evolving into the more popular alternative rock, rap music, later called hip-hop, emerged as the new musical style among African Americans. This dance-based music was inspired first by traditional R & B and by such artists as James Brown and Sly and the Family Stone. Close to disco, influenced by reggae, rap began as street music in the urban ghettos. It combined chanted vocals in rhyme (usually couplets), recorded R & B, hand-clapping, and increasingly complicated, aerobic-like dance routines, originally called break dancing. The deejay, or spinner, played a key role, stopping, starting, and reversing recordings as each piece progressed. Rap was soon transferred to the studio in the work of such early groups as the Sugarhill Gang, Fatback, and Kurtis Blow on small, independent labels like Enjoy, Sugarhill, and Clappers. In the studio, the background music ultimately would belong as much to studio technicians using synthesizers, sound effects, and musical quotes, as to the spinner, though spinner effects would remain in the work of most groups. Early rap, like all disco, was basically party music, but overt political themes soon began to appear. Brother D in "How We Gonna Make the

Black Nation Rise?" and Grandmaster Flash and the Furious Five (the most popular rap group of the early seventies) in "The Message" introduced themes which would become central to one of the most important groups of the eighties, Public Enemy, in their album *It Takes a Nation of Millions to Hold Us Back* (1988).

Public Enemy, formed in 1982, introduced a denser sound into rap, along with a delivery style of declamation and answer. In a virtual collage of music and street noises, the heavily intoned statements of lead singer Chuck D (Carlton Ridenour) were answered ironically or mockingly by group member Flavor Flav (William Drayton). As in virtually all hip-hop, group members used pseudonyms. (On one hand merely playful, on the other this practice also reflects a trademark of the street gangs, whose members adopt special names after initiation. Such gangs were a major part of rap's original audience, and many rap musicians have been gang members themselves.) The original members of Public Enemy—the other two were DJ Terminator X (Norman Lee Rogers) and Minister of Information Professor Griff (Richard Griffin)—came together at Adelphi College on Long Island and soon caught the attention of Rick Rubin of Def Jam, an important label for hip-hop music. In *Nation of Millions* PE would praise Louis Farrakhan, controversial leader of the Black Muslim movement, in "Bring the Noise," while other songs—"Countdown to Armageddon," "Rebel Without a Pause," "Prophets of Rage"—suggested that the anger of the ghetto riots of the sixties (when PE group members were growing up) was barely contained in the eighties. The fact that this album should have come out when it did, toward the end of the Reagan years in the White House, is a significant point. Reagan was not only unpopular with most African Americans, but his administration reversed or slowed down most programs devised in the sixties and seventies that attempted to remedy the problems of urban poverty and racism. The president of the majority, as Reagan fancied himself, made little effort to speak on the behalf of any minority, least of all African Americans.

The controversial edge to *Nation of Millions* was not dulled by comments made the year following its release by Professor Griff. In an interview in the *Washington Post*, he blamed Jews for "the majority of wickedness" in the world, echoing similar remarks of Louis Farrakhan's. Though Griffin was ultimately dropped by the group, the incident led Chuck D to write "Welcome to the Terrordome" (1990), in which he compared his situation in the controversy to

Jesus being persecuted by the Jews. The analogy led to charges of anti-Semitism against him.

The confrontational edge to PE's lyrics and musical style was a major influence in the development of an even more controversial form of rap music, known as "gangsta rap." With roots in ghetto gang life and lyrics replete with street language, gangsta rap rose to predominance in the rap music world by the mid-1990s. The first important gangsta group, however, was formed in Los Angeles in 1986. N.W.A. ("Niggaz with Attitude") borrowed techniques from PE and other earlier rap groups and applied them to songs that reflected gang life. Their second album, *Straight Outta Compton* (1989), went platinum, but raised the sort of controversy associated with this form of rap with songs like "Gangsta Gangsta" and, especially, "Fuck tha Police." The latter provoked criticism from the F.B.I. and was banned from radio. Individual members of the group frequently faced assault charges, but three went on to solo careers— Ice Cube, Dr. Dre, and the late Eazy-E (who died of AIDS in 1995).

Performers such as Ice-T, Snoop Doggy Dogg, and the late Tupac Shakur soon joined the growing list of gangsta rappers. Too frequently, however, they seemed to be justifying, rather than attempting to remedy, the most negative aspects of contemporary urban black culture. Women's rights, gay rights, and parent groups united in opposition to gangsta rap's misogynistic, homophobic, and violent lyrics. Ice-T's "Cop Killer" (1992) brought negative comment from President George Bush and protests from police groups. The violence of gangsta lyrics carries over into the lifestyle of its artists and was demonstrated forcibly in the deaths of rappers Tupac Shakur (gunned down in a gang-style drive-by shooting in 1996) and Notorious B.I.G. These incidents, combined with the continuing criticism of gangsta rap lyrics, have led to a slight decline in its popularity and, more significantly, to censorship in various forms of gangsta rap lyrics. In many respects, gangsta rap, like the work of Public Enemy, continues a criticism of American society begun by the Black Panthers and other separatist groups of the late 1960s. However, the politics of this form of rap frequently get lost in its imagery of sex and violence.

Historically, African-American music has always been taken up by white musicians. This happened early in the century in the case of jazz, and, in the 1950s, on a large scale with R & B. The same phenomenon has occurred since the 1980s with rap music. At first almost exclusively the domain of black musicians and performers, within a decade of its appearance rap had become an interracial musical form. This shift occurred chiefly because of rap's commercial success among young white males.

In 1986, Aerosmith, a white hard rock group formed in the heavy metal heyday of the seventies, collaborated with black rappers Run-D.M.C. on "Walk This Way." More than any other rap group of the time, Run-D.M.C. (formed in 1981) was responsible for popularizing rap music with a rock-oriented white audience. In addition, they were the group that set the rap "look," including hats, gold chains, baggy pants, and laced-down sneakers. Thus their collaboration, more or less fortuitous, with one of the premier white rock groups of the eighties became a cultural event. It blessed the passage of rap from African America to white.

The year 1986 also saw the debut album of the Beastie Boys (also formed in 1981), an all-white rap group with punk rock roots. *Licensed to Ill* (#1 on the album chart) featured their popular single, "(You Gotta) Fight for Your Right to Party" (#7 [1987]) later parodied by Public Enemy in "Party for Your Right to Fight" (*Nation of Millions* [1988]). Soon lesser musical talents would follow in the Beastie Boys' footsteps, and sanitized rap would become a pervasive sound on the airwaves.

More recently, music in rap style has been a basic feature of white musical artists as diverse as Rage Against the Machine and Beck. The mostly white Rage (lead singer Zack De la Rocha is part-Chicano) combines rap-style lyrics with a heavy political message and hardcore rock guitar. Their music echoes protest themes of the 1960s, as in "Take the Power Back" and "Freedom" from their self-titled album of 1992 or in "Vietnow" from *Evil Empire* (1996). (The cover of the first of these albums features a reproduction of the famous sixties photo of a Buddhist monk immolating himself to protest the corrupt Diem government of South Vietnam, overthrown in 1963.) Beck, an eclectic electronic composer whose variegated music is largely a product of the studio, uses rap-style lyrics in funky songs that occasionally comment, as in "The New Pollution" (*Odelay* [1996]), on environmental or other social issues.

WOMEN IN RAP AND ROCK

Another, perhaps ultimately more significant, crossover in the history of rap is the appearance by the late 1980s of women's rap groups. This development parallels the emergence of major female talents in rock music as a whole, and has led, by the 1990s, to a new status for women in the field of popular music. In rap, the major breakthrough came with Dana Owens, known as Queen Latifah (Arabic for "delicate" or "sensitive"). In her debut album of 1989, the Queen celebrated girl love in "Ladies First," a notable departure from the standard take on women in rap. The impact of its subject matter compares to that of Aretha Franklin's "Respect" in the R & B world of the sixties. Queen Latifah's second album, *Nature of a Sista'* (1991), would develop a different, more soul-related program. Her third, *Black Reign* (1994, #15 R & B), from Motown Records, would become the greatest commercial success of the group. Queen Latifah remains an eloquent and popular spokesperson for black women. Her acting career in movies and television, including a starring role in the popular sitcom "Living Single," has added significantly to her reputation.

The major turning point for women in rock music came by the end of the seventies. Debbie Harry of Blondie and Stevie Nicks of Fleetwood Mac led the way with #1 hits in the singles and album categories. Fleetwood Mac, with Nicks as lead vocalist after 1974, was especially successful with their broad, blues-based musical style. Their album *Rumours* (1977) sold over 17 million copies, won a Grammy, and scored four Top Ten hits on the singles chart in the year of its release. It became one of the best-selling albums of all time.

Chrissie Hynde and the Pretenders claimed the hard rock turf for women with their self-titled debut album of 1980. Hynde, born in Akron, Ohio, emigrated to England in the mid-seventies and ultimately joined with three male Brits to form the group. Their first release went to first place in the United Kingdom and Australia and to #14 on the album chart in the United States. As lead vocalist, chief composer, and rhythm guitarist for the group, Hynde operated successfully within the predominantly male hard rock arena.

Joan Jett preceded Chrissie Hynde by four years with the debut album of her group the Runaways, a punk and heavy metal all-girl band formed in Los Angeles in 1975. While musically the group had its weaknesses, it was one of the very first hard rock groups made up entirely of women. The experience she gained there certainly benefited Jett in her solo career in the 1980s. Jett went quickly to the top of the singles chart with "I Love Rock 'n' Roll" from her second solo album (1981), for which the song provided the title. This was an unprecedented degree of success for a female hard rocker. Although Jett, like Chrissie Hynde, would not sustain her popularity, her achievement was a high-water mark for women. Both artists inspired important all-female groups of the seventies and eighties like the Go-Go's and the Bangles.

The most written-about, and by far most successful woman in popular music of the eighties, however, was not a hard rocker, but a singer who never composed her own music and who assumed so

Madonna (1987)

many different personas that (like Bette Midler before her) it was virtually impossible to say who the real person was. That singer—less rock star than pop star—was Madonna.

Entering the music world by way of dance music in the early eighties, Madonna soon capitalized on the developing medium of Music TeleVision (MTV) and her own strong sense of what would attract the greatest amount of attention, to become one of the best-selling female singers of all time. Throughout the 1980s and early nineties, in recordings, concert tours, television and movie appearances, and books, Madonna was a consistently controversial and popular figure. Praised by some for her courage in dealing with taboo subject matter and her support for women and gays, she was also condemned for using sexuality and feminine stereotypes to promote her image and sell her records. "Papa Don't Preach" (#1, 1986) defended the right of young unmarried women to keep their children, and "Vogue" (#1, 1990) revived a gay dance craze as Madonna was urging support for AIDS research. At the same time, Madonna's videos and concert performances often exploited sensational imagery for little more than its shock value. In purely musical terms, Madonna has never made a contribution comparable to that of a Janis Joplin, Laura Nyro, or Stevie Nicks. What she has done, however, is to show the music world that women can be as canny as men in the pursuit of celebrity and financial success and can do it without compromising unduly what they choose to sing or say. Her achievement in this regard—like Barbra Streisand's in the sphere of romantic ballads and show music—has been an example for all women after her, significantly raising the stakes for them in the music world of the 1990s. And, in that world, women as solo performers or as members of musical groups are more important than they have ever been. In fact, women have become the most popular performers and recording artists of the latter half of the 1990s, as grunge and other predominantly male musical trends have faded from popularity. The most popular musical tour of 1997 was the all-female, folk-oriented Lilith Tour, and female artists head the charts in virtually all categories.

"Confessional"-style music of the kind originated in the sixties by Laura Nyro and Joni Mitchell has had a huge revival in the nineties among such disparate talents as the Indigo Girls, Alanis Morissette, Tori Amos, Fiona Apple, Sarah McLachlan, Jewel, k. d. lang, and Melissa Etheridge. At the cutting edge of this trend, in 1992 k. d. lang announced publicly that she was a lesbian. The effect was to boost her popularity to new heights. Melissa Etheridge's public outing in 1993 was followed by the triple platinum *Yes I Am* (#16), including her hit single "I'm the Only One" (#11, 1994). Such openness about sexuality and other life experiences typifies all the singers in the confessional mode. Meanwhile, female pop and R & B singers like Mariah Carey, Janet Jackson (sister of Michael), and Whitney Houston have achieved unprecedented levels of popularity, challenging records held by some of the biggest names in the history of American popular music. In rock music, Hole, featuring lead singer Courtney Love, widow of Nirvana's Kurt Cobain, became one of the most respected groups of the nineties. A mixed gender group, Hole's music fell into the alternative category and, with the album *Live Through This* (1994), won critical as well as audience acclaim.

Rock music in general has been one of the most significant and enduring of the legacies of the 1960s. During that decade it consolidated its hold on the vast majority of American young people. Since then, it has continued to be a significant factor in the lives of succeeding generations. Pervasive to every entertainment medium in this country—radio, TV, movies, even musical theater—it has also spread throughout the world to become one of our most important contributions to contemporary culture.

SIXTIES MOVIES: FROM HISTORY TO FANTASY

Equally important to the interpretation of the sixties in the popular imagination have been movies about major personalities and events of the decade. With themes ranging from nostalgic regret to angry idealism to pure fantasy, these films attempt, with varying degrees of success, to recapture vital aspects of the history of the 1960s and 1970s.

One such film—and the only one of this group to date from before the 1980s—is George Lucas's *American Graffiti* (1973). Hot on the heels of the major fifties revival of the early seventies, *American Graffiti*, set in 1962, is a paean to the car culture of southern California and the music that teenagers of that period liked to listen to. The theme of the film, like that of so many imaginative treatments of the sixties, is lost innocence. The world that Curt (Richard Dreyfuss), Steve (Ron Howard), John (Paul Le Mat), Terry, a.k.a.

Toad (Charles Martin Smith), and Bob (Harrison Ford) inhabit has none of the tensions that would surface later in the decade. Their focus—and the film is very much *guy*-focussed—is cars and girls, girls and cars, and their music comes from the fifties. Songs like "Rock Around the Clock" and "Teen Angel" and "Chantilly Lace" and "Runaway" dominate the sound track, and Terry at one point laments the death of Buddy Holly and the advent of surfer rock (which, ironically, is also mostly about girls and cars). With a tight time frame of one night's events and a modest plot, turning chiefly on whether Curt and Steve will really decide to take off for an eastern college the next morning—the film, like the characters it depicts, is all surface, with only occasional hints of greater depth. As a document of the early sixties, it has considerable accuracy, from the drive-in restaurants the kids frequent, to the cars they drive up and down the Modesto, California strip, to the cameo appearance of one of the leading West Coast deejays, "Wolfman" Jack. Only at the very end of the film, as the credits appear on the screen, do we learn that Curt will eventually end up in the protest movement, that Steve will go into the real estate business, and that Terry will die in Vietnam. Shot on a budget of about $700,000 in only 28 nights, *American Graffiti* is one of the most honest portrayals of early sixties adolescent culture in American film. George Lucas—a product, like his friend and mentor Francis Ford Coppola, of the UCLA Film School—would go on to do the celebrated Star Wars Trilogy, three of the most popular films of all time, but to date he has never returned to the subject matter of his first feature film.

Nostalgia for the sixties is expressed in a different way in another fictional film of ten years later, Lawrence Kasdan's *The Big Chill* (1983). Here we have a group of baby boomers now in their thirties, looking back with mixed feelings on their 1960s experiences. All of them have found a big difference between the dreams of their growing-up period and the reality of the post-sixties world. Friends since college, they have gathered for the funeral of one of their group who, in a state of despair, has committed suicide. Their attitudes range from the cynicism of the former radical, Sam (Tom Berenger), who is now the star of a TV sitcom, to the resignation of Karen (JoBeth Williams), who has given up a writing career for housework, to the complacency of Harold (Kevin Kline), never an activist, now a family-oriented businessman. Virtually all of the characters have experienced an overwhelming sense of loss—not only of their dead friend, but also of their hopes and dreams. What is to come for them is much less clear than what they feel they have left behind.

The Big Chill represented a life review not only for its characters, but also for its director. Lawrence Kasdan had lived through the sixties and was engaged for years afterward in an ongoing assessment of what had happened to him and his generation. As director, cowriter, and executive producer of *The Big Chill*, he was working out more than simply a good script. He assembled an outstanding cast of actors at the beginnings of their careers. Besides Berenger, Kline, and Williams, the cast includes Glenn Close, Jeff Goldblum, William Hurt, and Meg Tilly. *The Big Chill* is a thoughtful, sometimes poignant, sometimes funny exploration of the generational theme so important to the sixties. The sound track—including the Rolling Stones' "You Can't Always Get What You Want," Percy Sledge's "When a Man Loves a Woman," Creedence Clearwater Revival's "Bad Moon Rising," and Smokey Robinson and the Miracles's "Tracks of My Tears"—reflects the experiences and moods of the characters as their story progresses.

Generational conflict of another sort informs Sidney Lumet's *Running on Empty* (1988). This film tells the story of a pair of sixties radicals, Annie and Arthur Pope (Christine Lahti and Judd Hirsch), who are trying desperately to evade their past by constant changes of identity and residence. Fifteen years before, they blew up a laboratory where napalm was made, seriously injuring a man inside. Since that time, they have been on the FBI's Most Wanted list and have been living an underground existence. In the opening sequence of the film, the Popes leave behind even the family dog in their urgency to escape detection. This pattern of deconstructing their lives might presumably continue indefinitely, but their older son Danny (the late River Phoenix), now 17, has grown tired of the constant changes their life requires. Talented at music, he is encouraged by a high school teacher to pursue a scholarship to study piano. He falls in love with Lorna (Martha Plimpton), the teacher's daughter, whose family has the kind of ordinary life that Danny longs for. A crisis occurs for his parents when he needs grade records for his application to music school. They also become involved in a bank robbery with an old cohort from the underground.

Interesting though the situation is, with many real-life parallels that suggest themselves (most recently, the case of Katherine Ann Power, who lived under assumed identities for more than two decades), the most compelling aspect of the story is the frustration that Danny feels in being unable to live a normal life. The outcome of the film suggests that it is never possible to live forever in the past and, furthermore, that we are always accountable for whatever we do. Danny's parents (and his younger brother) continue to flee from the past, though it is clear, by the end, that they are now "running on empty." Danny, however, does not leave with them. Instead, he stays on with Lorna and her family, presumably to build a new life for himself. The soundtrack includes music by James Taylor ("Fire and Rain") and Roy Orbison ("Pretty Woman").

In addition to fictional films about the sixties experience, a number of films from the eighties and nineties deal with historical characters and incidents of the period. These are "based-on-a-true-story" movies—that is, somewhat fictionalized accounts. However, even with inaccuracies or distortions of fact, such films have value in recreating the background of history: the milieu and circumstances in which events occurred and the personalities of figures who too frequently are faceless. Often, these films raise the same questions that occur in written history, but present them in visual or dramatic terms.

Journalist Tom Wolfe's novelistic account of the Mercury 7 Astronauts and the beginnings of the United States's space program provided the title and basic content of Philip Kaufman's *The Right Stuff* (1983). Covering the period from 1947, when Chuck Yeager (Sam Shepherd) breaks the sound barrier for the first time, to 1962, when Astronaut John Glenn (Ed Harris) circles the earth in a space capsule, the film recreates an important phase of the history of the U.S. space program with considerable accuracy of detail. Its theme—that Yeager and Glenn showed heroism not only in what they did but in their doing it alone—suggests that individualism is dead and that heroes in the modern world are more often manufactured than real. Even so, the Mercury Astronauts emerge with believable personalities through the strong script and performances of the cast, including Scott Glenn as Alan Shepard, Dennis Quaid as Gordon Cooper, Fred Ward as Gus Grissom, Charles Frank as Scott Carpenter, Levon Helm as Jack Ridley, and Scott Wilson as Scott Crossfield. This is a story of lives, not just heroics, so the wives of the Astronauts (and Yeager) and numerous minor characters have distinctive personalities. Few films on such subjects have managed to take us so convincingly behind the events they depict and still maintain a documentary feeling on the surface.

Two films by Oliver Stone released in 1991—between the second and third films in his Vietnam trilogy—give us a take on two very different aspects of the history of the 1960s. *JFK* recounts the efforts of New Orleans District Attorney Jim Garrison to prove the existence of a conspiracy in the assassination of John Kennedy. *The Doors* is a biographical account of the development and ultimate demise of the Los Angeles rock group and its charismatic lead singer, Jim Morrison.

The Doors—the first of the two to be released—follows the career of Jim Morrison from the time The Doors formed as a group in 1965 until his death from heart failure in Paris in 1971. With Morrison look-alike Val Kilmer in the role of the singer (Kilmer also does most of the singing), the film recreates memorable incidents from the history of The Doors. Especially in its performance sequences, it dramatizes effectively the spirit of the counterculture and the rebelliousness of the youth culture of the sixties.

JFK, through its focus on the investigation of Jim Garrison (Kevin Costner) into the Kennedy assassination, raises questions that have existed since Kennedy's death in Dallas, Texas, in November of 1963. Mixing documentary footage, recreated scenes, and fictional narrative, *JFK* was widely criticized at the time of its release for pushing its thesis too far. Scenes that imply the involvement of Lyndon Johnson in the conspiracy (though rumored at the time) were especially singled out in this discussion.

On the other hand, as Robert A. Rosenstone has pointed out, Stone's film does no more—indeed, much less—than most American films of its genre have done. It creates a story, reaches a conclusion, gives us a hero, and makes historical issues "personalized, emotionalized, and dramatized." In these terms, the film deserves praise not only for the faithfulness of its recreation of the atmosphere of the time, but also for raising the same questions about the assassination that have been seriously considered by historians and governmental commissions. As Rosenstone puts it, "a historical film . . . is not a window onto the past but a construction of a past; like a history book, a film handles evidence from that past within a certain framework of possibilities and a tradition of practice. For neither the writer of history nor the director of a film is historical literalism a possibility."

Perhaps because of the widespread criticism he received for *JFK*, Stone's next foray into the historical film (after completing his Vietnam trilogy with *Heaven and Earth*) was a more literal

recreation of historical events. *Nixon* (1995) covers the career of
the Republican president from his beginnings in California to his
resignation in 1974. Carefully researched, with a convincing performance by British actor Anthony Hopkins as Nixon, the film has a
psychological accuracy that makes the viewer feel that Nixon had
to be this way and no other. The script is based on the record provided by major players in the Watergate story and by such documentary historical evidence as the much-disputed Watergate tapes:
conversations among Nixon and his advisers recorded in the White
House at the height of the crisis the affair created. *Nixon* also
seems more historically accurate because of the literalness of its
cinematic style. Compared with *JFK*, the story of Nixon is told with
a greater aura of realism, though nearly as many liberties are taken
with historical fact. Taken together, these films—along with Stone's
distinguished Vietnam trilogy—make him the American director
who has done most with this historical period. The sixties were the
time when he matured and experienced what he would later write
about and film. The decade has found an eloquent spokesperson in
Oliver Stone.

The civil rights and Black Power movements have also received
serious treatment in three recent historical films: *Mississippi Burning* (1988), *Ghosts of Mississippi* (1996), and *Malcolm X* (1992).
Set in the most determinedly segregationist state of the South in the
summer of 1964, shortly after the murder of three civil rights workers from CORE, *Mississippi Burning* chronicles the investigation by
two FBI agents into the tragedy. One agent, played by Gene Hack-
man, is a southerner; the other, played by Willem Dafoe, comes
from the North. Together, they track down the suspects and bring
them to trial on a federal charge of interference with the victims'
civil rights.

While the FBI under J. Edgar Hoover was notoriously unsympathetic to the civil rights cause (and in 1964 had not one black
agent), the law enforcement agency was actively involved in this
case. If to some extent the film exaggerates the degree of that involvement, it recreates with great accuracy and feeling the Deep
South of that era, with all its bigotry and hatred. This, combined
with excellent performances (including Frances McDormand as the
wife of one of the murderers), makes *Mississippi Burning* a worthwhile dramatization of the period. However, in focusing on the
white agents and the racists they pursue, the film leaves African
Americans almost invisible.

Stronger in this regard is the detailed account of the gradual involvement of a white district attorney in a case that would never serve his political or personal interests. Rob Reiner's *Ghosts of Mississippi* recounts the story of the bringing to justice of the murderer of NAACP representative Medgar Evers, shot in the driveway of his home in June 1963 by a Mississippi racist named Byron De La Beckwith. Evers's widow Myrlie pursued the punishment of her husband's murderer over a period of some three decades. Acquitted twice by all-white juries, De La Beckwith (James Woods) is eventually brought to justice by Bobby DeLaughter (Alec Baldwin). Unfortunately, however, the film falls into clichés, including that of the white savior to whom Evers's widow (Whoopi Goldberg) is eternally indebted, and courtroom scenes that are too much like those in *To Kill a Mockingbird.*

Spike Lee's biographical *Malcolm X*, based on Malcolm's posthumous autobiography (written with Alex Haley), is a much more successful portrayal of a much more difficult subject. The story begins in the 1940s in Boston, where Malcolm (Denzel Washington), following the murder of his father by a group of white racists, goes to live with his aunt. There, and later in Harlem, Malcolm (then known as Malcolm Little) carves out a niche as a petty thief and street hustler. Eventually, he ends up in prison, where he comes under the influence of the Black Muslim movement and its founder Elijah Muhammad. (In the film his introduction comes by way of a fellow prisoner. In real life, Malcolm's brother led the way.)

As an ex-con, Malcolm makes his way to Chicago. Within a few years, he becomes Elijah Muhammad's most eloquent spokesman and second lieutenant. Malcolm is eventually disillusioned with the leader of the Black Muslims when he learns that Elijah, contrary to Muslim teachings, supports several women who have borne his children. Malcolm's assassination—here attributed to a collusion between the Muslims and the FBI—forms the climax of the film.

Lee, the only African-American director working regularly in American films, does not lighten Malcolm's message very much, though he does soften his rhetoric. He also dilutes his separatist position, a fundamental feature of Black Muslim ideology and of Malcolm's personal vision. While it is true that Malcolm modified his separatism somewhat not long before his death, he still regarded the future of African Americans—or Afro-Americans, in his term—as separate from white America. Like most epic-style biographical films of historical figures, *Malcolm X* is overly reverential. It also requires some prior knowledge of the autobiography. Nonetheless, Lee's film is both honest and credible in its portrayal of one of the most important figures in the civil rights movement of the sixties. Unfortunately, Malcolm's unpopularity with white Americans during his lifetime seemed to carry over in the attendance figures for Lee's film, which did not do very well at the box office.

More popular than any of these films—and perhaps more influential in shaping contemporary opinion on the 1960s—is *Forrest Gump* (1994), directed by Robert Zemeckis and based on the novel by Winston Groom. This film is a historical fantasy about the experiences of the title character (played by Tom Hanks) as he makes his way through life, encountering many of the major figures of the fifties and sixties on his way. Incredibly enough, these include such important icons of the period as Elvis Presley, John Kennedy, and John Lennon. Special effects are responsible for the scenes in which Forrest (a white southerner named for a Confederate general) appears with these celebrities. Zemeckis had previously directed the *Back to the Future* films and *Who Framed Roger Rabbit?*, all of which were heavy with such effects.

Between the specially created scenes, however, comes a story that is by turns maudlin and inexplicable, recounting Forrest's life-long devotion to his girlfriend Jenny (Robin Wright) and his Vietnam C.O. Lieutenant Dan Taylor (Gary Sinise), who has become a paraplegic. However, the film is so reductive of the historical events of the sixties, and so inconsistent in its interpretation of

Forrest Gump (Tom Hanks) afloat in the tide of history (1994)

these events, that the brief, technically brilliant recreations of the times in which Forrest appears side by side with historical notables cannot redeem the mediocrity of its vision.

In the end, the message of the film seems to be that we must be passive to historical events, going along with whatever happens. "Life," Forrest asserts in an often-quoted speech, "is like a box of chocolates. You never know what you're gonna get." The film is also notably unsympathetic to the antiwar movement (portraying the only SDS character as a sexist pig) and the counterculture. Were it more serious in its history, it would be the best representative to date of the revisionism that has produced a more conservative version of sixties history than that which came from the seventies and eighties. The attitude it supports unfortunately coincides with the general passivity toward politics and history characteristic of generation-Xers. If popularity is any measure, this attitude has become general. *Forrest Gump* grossed $301 million in the year of its release (second only to Disney's *The Lion King*) and netted both Hanks and Sinise Academy Awards for their performances. In winning the best actor award, Hanks repeated the same achievement two years in a row, having won another Oscar in 1994 for his role in a film with a different political vision, *Philadelphia* (1993), in which he portrayed an AIDS-afflicted gay attorney who sues his firm for firing him.

SIXTIES LEGACIES IN TV AND THE MEDIA: PROGRESS AND PROBLEMS

The sixties experience—the subject of so many interpretations in American film—has also occupied the broadcasting industry. All major networks have at various times commemorated major events of the era with biographical specials and documentaries. Of the latter, perhaps the most outstanding have been the 13-part *Vietnam: A Television History* (1983) and the 6-part *Making Sense of the Sixties* (1991) from PBS, both based on extensive research and interviews with participants.

Of developments in broadcasting that owe something to the sixties, talk shows, television "magazines," and interactive television and radio broadcasts would all rank high. Television talk shows, in which a host interviews authorities or celebrity guests, first became important in the sixties and have remained one of the most popular forms of broadcasting since then. TV magazines—

news-oriented programming which provides coverage similar to that of a print magazine—ultimately derive from daytime programs like the NBC "Today" show, with their emphasis on "soft" news. Since the seventies, programs like "20/20," "Dateline," and "Hard Copy" have become increasingly popular forms of nighttime television. Interactive radio and TV broadcasting, in which listeners phone in comments that are aired as they speak, was a feature of alternative broadcasting of the sixties and has now become another popular form of broadcasting nationwide.

Music videos—a nascent form of television in the sixties (in the form of clips to promote songs)—became more popular in the seventies. Since 1981 and the debut of MTV, they have become a major force both nationally and internationally in forging taste and sales among the crucial age group from 12 to 24. With rock, hip-hop, and other forms of popular music more than ever dependent upon commercial success for their survival, MTV has positioned itself to determine what will be listened to by a large and important segment of the music-buying public. Furthermore, the success of MTV has made popular music a visual as well as an aural experience, with music videos now being charted and given awards on an annual basis just like recordings and films.

Cable TV has developed in the past several decades into a serious competitor of the original Big Three networks. With programming that now includes virtually anything for which there is an audience, from home and garden shows to ultimate fighting and pornography, cable TV has taken an increasingly larger share of the viewing audience. The same thing is true of the Fox network, an independent that has seriously challenged the ratings of the three major networks with popular shows like "Melrose Place" and "Beverly Hills 90210."

Unfortunately, the commercial connections that now exist among all forms of entertainment have created special problems as the new millennium approaches. The 1950s saw the triumph of the record and broadcasting companies over music publishers as rock 'n' roll first became popular with a white middle-class audience. The 1960s and 1970s saw the expansion of musical venues and an increasing number of tie-ins between recordings, concert tours, and publications. Since the 1980s, previously independent forms of entertainment—TV networks, radio stations, news magazines, cable TV, even theme parks—have become part of vast media conglomerates like Time-Warner and Disney. This trend has significantly reduced diversity in the channels disseminating various forms of popular culture. At the same time, the commercial tie-ins in TV programs and movies have dramatically increased, erasing the distinction between advertising and entertainment.

In informational broadcasting, the reporting of "hard news" has declined in favor of human interest and celebrity stories. Readership of newspapers and news magazines has also seriously declined, especially among generation-Xers. This in turn has led to cuts in reporting and editorial staffs and a greater emphasis on more sensational news. In general, it is more difficult to find serious reporting of the news in any of the popular media now than it was in the 1960s and 1970s.

SIXTIES LEGACIES AND THE NEW MILLENNIUM

In every sphere of American popular culture, including many not dealt with here, the sixties live on as the current century reaches its close. But history as recent as that which is charted in this book is far from closed. Newly revealed documents and historical data change our interpretation of major events and personalities. Issues of public policy and personal choice that the sixties generation hoped to resolve have resisted closure or have been reopened in the hope of new resolutions. What the future holds for our popular music, movies, and media is difficult to predict—though we know that they will continue to be tied to commercial forces that both shape and reflect popular taste.

BIBLIOGRAPHY

Because of the diversity of the materials used in the writing of this book, I have divided the following between those sources that have been generally helpful and those that have bearing on particular chapters. Needless to say, the sheer plenitude of scholarly and popular books and articles about the sixties has forced me to exert a high degree of selectivity. Keeping in mind the needs of students who might want to pursue topics further, I have tried to strike a balance between sources that are essential to a general understanding of the subject and those that are especially germane to interpretations offered in this text. While recordings, films, and videotapes have been important resources and, indeed, form the subject of much of this book, I have not made special lists of these. My assumption is that the references listed below will guide students into this material better than any list—of necessity short—that I might make. I have also generally not listed any work that I have referred to at length in my text.

For a **general overview of the history of the decade**, synthesizing political and social history, James T. Patterson's *Grand Expectations: The United States, 1945-1974* (1996) is essential. With a wealth of detail and careful documentation, it covers the period from the end of World War II to the resignation of Nixon and the early seventies recession. Another excellent, though shorter, book is David Farber's *The Age of Great Dreams: America in the 1960s* (1994). Other good general treatments of the sixties and the postwar period (or important aspects thereof) include: Godfrey Hodgson, *America in Our Time: From World War II to Nixon— What Happened and Why* (1978); Charles R. Morris, *A Time of Passion: America 1960-1980* (1984); William H. Chafe, *The Unfinished Journey: America Since World War II* (1986); James Gilbert: *Another Chance: Postwar America 1945-1985* (1986); and Michael Barone, *America from Roosevelt to Reagan* (1990). From the large body of personal recollections and memoirs of the period,

Todd Gitlin's *The Sixties: Years of Hope, Days of Rage* (rev. ed., 1993) is one of the best and most interesting. Another is Richard Goodwin's *Remembering America: A Voice from the Sixties* (1989). The PBS series *Making Sense of the Sixties* (first shown in 1991 and available on videocassette) provides a valuable introduction to the sights and sounds of the decade, with interviews of people, famous and not famous, who were participants. Many important documents are gathered in Albert and Albert, *The Sixties Papers: Documents of a Rebellious Decade* (1984). Popular magazines like *Life*, *Time*, and *Newsweek* are important sources of contemporaneous information on personalities, events, and popular culture. *Life* in particular has proved a valuable resource for this book.

On **popular culture**, a useful introduction to basic theory (including discussion of the origins issue and distinctions among forms) occurs in Jack Nachbar and Kevin Lause, *Popular Culture: An Introductory Text* (1992), especially "An Introduction to the Study of Popular Culture: What Is This Stuff That Dreams Are Made Of?" from which my first chapter borrows certain terms. More advanced popular culture history and theory will be found in such sources as Raye Brown, *Popular Culture and the Expanding Consciousness* (1973), and Russell Nye, *New Dimensions in Popular Culture* (1972). In the related area of cultural studies, the work of French historian Michel Foucault has been extremely influential. *The Foucault Reader* (ed. Paul Rabinow, 1984) presents a representative cross-section of his work.

On **music**, the student should begin by listening to a great deal of sixties music. With the advent of the CD and new techniques of recording, virtually all major and much minor music of the decade is now readily available in commercial form. Another excellent source is *Rolling Stone* magazine, which began publication in 1967. The *Rolling Stone Illustrated History of Rock & Roll* (rev. ed., 1980), by various hands, remains the best general treatment of the subject. *The New Rolling Stone Encyclopedia of Rock & Roll* (rev. ed., 1995), is an excellent factual source. *The Rolling Stone Interviews*, collected in several volumes, are a good source of primary comment on music of the sixties by its makers. Russell and David Sanjek's *American Popular Music Business in the 20th Century* (1991) provides an authoritative overview of the commercial aspect of popular music, including that of the sixties. Philip H. Ennis's *The Seventh Stream: The Emergence of Rocknroll in Amer-*

ican Popular Music (1992) visits the same territory and also documents in detail the covers and crossovers that contributed to the growing popularity of rock 'n' roll. Various books compiled by Joel Whitburn from the *Billboard* charts provide essential data on what was popular in the major musical categories. Dave McAleer's *The All Music Book of Hit Singles: Top Twenty Charts from 1954 to the Present Day* (1996) combines *Billboard* data with United Kingdom chart information. The Internet is frequently a valuable source of song lyrics and other information about major musical groups and solo performers both.

On **movies**, the best introduction is Robert Sklar, *Movie-Made America: A Cultural History of the American Movies* (rev. ed., 1994), which covers the entire field. Reviews by film critics important in the sixties—for instance Pauline Kael of *The New Yorker* magazine—are another excellent source of information, as are contemporaneous film reviews in newspapers like the *New York Times*. Gene Brown's *Movie Time: A Chronology of Hollywood and the Movie Industry from Its Beginnings to the Present* (1995) is useful for facts and statistics on the industry. The Internet Movie Data Base (http://us.imdb.com) provides credits and other valuable information about thousands of films. Again, students are encouraged to look at as many films of or about the decade as possible. With the advent of the videocassette, and the general availability of these for rental, virtually all major American films of the sixties and seventies are readily at hand for home viewing. Many have also been re-edited and have improved soundtracks.

On **broadcasting**, Erik Barnouw's three-volume *A History of Broadcasting* (1966-1970) remains a valuable source. See also his *Tube of Plenty: The Evolution of American Television* (2d ed. rev., 1990). *Stay Tuned: A Concise History of American Broadcasting*, 2d ed. (1990) by Christopher H. Sterling and John M. Kittross deals with the entire subject in one volume and contains useful statistical data. For ratings of television shows, see Tim Brooks, *The Complete Directory to Prime Time Network TV Shows, 1946-Present* (2d ed. rev., 1981). In addition, students should also read Raymond Williams, *Television: Technology and Cultural Form*, 2d ed. (1992), by one of the major figures in the field of cultural studies. Also valuable, for both radio and television history, are memoirs and biographies of well-known broadcasters. For those who have access to it, the Museum of Broadcasting in New York City is an extensive collection of television material dating back to the early

days of the medium. Radio material of similar value is available
through the Robert M. Vincent Voice Library at Michigan State
University and the Popular Culture Library of the Bowling Green
University in Ohio (which also houses an impressive collection of
popular music in its Sound Recording Archive). Similar collections
are to be found in many college and university libraries.

Chapter 2. In addition to sources cited previously, the following have been especially helpful. On the 1950s in general, two excellent books are David Halberstam, *The Fifties* (1993) and Douglas
T. Miller and Marion Nowak, *The Fifties: The Way We Really Were*
(1977). For other significant aspects of the period, see Stephen J.
Whitfield, *The Culture of the Cold War* (1991), Stephanie Coontz,
*The Way We Never Were: American Families and the Nostalgia
Trap* (1992), and W. T. Lhamon, Jr., *Deliberate Speed: The Origins
of a Cultural Style in the American 1950s* (1990). The intellectual
roots of the sixties are evaluated in Andrew Jamison and Ron Eyer-
man, *Seeds of the Sixties* (1995). On the malling of America, see the
special issue of the *American Historical Review* with a *Forum*
devoted to this topic (*AHR* 101 [October 1996]: 1049–1121).

Andre Millard's *America on Record: A History of Recorded
Sound* (1995) is valuable for the evolution of recording techniques.
Books on Elvis are legion, but few people have written as tellingly
on him as Greil Marcus in *Mystery Train: Images of America in
Rock 'n' Roll Music* (3d ed. rev., 1990). See also his *Dead Elvis: A
Chronicle of a Cultural Obsession* (1991).

On the impact of television, see Ella Taylor, *Prime-Time Families: Television Culture in Postwar America* (1989), esp. Ch. 2;
Karal Ann Marling, *As Seen on TV: The Visual Culture of Everyday
Life in the 1950s* (1994); and Nina C. Leibman, *Living Room Lec-
tures: The Fifties Family in Film* (1995), which includes material
on movies. On the studio system and Hollywood in general, see
David Bordwell, Janet Staiger and Kristin Thompson, *The Classical
Hollywood Cinema: Film Style & Mode of Production to 1960*
(1985); Thomas Schatz, *The Genius of the System: Hollywood
Filmmaking in the Studio Era* (1988); and Ronald L. Davis, *The
Glamour Factory* (1993).

Chapter 3. On the civil rights movement, see the works of
Martin Luther King, *Stride Toward Freedom: The Montgomery
Story* (1958), *Why We Can't Wait* (1963), and *Strength to Love*
(1964). On Malcolm X, see *The Autobiography of Malcolm X* (with
Alex Haley) (1965). Taylor Branch's *Parting the Waters: America*

in the King Years, 1954-1963 (1988) is an excellent study of the life of King through those years and of the movement he headed. His *Pillar of Fire: America in the King Years, 1963-65* (1998) extends the biography to the peak year of King's career.

Paul Williams's *Bob Dylan, Performing Artist: Book One (1960-1973)* (1990) is the best commentary on Dylan's music from its beginnings to the early seventies. Also useful, for biography as well as criticism, is Robert Shelton, *No Direction Home: The Life and Music of Bob Dylan* (1986). For Dylan's song lyrics, see Bob Dylan, *Lyrics, 1962-1985* (1994), which also includes drawings and writings. On African-American stereotypes in film and other popular media, see Jack Temple Kirby, *Media-Made Dixie* (1978) and J. Fred MacDonald, *Black and White TV* (1983).

Chapter 4. Three especially worthwhile accounts of the Vietnam War are George Herring, *America's Longest War: The United States and Vietnam, 1950-1975*, 2d. ed (1986), Stanley Karnow, *Vietnam: A History* (1991), and Marilyn Young, *The Vietnam Wars, 1945-1990* (1991). Terry Anderson, *The Movement and the Sixties* (1995) is very useful for the resistance to the war, as is Todd Gitlin's *The Sixties*, cited above. Chester J. Pach, Jr., "And That's the Way It Was: The Vietnam War and the Network Nightly News" (in *The Sixties: From Memory to History*, ed. David Farber, 1994) disputes the frequently uttered criticisms of network coverage of the war. *The Vietnam War and American Culture*, ed. John Carlos Rowe and Rick Berg (1991) assesses the impact of the war on various aspects of American life, including music.

Chapter 5. On the Haight, see Charles Perry, *The Haight-Ashbury* (1985). On LSD and hippie drug culture in general, see Jay Stevens, *Storming Heaven: LSD and the American Dream* (1987). Timothy Leary's *The Psychedelic Experience* (1964) and *The Psychedelic Reader* (1965) provide his viewpoint on LSD. For an early overview of the counterculture, see Theodore Roszak, *The Making of the Counterculture* (1969). Stewart Brand's *The Whole Earth Catalog* (beginning 1968) is a good source of information on rural commune life.

A recent reassessment of the sexual revolution is Beth Bailey, "Sexual Revolution(s)," in *The Sixties: From Memory to History*, cited above. The underground press is best accessed through various microfilm collections. Abe Peck, *Uncovering the Sixties: The Life and Times of the Underground Press* (1985), surveys its impact.

For religious exoticism in the sixties see Sydney E. Ahlstrom, *A Religious History of the American People*, II, Ch. 61, "Piety for the Age of Aquarius: Theosophy, Occultism, and Non-Western Religions" (1975). See also Martin E. Marty, *Pilgrims in Their Own Land: 500 Years of Religion in America* (1986), esp. Ch. 19, "Always a Horizon." *Big Sky Mind: Buddhism and the Beat Generation*, ed. Carole Tonkinson (1995) anthologizes beat writings which show the importance of Buddhism (carried to the counterculture by figures like Allen Ginsberg) to the earlier antiestablishment group.

The best source to capture the spirit and mood of Woodstock is the documentary of the event (1970), re-edited and given a new soundtrack on the occasion of the twenty-fifth anniversary. The latter gave rise to numerous (though sometimes fanciful) reassessments in various popular magazines. A. E. Hotchner's *Blown Away: The Rolling Stones and the Death of the Sixties* (1990) is the best single source on Altamont. *I Want to Take You Higher: The Psychedelic Era 1965-1969*, ed. James Henke (with Parke Puterbaugh) (1997) catalogs an important exhibit on the subject at the Rock and Roll Hall of Fame and Museum, Cleveland.

Chapter 6. The most detailed sources on Nixon and his presidency are Stephen Ambrose, *Nixon: The Triumph of a Politician, 1962-1972* (1989) and *Nixon: Ruin and Recovery, 1973-1990*. Seth Kagin and Philip Dray, *Hollywood Films of the Seventies: Sex, Drugs, Violence, Rock 'n' Roll, and Politics* (1984) is a useful survey of major American films of the period, including many from the late sixties.

Chapter 7. On the women's movement and the politics of personal identity, see William Chafe, *The Paradox of Change: American Women in the 20th Century* (1991) and Sara Evans, *Personal Politics: The Roots of Women's Liberation in the Civil Rights Movement and the New Left* (1979). Mim Udovitch, "Mothers of Invention: Women in Rock Talk About Scents, Sensibility and Sexism" (*Rolling Stone*, October 6, 1994) includes a useful time line of women in rock music, from the mid-forties to the nineties. The thirtieth anniversary issue of the same magazine (November 13, 1997) is devoted to *Women of Rock*, with extensive articles and interviews detailing this subject. Molly Haskell, *From Reverence to Rape: The Treatment of Women in the Movies*, 2d ed. (1987) is a comprehensive, though brief, history from the 1920s to the latter part of the 1980s. On the treatment of gay characters in film, see

Vito Russo, *The Celluloid Closet: Homosexuality in the Movies* (rev. ed., 1985). Also useful is James Robert Parish, *Gays and Lesbians in Mainstream Cinema* (1993), a collection of plot summaries and short critiques for 272 films. On the films of Andy Warhol and their place in the sixties, see David Bourdon, *Warhol* (1989) and Michael O'Pray, ed., *Andy Warhol Film Factory* (1989). The Warhol Museum in Pittsburgh has an extensive archive of Warhol's films, most of which are not available elsewhere.

CREDITS

Short quotes

From Robert M. Collins, *The Sixties: From Memory to History*. University of North Carolina Press, 1994.

From *White Collar*, by C. Wright Mills. Copyright © 1951 by C. Wright Mills. An Oxford University Press book.

From *The Vietnam War and American Culture* edited by John Rowe and Rick Berg. Copyright © 1991 by Columbia University Press.

From *The Feminine Mystique* by Betty Friedan. Copyright © 1983, 1974, 1973, 1963 by Betty Friedan. W.W. Norton & Company, Inc.

From Mary Welsh Hemingway, *How It Was*. Alfred A. Knopf, Inc., 1976.

From *Visions of the Past* by Robert Rosenstone. Copyright © 1995 by the President and Fellows of Harvard College. Harvard University Press.

From Greil Marcus, *Rolling Stone Illustrated History of Rock N Roll*, 3rd edition. Rolling Stone Press, 1992.

Photos

p. 28 . . . . Michael Ochs Archives / Venice, CA
p. 60 . . . . © Lisa Law / The Image Works
p. 65 . . . . Michael Ochs Archives / Venice, CA
p. 82 . . . . LIFE Magazine
p. 96 . . . . Oliver Stone, "Platoon" / Photofest
p. 106 . . . © Lisa Law / The Image Works
p. 125 . . . © Copyright 1967 Embassy / Lawrence Turman, Inc. / Courtesy The Kobal Collection
p. 154 . . . The Cannon Releasing Corporation, "Joe" by David Gil and directed by John Avildsen. Joe Curran (Peter Boyle) at a bar in the East Village / The Kobal Collection, NY
p. 178 . . . Factory Films 1965 / Courtesy The Kobal Collection
p. 201 . . . Visages
p. 210 . . . Photofest

INDEX